PORTFOLIO THEORY

WITH APPLICATION
TO BANK ASSET MANAGEMENT

This is a Volume in
ECONOMIC THEORY, ECONOMETRICS, AND MATHEMATICAL ECONOMICS

A series of Monographs and Textbooks

Consulting Editor: KARL SHELL

A complete list of titles in this series appears at the end of this volume.

PORTFOLIO THEORY

WITH APPLICATION TO BANK ASSET MANAGEMENT

Giorgio P. Szegö
Istituto Universitario di Bergamo
Bergamo, Italy

1980

ACADEMIC PRESS
A Subsidiary of Harcourt Brace Jovanovich, Publishers
New York London Toronto Sydney San Francisco

ACADEMIC PRESS, INC.
111 Fifth Avenue, New York, New York 10003

United Kingdom Edition published by
ACADEMIC PRESS, INC. (LONDON) LTD.
24/28 Oval Road, London NW1 7DX

Library of Congress Cataloging in Publication Data

Szegö, G. P.
Portfolio theory: With application to bank asset management.

(Economic theory, econometrics, and mathematical economics)
Bibliography: p.
Includes index.
1. Bank investments--Mathematical models.
2. Bank management--Mathematical models. I. Title.
HG1616.I5S95   332.1'068'1   79-8854
ISBN 0-12-680780-9

PRINTED IN THE UNITED STATES OF AMERICA

80 81 82 83   9 8 7 6 5 4 3 2 1

To Emilia Szegö,
my wife

CONTENTS

PREFACE

One of the most fascinating problems in the area of finance is the management of bank assets and liabilities. Indeed, all other financial problems, like portfolio selection, capital budgeting, and investment analysis, can be regarded as particular cases.

The "bank asset management" problems can be subdivided into a series of steps or partial problems, proceeding in a logical fashion. We first recall what can be called, analogously to what is done for firms, the problem of the capital structure of a bank, i.e., the optimal composition of the capital/debt structure. The capital is accumulated by issuing shares, the debt by accepting deposits from customers. There is, even for the problem of the optimal capital/debt ratio, a wide variety of behavior, which changes mostly from country to country, the major factors affecting this decision being the tax structure of the country and the behavior of the depositors.

The total amount of capital available, which clearly is not a fixed quantity but changes according to the interest rates that the management thinks reasonable to pay, is then invested essentially into three different categories of assets: capital investments (buildings, etc.), loans to customers, and additional risk-free investments (bonds, etc.). To each kind of liability and asset there also corresponds a technical operational cost (personnel, etc.), a different time structure, and a different risk structure.

We can therefore say that the "financing" problems of a banking firm are different from those of other kinds of firms because most of the debt is in the form of deposits that can either be instantaneously recalled by the lender (demand deposits) or withdrawn at a specified short notice. Thus the financing of a banking firm has a certain degree of risk, which may be compared to that of a mutual fund, but is (in theory) higher than that of a manufacturing firm. As far as the "production" side of the banking firm is concerned, we can say that the main source of risk is default on loans since clearly their interest rates are fixed in advance. Thus the major (theoretical) difficulty in the banking area is the difference between the length of debt contracts (which is very short) and that of the asset investments (which is medium or long). One of the major problems in bank asset and liability management is that of taking into account the liquidity of the various assets, which is the loss that one has to account for when the bank must suddenly sell assets or raise additional capital to compensate for the withdrawal of a deposit or the default on a loan.

The problem that we are investigating is one typical of decision under uncertainty in a financial environment.

The method proposed for its solution is an extension of the mean-variance approach, which has allowed us to obtain many analytical results and a complete insight into the portfolio selection problem.

Since this approach is of some theoretical difficulty, in the first chapter of this book we give a short but complete presentation of the formalization of decision-making under uncertainty: the utility function theory. This will allow the reader to understand the exact range of applicability of the approach and the reason for some claim that the mean-variance approach is for risk-lovers.

Most of the monograph (Chapters 2–14) is devoted to the construction and complete analysis of a Markowitz-type portfolio selection model. Chapters 15 and 16, which use the results obtained in the previous chapters, are devoted to problems of portfolio selection in an inflationary or multicurrency environment and to the bank asset management problem, respectively.

The long research presented in this book was, in its more theoretical aspects, financed by C.N.R. Comitato Scienze Economiche, Sociologiche e Statistiche and in its application to multicurrency analysis and banking by the Ente per gli Studi Monetari, Bancari e Finanziari "Luigi Einaudi." The encouragement and patience throughout the very long research and writing of the book and the partial financing of this volume by the "Ente Einaudi" are gratefully acknowledged.

I am deeply thankful to my co-workers Dr. E. Cavalli, Dr. P. Mazzoleni, Dr. S. Stefani, and Dr. G. Zambruno for the technical revision of parts of the manuscript, to Dr. J. J. McKeown of the N.O.C., who polished the English, and finally to M. Hunter of the N.O.C., who provided a typewritten manuscript through a painstaking graphical analysis of my handwritten notes.

I wish to express my personal appreciation and thanks to the staff of Academic Press who did more than their usual share in helping to overcome many technical production problems.

GIORGIO P. SZEGÖ

NOTATION

Throughout this volume, when not otherwise stated, we shall denote matrices or spaces by capital Latin letters, column vectors by lowercase Latin letters, and scalars by Greek letters.

In particular,

V is the $n \times n$ variance–covariance matrix of the returns on the investments. Thus

$$v_{ij} = \sigma_i \sigma_j \rho_{ij}, \qquad \mathrm{i}_j = 1, \ldots, n,$$

where σ_i is the standard deviation on the return on the ith investment and ρ_{ij} the correlation coefficient between the ith and the jth investments.

x is the n-dimensional allocation vector. Thus x_i is the fraction of the available capital invested in the ith investment, $i = 1, \ldots, n$.

r is the n-dimensional expected return vector. Thus r_i is the expected return on the ith investment, $i = 1, \ldots, n$.

e is the n-dimensional unit vector. Thus $e_i = 1$ for all $i = 1, \ldots, n$.

$\emptyset$ is the n-dimensional zero vector. Thus $\emptyset_i = 0$ for all $i = 1, \ldots, n$.

The transpose of a (column) vector b is the row vector b'.

We shall also use the quadratic form notation for inner products. Thus $a'a = \Sigma_{i=1}^{n} a_i^2$. When not misleading, we shall use a simplified notation for summation by writing Σ or Σ_i in place of $\Sigma_{i=1}^{n}$.

The scalars α, β, and γ are defined by the relationships

$$\alpha = r' V^{-d} r, \qquad \beta = r' V^{-1} e, \qquad \gamma = e' V^{-1} e,$$

while by B^n and $\mathscr{X}^n$ we denote the boundaries of the region of admissible portfolios respectively in the planes (ν, π) or (σ, π) and in the n-dimensional Euclidean space X, defined by the component of the allocation vector x.

By ν_ν, π_ν, r^ν, and x^ν we denote the corresponding values relative to the minimum variance portfolio (or vertex portfolio).

By d or r^d we denote the "risk premium" vector or "excess return" vector. Thus $d = r^d = r - r^\nu e$. In some special case r^ν is equal to ρ or ρ^-.

When not otherwise stated in the text, the same set of symbols that we have introduced, with a tilde above, refers to the corresponding values of the case of $n + 1$ investments. Thus $\tilde{V}$, $\tilde{r}$, $\tilde{x}$, $\tilde{e}$, and $\tilde{\emptyset}$ are the $(n + 1) \times (n - 1)$ variance–covariance matrix, and the $(n + 1)$-column vectors relative to a set of $n + 1$ investments, while $\tilde{\alpha}$, $\tilde{\beta}$, and $\tilde{\gamma}$ denote the scalars that we have defined above relative to the set of $n + 1$ investments. In an analogous fashion, we have denoted by $\underset{\sim}{V}$, $\underset{\sim}{r}$, $\underset{\sim}{x}$, $\underset{\sim}{e}$, and $\underset{\sim}{\emptyset}$ data relative to a set of $n - 1$ investments.

PORTFOLIO THEORY

WITH APPLICATION
TO BANK ASSET MANAGEMENT

CHAPTER 1

INVESTMENT DECISIONS UNDER UNCERTAINTY

Portfolio theory is the area of finance which deals with the theoretical problems connected with the allocation of a given amount of money among n different available investments.

If no particular restrictions are made, the sum to be allocated can be either positive or negative. Indeed, in addition to a given wealth or endowment, the investor is allowed to borrow at a certain interest rate. Similarly, short sales of investments may be allowed. This will imply that the amount of money invested in certain securities may be negative.

Portfolio theory therefore consists of the analysis of the theoretical aspects connected with decision making related to the portfolio selection problem as originally formulated by Markowitz (1952). The success achieved in the investigation, which started only about ten years ago, of the mathematical and statistical foundations of the portfolio selection problem allows us to claim that portfolio theory is a branch of financial studies whose applicability goes well beyond the portfolio selection problem in the strict sense.

The original mathematical model of the portfolio selection problem was absolutely static, and in addition it made the crucial assumption that at the decision instant the investor did not own any share of the n available investments, but only the capital to invest. Because of this assumption, the model could not be used to investigate the problem of portfolio management in which at each decision instant the investor must reassess the composition of his optimal portfolio and possibly change it by selling parts of his investment in some and using the proceeds of the sales to buy shares of some other security.

While most of this book is devoted to the theoretical aspects of the portfolio selection problem in its original formulation, the last chapter approaches the problem of portfolio management and analyzes in detail a specific model in which the ideas of portfolio theory are applied to the problem of bank asset management. While the model proposed is still static, it deals with a general one-period model at the beginning of which the investors already own a portfolio of securities.

This one-period portfolio management problem can then be expanded into a more realistic multiperiod portfolio management model.

The basic theoretical difference between a portfolio selection and a portfolio management model lies in the need to introduce in the latter a set of transaction and market costs that crucially affect the decisions of changing the composition of the portfolio at each decision instant and that alter rather essentially the form and the properties of the mathematical model. In the case of portfolio selection as well as in the case of portfolio management problems and in the case of one-period models as well as in the case of multiperiod or dynamic models, the first problem that arises is the analysis and, in some cases, the choice of the various relevant time intervals.

The first time interval that must be defined is the *planning interval*. This is the time horizon on which the investor makes his choice. As examples of such planning interval, we may recall the expected lifetime of the investor or the expected time of his retirement. Along this planning interval the investor may be interested in a regular cash flow and in the final wealth at the end of the interval (bequest) or possibly only in the final wealth.

The second interval, which in theory is particularly important in discrete time models, but in practice must also be defined in the continuous time case, is the *decision interval*, i.e., the time interval that elapses between two different decision instants. The decision interval can be either constant, i.e., fixed beforehand or variable and changing according to the market situation.

We must next consider three different time intervals that are connected with the particular nature of the investments, i.e., the *trading interval*, the *interval to maturity*, and the *interest payment interval*. The trading interval is the shortest interval that can exist between two successive orders to the markets; it clearly depends not only on the investments, but also on the investor, and it induces a lower limit to the decision interval, which obviously can never be shorter than the trading interval. The interval to maturity is the lifespan of the investment. This lifetime could be infinite, as in the case of shares; it could last for many years, as in the case of most bonds, and go down to half-day as in some money market operations, which are possible nowadays due to the high-speed communication links among financial institutions. The interest payment (or coupon) interval is the interval between the payment of two interest intervals. If this coupon interval is shorter than decision interval, one must discount the payment of the interest, thus introducing another source of uncertainty in order to be able to compare investments with different coupon intervals.

The final type of interval that we must consider is the *sampling interval*, which is the time interval between different observations of the price and/or return on the different investments. Since, as will be shown from the time series of the observations of such data, the investor will derive different statistics for the description of the random variables (the return on the investments), the correct choice of the sampling interval is a crucial decision for practical applications.

In the original portfolio selection model the investment decisions were made in a totally myopic fashion, and all time intervals that we have described were reduced to a single interval, or time horizon, allowing only the sampling interval to be shorter if necessary.

The first problem to be solved in portfolio theory is that of the time horizon, i.e., of the identification of the unit time interval between the instant at which the investment decision is taken and the future instant at which the interest on the investment is obtained and the return on the investment can be computed. Thus the return $R_{i,t}$ on the ith investment $i = 1, \ldots, n$ in the unit time interval beginning at time t and ending at time $t + 1$ is defined by the formula

$$(1.1) \qquad R_{i,t} = \frac{P_{i,t+1} - P_{i,t} + I_{i,t+1}}{P_{i,t}} = \frac{P_{i,t+1}}{P_{i,t}} + \frac{I_{i,t+1}}{P_{i,t}} - 1,$$

where $P_{i,t+1}$ is the selling price at the instant $t + 1$ of the ith investment, $P_{i,t}$ its purchase price, and $I_{i,t+1}$ the interest paid in the interval $(t, t + 1)$.

During the time interval $(t, t + 1)$ no decision can be taken. Clearly in this model there is no time effect, but just a terminal state: the instant $t + 1$. Now in order that the formula (1.1) contain only comparable quantities, all investments must terminate at time $t + 1$. A consequence of this fact is that there can be only one riskless asset, i.e., the asset for which both $P_{i,t+1}$ and $I_{i,t+1}$ are fully known with certainty at the decision instant. All investments that are "riskless" in a period that does not coincide with the particular unit period $(t, t + 1)$ we have considered are risky. For instance, if the unit time interval is one year, a bond that has five years to maturity is a "risky" investment since we do not know with certainty at time t what $P_{i,t+1}$, the market price of that bond at the end of the first year, i.e., four years to maturity, will be. Similarly, we must consider as uncertain the return on an investment that has a life span shorter than one year and in particular an investment that reaches its maturity sometime during the period $(t, t + 1)$. In this case we must make an estimate of the proceeds of this investment at the end of the time interval, i.e., evaluate $P_{i,t+1} + I_{i,t+1}$ under the assumption that we reinvest these proceeds from the instant at which maturity was reached to the time $t + 1$. Note that in the case of investments with a life span shorter than the unit time horizon, we can define a lower bound on the return from the investment by assuming that in the time interval between maturity and the instant $t + 1$ the return on the investment will be zero.

Thus the return at the end of the time horizon $t + 1$ $(P_{i,t+1} + I_{i,t+1})$ on any investment $i = 1, \ldots, n$ that reaches its maturity before the instant $t + 1$ can be at least as great as its return computed at the time of its maturity. This follows from the fact that the investor has always at his disposal at least a riskless investment with zero return. This property does not hold for the case of investments with maturity after the instant $t + 1$. These remarks suggest that it may be convenient to use as a time horizon for a portfolio selection model the time interval corresponding to the shortest life span of all investments.

It must be clear by now that from the mathematical point of view the properties of completely risky securities, like shares, and of bonds with a life span longer than the time horizon are the same. Similarly, we can conclude that for each time horizon there exists one and only one riskless rate since a rational market will not allow for more than one riskless interest rate in the same time span.

From the preceding considerations it may by now be obvious that the portfolio selection model is rather crude and that the decision regarding the time horizon is crucial for the applicability of the model. In the case in which the investor must indeed take into account the intrinsic difference between bonds with different life spans and shares, the advisable procedure is to repeat the portfolio selection process with different time horizons.

In the preceding argument we have used the word "risky" to mean essentially the variability of returns. Indeed, throughout our analysis we use variability, which has a precise statistical definition, as a proxy for risk. Usually we do not take into account the more unsystematic risk of default or bankruptcy, which is related to variability but does not coincide with it. The suggestion of identifying risk with variability of returns is one of the major contributions of Markowitz, and its simplicity made this assumption very popular in spite of various arguments against it (see Notes and References).

Since for almost all investments the return variable $R_{i,t}$ is not known with certainty at the decision instant, we define next the random variable R_i, which defines the return from the ith investment, $i = 1, \ldots, n$. The probability distribution of R_i can be obtained from the historical data on the past returns $R_{i,t-1}, R_{i,t-2}, \ldots$, possibly modified by some subjective estimates.

We are therefore left with the problem of allocating a given capital W_0 among n different investments characterized by random returns $R_i (i = 1, \ldots, n)$. How to do it? Usually the technique of solving an allocation problem is an optimization method, i.e., dividing the given resources among the various possible uses in order to maximize some overall goal function.

In our problem the situation is complicated by the fact that the outcome of the decision process, i.e., the total return on all investments, is a random variable; thus the goal function must provide a means of choosing between probability distributions of random variables. Therefore, before proposing a definite solution technique, we must investigate the general approaches to the problem of decisions that are characterized by the uncertainty of their outcomes.

The scheme of the theory is as follows: we postulate the existence of a set of possible actions that the decision maker can take, each of which has certain consequences. The decision maker then develops a preferential ordering of all possible consequences or "outcomes" of the decisions in such a way that, given two consequences, i.e., any pair of elements of the ordering, he can decide which of the two he prefers or whether he is indifferent to both. Preference ordering has many properties, the most important of which is the following:

(1.2) **Transitivity property**

If the outcome A is preferred to B and B to C, then A is preferred to C.

The formalization of the theory of decisions under uncertainty has been characterized by a very recent and rapid development. The major breakthrough in the area is possibly due to the introduction of the axiomatic treatment of decision making under uncertainty proposed first by Von Neumann and Morgenstern. This axiomatization has thrown new light on the rule of maximization of expected utility, i.e., Bernoulli's principle. Here each possible outcome of the decision is associated with a real number, the utility, the expected value of which measures the preferences of the given set of outcomes.

In order to proceed formally, we must first introduce a preference ordering on the set Ω of the probability densities of the possible outcomes with

$$\Omega = \{f_i(x),\ i \in I\}, \tag{1.3}$$

where x is a random variable, $f_i(x)$ represents the probability density function associated with the ith choice and I is an index set.

The ordering can be represented by a utility function $u(x)$ such that to each outcome probability distribution $f(x)$ we associate a real-valued function $U(f)$ such that

$$U(f_i) \geq U(f_j) \qquad \text{if and only if} \quad f_i \gtrsim f_j, \tag{1.4}$$

where the symbol $\gtrsim$ is the preference symbol, denoting either that f_i is preferred to f_j or that we are indifferent to f_i and f_j.

If we are faced with different alternative risky options f_i, $i \in I$, the optimal choice will be the decision which maximizes the expected utility, provided that the following three axioms hold.

(1.5) **Axiom I**

The preference ordering is complete, i.e., for each pair $f_i, f_j \in \Omega$ we have that

(1.6) $$\text{either} \quad f_i \gtrsim f_j \quad \text{or} \quad f_j \gtrsim f_i,$$

and

(1.7) $$f_i \gtrsim f_j \quad \text{and} \quad f_j \gtrsim f_k \quad \text{imply} \quad f_i \gtrsim f_k.$$

(1.8) **Axiom II**

For all $f_i, f_j, f_k \in \Omega$, $i, j, k \in I$, the sets

(1.9) $$\{\alpha : \alpha f_i + (1 - \alpha) f_j \gtrsim f_k\} \quad \text{and} \quad \{\alpha : \alpha f_i + (1 - \alpha) f_j \lesssim f_k\},$$

where α is a real number, are closed.

(1.10) **Axiom III**

If $f_i \sim f_j$, i.e., we are indifferent to the choice between f_i and f_j, then

(1.11) $$\tfrac{1}{2} f_i + \tfrac{1}{2} f_k \sim \tfrac{1}{2} f_j + \tfrac{1}{2} f_k \quad \text{for all} \quad f_k \in \Omega.$$

An important consequence of this axiomatic system is the following:

(1.12) **Theorem**

For all $f_i, f_j \in \Omega$, if $f_i \sim f_j$, then

(1.13) $$\mu f_i + (1 - \mu) f_j \sim f_i \quad \text{for all real numbers } \mu,\ \mu \in [0, 1].$$

Proof

Axiom II ensures the continuity of the ordering with respect to the distributions, i.e., if

(1.14) $$\lim_{n \to \infty} \mu_n = \mu$$

and for each real number μ_n

(1.15) $$\mu_n f_i + (1 - \mu_n) f_j \gtrsim f_k,$$

then we have

(1.16) $$\mu f_i + (1 - \mu) f_j \gtrsim f_k.$$

Similarly, for the orderings $\lesssim$ and $\sim$.

On the other hand, the successive application of Axiom III leads to the result that if $f_i \sim f_j$, then

$$\rho_n f_i + (1 - \rho_n) f_j \sim f_i \tag{1.17}$$

with

$$\rho_n = \sum_{k=1}^{m(\rho)} \frac{\alpha_k}{2^k}, \qquad \text{where} \quad \alpha_k = 0 \quad \text{or} \quad \alpha_k = 1. \tag{1.18}$$

If we choose ρ_n in such a way that

$$\lim_{n \to \infty} \rho_n = \mu, \tag{1.19}$$

from (1.16) written for the ordering $\sim$, (1.13) follows.

By means of the axiomatic system (1.5)–(1.10) it is possible to identify a real-valued function U such that

$$U(f_i) \geq U(f_j) \qquad \text{if and only if} \quad f_i \precsim f_j \tag{1.20}$$

and

$$U(\alpha f_i + (1 - \alpha) f_j) = \alpha U(f_i) + (1 - \alpha) U(f_j). \tag{1.21}$$

While (1.20) implies that U maintains the preference ordering, (1.21) implies that U is linear. This can be done by associating to each probability density $f(x)$ a real number U such that

$$U = U(f(x)) = \int_{-\infty}^{+\infty} u(x) f(x)\, dx = \int_{-\infty}^{+\infty} u(x)\, dF, \tag{1.22}$$

where F is the cumulative probability function of the random variable x. The variable $u(x)$ represents the utility applied to each elementary value of the random variable. Expression (1.22) defines the principle of expected utility, or Bernoulli's principle, and can be expressed also in the form

$$U(f(x)) = E(u(f(x))) \tag{1.23}$$

since (1.22) defines the expected value of the utility function $u(x)$ applied to the probability density function $f(x)$.

It can be proved that the utility function $u(x)$ has the following properties:

(1.24) **Property**

The utility function $u(x)$ is unique up to a positive linear transformation.

(1.25) **Property**

The utility function $u(x)$ is a nondecreasing function; thus $du/dx \geq 0$.

(1.26) **Property**

The sign d^2u/dx^2 defines the aversion or propensity to risk. Thus convexity of $u(x)(d^2u/dx^2 < 0)$ implies risk aversion, while concavity $(d^2u/dx^2 > 0)$ implies risk propensity.

Having investigated the basic properties of utility functions, we shall next use the concepts that we have developed in order to solve our original problem of investment under uncertainty. The first step toward this is to define the concept of an efficiency criterion. This is a decision rule that allows us to divide all possible investment choices into two mutually exclusive sets—an efficient set and an inefficient set. The efficient set will contain all decisions that are desirable for the class of investor characterized by the particular criterion and will dominate the inefficient set with respect to it. Once an efficiency criterion has allowed the identification of the efficient set, some more precise efficiency criteria will have to be used recursively in order to further reduce the efficient set down to a point.

The first efficiency criterion to be used is the so-called general criterion (GC), or first degree stochastic dominance. This criterion can be used no matter what the form of the utility function is, as long as $du/dx \geq 0$, i.e., as long as we make no assumption about the propensity or aversion to risk on the part of the investor. Indeed, from property (1.20) we have

(1.27) **Definition**

Given two options f_i and f_j, we say that f_i is preferred to f_j according to the general criterion if and only if

$$E(u(f_i)) \geq E(u(f_j)) \qquad \text{for all} \quad i, j \in I. \tag{1.28}$$

In this case we shall say that all choices f_i such that (1.28) holds belong to the efficient set according to the general criterion, i.e., dominate f_j.

It follows that

(1.29) **Theorem**

Given two cumulative distributions F_i and F_j, f_i will be preferred to f_j according to the general criterion if and only if

$$F_i(x) \leq F_j(x) \qquad \text{for all} \quad x \tag{1.30}$$

and there exists at least one x_0 such that (1.30) holds with the strong inequality sign.

Proof

We shall first show that for each cumulative probability distribution F_i and F_j and each nondecreasing utility function $u(x)$ we have

$$\Delta E(u) = E(u(f_i)) - E(u(f_j)) = \int_{-\infty}^{+\infty} [F_i - F_j]\, du(x) \tag{1.31}$$

if such integral exists. Indeed,

(1.32)

$$\Delta E(u) = \int_{-\infty}^{+\infty} u\, dF_i - \int_{-\infty}^{+\infty} u\, dF_j = \int_{-\infty}^{+\infty} d[u(F_i - F_j)] + \int_{-\infty}^{+\infty} [F_j - F_i]\, du,$$

where we have used integration by parts. We can show that the first term on the right-hand side of (1.32) is equal to zero by defining a sequence of functions $u_n(x)$ that converge to $u(x)$ in the following way:

$$u_n(x) = \begin{cases} u(-n) & \text{for} \quad x < -n \\ u(x) & \text{for} \quad -n \leq x \leq n \\ u(n) & \text{for} \quad x > n. \end{cases} \tag{1.33}$$

Thus

$$\int_{-\infty}^{+\infty} d[u(F_i - F_j)] = \lim_{n \to \infty} \int_{-\infty}^{+\infty} d[u_n(F_i - F_j)] = 0. \tag{1.34}$$

Having proved (1.31), it immediately follows that condition (1.30) is sufficient. Indeed, if

$$F_j - F_i \geq 0, \tag{1.35}$$

then

$$\int_{-\infty}^{+\infty} [F_j - F_i]\, du \geq 0 \tag{1.36}$$

if $u(x)$ is nondecreasing. On the other hand, if

$$F_j(x_0) - F_i(x_0) > 0, \tag{1.37}$$

from the right-hand continuity of F_i and F_j there exists an interval $[x_0, x_0 + \beta]$ in which

$$F_j(x) - F_i(x) > 0. \tag{1.38}$$

In order to prove that there exists some u_0 for which we have $\Delta E(u_0) > 0$, we choose u_0 as follows:

$$u_0(x) = \begin{cases} x_0 & \text{for} \quad x \leq x_0 \\ x & \text{for} \quad x_0 \leq x \leq x_0 + \beta \\ x_0 + \beta & \text{for} \quad x \geq x_0 + \beta. \end{cases} \tag{1.39}$$

Then u_0 is a utility function, and from (1.38) we obtain

$$\int_{-\infty}^{+\infty} (F_j - F_i)\,du = \int_{x_0}^{x_0+\beta} (F_j - F_i)\,dx > 0. \tag{1.40}$$

We shall now prove necessity. For that we shall assume that for some x_1, $F_j(x_1) - F_i(x_1) < 0$, there exists an interval $A = [x_1, x_1 + \varepsilon]$ such that from the continuity of F_i and F_j at the right of A we have

$$F_j(x) - F_i(x) < 0. \tag{1.41}$$

Consider next a utility function $u_1(x)$ defined as

$$u_1(x) = \begin{cases} x_1 & \text{for} \quad x \le x_1 \\ x & \text{for} \quad x_1 \le x \le x_1 + \varepsilon \\ x_1 + \varepsilon & \text{for} \quad x \ge x_1 + \varepsilon. \end{cases} \tag{1.42}$$

Then

$$\int_{-\infty}^{+\infty} (F_j - F_i)\,du = \int_{x_1}^{x_1+\varepsilon} (F_j - F_i)\,dx < 0, \tag{1.43}$$

but then from (1.31) it would follow that $f_j \gtrsim f_i$, which is against the hypothesis of the theorem.

From Theorem (1.29) it follows that the general criterion can be applied only when two cumulative distributions F_i and F_j do not intersect. This is indeed a necessary and sufficient condition for dominance. When this condition is satisfied, the dominating cumulative distribution will lie completely to the right of the dominated cumulative distribution.

We can interpret condition (1.30) in terms of probabilities. Indeed, from (1.35) we have

$$P_{f_i}(x \le k) \le P_{f_j}(x \le k) \qquad \text{for all} \quad k, \tag{1.44}$$

or in other words,

$$1 - F_j \le 1 - F_i. \tag{1.45}$$

Thus the probability of obtaining a return $x \ge k$ is lower in f_j than in f_i. This clearly is a condition for preferring f_i to f_j, independently of the risk preference.

Clearly, the general criterion can be related immediately to the first moment of the distributions of returns. Indeed, f_i dominates f_j with respect to the general criterion if and only if

$$E(u(f_i)) \ge E(u(f_j)) \qquad \text{for each nondecreasing } u(x). \tag{1.46}$$

In particular, (1.33) must hold for the linear utility function $u(x) = x$. Thus from (1.46)

$$\pi_{f_i}(x) \geq \pi_{f_j}(x), \tag{1.47}$$

where we have denoted by $\pi_{f_i}(x)$ and $\pi_{f_j}(x)$ the expected value of x under the options f_i and f_j, respectively. This property explains the fact that the general criterion is also called first degree stochastic dominance.

A second criterion which can be used to further specify the efficient set is the so-called risk aversion criterion, or second degree stochastic dominance. This criterion can be applied only when the utility functions are concave, i.e., under the assumption that $d^2u(x)/dx^2 \leq 0$, which implies that the marginal utility of money declines. Indeed, this is always the case for risk averters.

(1.48) **Definition**

Given two investment options f_j and f_j, we say that f_i is preferred to f_j according to the risk aversion criterion if and only if

$$E_i(u(x)) \geq E_j(u(x)), \tag{1.49}$$

where $E_k(u(x))$ denotes the expected utility associated with f_k.

For this criterion we have

(1.50) **Theorem**

Given two cumulative distributions F_i and F_j, f_i will be preferred to f_j according to the risk aversion criterion if and only if

$$\int_{-\infty}^{x} [F_j(t) - F_i(t)]\, dt \geq 0 \qquad \text{for all} \quad x \tag{1.51}$$

and there exists at least one x_0 such that (1.51) holds with the strong inequality sign.

Proof

The fact that condition (1.51) is necessary follows again from (1.31). Assume for the moment that there exists some value x_0 such that, contradicting (1.51),

$$\int_{-\infty}^{x_0} (F_j - F_i)\, dt < 0. \tag{1.52}$$

Consider next the utility function $u_2(x)$, defined as

$$u_2(x) = \begin{cases} x & \text{for} \quad x \leq x_0 \\ x_0 & \text{for} \quad x \geq x_0. \end{cases} \tag{1.53}$$

Now $u_2(x)$ is nondecreasing and concave, but from (1.51)

$$\Delta E(u_2) = \int_{-\infty}^{+\infty} (F_j - F_i)\, du_2 = \int_{-\infty}^{x_0} (F_j - F_i)\, dt \leq 0. \tag{1.54}$$

Thus the condition is necessary.

Let us proceed with the proof that condition (1.51) is sufficient. To do that, let us define the two characteristic functions

$$\begin{aligned} I_A(x) &= 1, \quad & I_B(x) &= 0, \quad & \text{if} \quad F_j(x) &\geq F_i(x), \\ I_A(x) &= 0, \quad & I_B(x) &= 1, \quad & \text{if} \quad F_j(x) &< F_i(x), \end{aligned} \tag{1.55}$$

and a transformation $T(x)$ defined through the equation

$$\int_{-\infty}^{T(x)} I_A(t)|F_j - F_i|\, dt = \int_{-\infty}^{x} I_B(t)|F_j - F_i|\, dt. \tag{1.56}$$

Since

$$\lim_{x \to \infty} \int_{-\infty}^{x} |F_j - F_i|\, dt = 0, \tag{1.57}$$

we have

$$\int_{-\infty}^{x} (F_j - F_i)\, dt = \int_{-\infty}^{x} I_A(t)|F_j - F_i|\, dt - \int_{-\infty}^{x} I_B(t)|F_j - F_i|\, dt, \tag{1.58}$$

which is nonnegative by assumption.

Now the first term on the right-hand side of (1.58) is a nondecreasing function of x, and equality (1.56) holds if $T(x) \leq x$ for all x. It is also easy to show that the transformation $T(x)$ is almost everywhere continuous, differentiable, and nondecreasing.

Differentiating (1.56) with respect to x, we obtain

$$I_A(T(x))|F_j(T(x)) - F_i(T(x))|T'(x) = I_B(x)|F_j(x) - F_i(x)| \tag{1.59}$$

for all x.

We shall prove next that

$$\int_{t \leq x} (F_j - F_i)\, du(t) \geq 0 \qquad \text{for all} \quad x. \tag{1.60}$$

We have

$$\begin{aligned} \int_{t \leq x} (F_j - F_i)\, du(t) &= \int_{t \leq x} I_A|F_j - F_i|\, du(t) \\ &\quad - \int_{t \leq x} I_B|F_j - F_i|\, du(t). \end{aligned} \tag{1.61}$$

If we substitute (1.59) into (1.61), we have

$$\text{(1.62)}\quad \int_{t\le x}(F_j - F_i)\,du(t) = \int_{t\le x} I_A|F_j - F_i|\,du(t) - \int_{t\le x} I_A(T(t))|F_j(T(t)) - F_i(T(t))|T'(t)\,du(t).$$

Now since the integrand in the second right-hand term of (1.62) is non-negative (this can be seen from (1.59)), we can prove that

$$\text{(1.63)}\quad \int_{t\le x} I_A(T(t))|F_j(T(t)) - F_i(T(t))|T'(t)\,du(t) \le \int_{t\le x} I_A(T(t))|F_j(T(t)) - F_i(T(t))|\,du(T(t)).$$

Indeed, since

$$\text{(1.64)}\quad du(t) = u'(t)\,dt$$

and

$$\text{(1.65)}\quad du(T(t)) = u'(T(t))T'(t)\,dt,$$

if we compare the two sides of (1.63), taking into account (1.64) and (1.65), they are equal with the exception of the terms $u'(t)$ and $u'(T(t))$. Now since $u(t)$ is concave, $u'(t)$ is decreasing; thus since $T(t) \le t$, it follows that

$$\text{(1.66)}\quad u'(t) \le u'(T(t))$$

and the inequality (1.63) holds.

Summarizing the results of Eq. (1.62), since $T(x) \le x$, we have

$$\text{(1.67)}\quad \int_{t\le x}(F_j - F_i)\,du \ge \int_{t\le x} I_A|F_j - F_i|\,du - \int_{t\le T(x)} I_A|F_j - F_i|\,du = \int_{T(x)\le t\le x} I_A|F_j - F_i|\,du \ge 0 \qquad \text{for all} \quad x.$$

Now

$$\text{(1.68)}\quad \Delta E(u) = \int_{-\infty}^{+\infty}(F_j - F_i)\,du = \lim_{x\to\infty}\int_{t\le x}(F_j(t) - F_i(t))\,du(t) \ge 0$$

for each concave utility function $u(x)$. This proves the sufficiency of the theorem, under the obvious condition that there exists some x_0 for which $F_i \ne F_j$.

The risk aversion criterion requires that given two options f_i and f_j in order that f_i dominate f_j, the cumulative difference between f_j and f_i must remain nonnegative on the whole range of x. Clearly, for the risk aversion criterion we also have

$$f_i \gtrsim f_j \qquad \text{implies} \qquad \pi_i \geq \pi_j, \tag{1.69}$$

which is equivalent to (1.47) but now is only a necessary condition. It must be pointed out, however, that (1.69) becomes also a sufficient condition for second degree stochastic dominance in the particular case in which the cumulative distributions F_i and F_j have only one intersection point. Indeed, we can prove the following extremely important result:

(1.70) **Theorem**

Let F_i and F_j be two distinct cumulative probability distributions. Denote by π_i and π_j their expected values. Assume that there exists $x_0 < \infty$ such that $F_i \leq F_j$ for $x \leq x_0$ and $F_i \geq F_j$ for $x \geq x_0$ and that at least one of the two inequalities is strongly satisfied for some value of x; then for concave utility functions $f_i \gtrsim f_j$ if and only if $\pi_i \geq \pi_j$.

Proof

We shall prove first that the conditions are sufficient. Indeed, using again the result (1.31) in the particular case for which $u(t) = t$, we have

$$\begin{aligned} \pi_i - \pi_j &= \int_{-\infty}^{+\infty} (F_j - F_i)\,dx \\ &= \int_{-\infty}^{x_0} (F_j - F_i)\,dx - \int_{x_0}^{+\infty} |F_j - F_i|\,dx \geq 0. \end{aligned} \tag{1.71}$$

Thus if $\pi_i \geq \pi_j$,

$$\int_{-\infty}^{x} (F_j - F_i)\,dt \geq 0 \qquad \text{for all} \quad x, \tag{1.72}$$

and from Theorem (1.50) it follows that $f_i \gtrsim f_j$, which proves sufficiency.

In order to prove the necessity of the conditions, assume that $\pi_i < \pi_j$. Then

$$\pi_i - \pi_j = \int_{-\infty}^{x_0} (F_j - F_i)\,dt - \int_{x_0}^{+\infty} |F_j - F_i|\,dt < 0; \tag{1.73}$$

hence there exists some $x_2 > x_0$ such that

$$\int_{-\infty}^{x_2} (F_j - F_i)\,dt = \int_{-\infty}^{x_0} (F_j - F_i)\,dt - \int_{x_0}^{x_2} |F_j - F_i|\,dt < 0. \tag{1.74}$$

On the other hand, for $x = x_0$ we have $\int_{-\infty}^{x_0} (F_j - F_i)\,dt > 0$, and the condition of Theorem (1.50) does not hold for all x. It follows that F_i does not dominate F_j for all concave utilities, which contradicts the hypothesis. Even if condition (1.69) holds also for second degree stochastic dominance, showing that the efficient set of the second degree stochastic dominance is a subset of the efficient set relative to the first degree stochastic dominance, it is not generally possible to obtain a similar necessary and sufficient condition for the second degree stochastic dominance involving the second moment of the probability distribution of returns. This fact may suggest that the variance or the standard deviation may not be a very precise measure of risk. Indeed, the risk aversion criterion in general involves all higher moments of the probability distribution and from a geometrical point of view can be investigated only in high dimensional space. This is a fact that limits the applicability of the risk aversion criterion in spite of its theoretical rigor and suggests for many practical applications the use of the mean variance technique. This technique satisfies the general criterion, but in general will identify, on the efficient set defined by the general criterion, an efficient subset that is different from that defined by the risk aversion criterion.

This mean variance criterion is defined as follows:

(1.75) **Definition**

Given two options f_i and f_j, we say that f_i is preferred to f_j according to the mean variance criterion if and only if

$$\pi_i \geq \pi_j \qquad \text{and} \qquad v_i \leq v_j, \tag{1.76}$$

where we have denoted by v_i and v_j the variance of x in the options f_i and f_j, respectively, and where at least one of the two inequalities (1.76) must be satisfied with the strong inequality sign.

Clearly, the mean variance criterion has a very immediate geometrical interpretation and, in particular, its efficient set can be represented on a plane with coordinates (v, π), the mean-variance plane. This accounts for the fact that in spite of the theoretical shortcomings the mean variance criterion is by far the most widely used efficiency criterion in the financial area.

It is important to point out, even if the formal statement will be given only at the end of the chapter, that if some conditions are satisfied, the mean variance efficient set identifies a subset of the second degree stochastic dominance efficient set. Thus the strategies that are mean variance efficient are also efficient according to the risk aversion criterion.

We can give two kinds of sufficient conditions that guarantee that the mean variance criterion can be used and will lead to meaningful results.

The first condition gives some restrictions on the probability distributions, the second on the form of the utility functions.

Let us proceed to the first result.

(1.77) **Theorem**

Let $F_i(x)$ and $F_j(x)$ denote two cumulative probability distributions associated with the returns from two alternative investments, and let (π_i, σ_i) and (π_j, σ_j) denote the corresponding expected returns and standard deviations. Assume that $\pi_i(x) \geq \pi_j(x)$ and $F_i(x)$ and $F_j(x)$ belong to the same family of (independent) two-parameter distributions and that the two parameters are independent functions of the mean and of the variance, respectively. Then if $F_i(x)$ and $F_j(x)$ intersect, we have $f_i \gtrsim f_j$ if and only if $\sigma_i \leq \sigma_j$.

Proof

The cumulative probability distributions $F_i(x)$ and $F_j(x)$ belong to the same family. By a reparametrization we have

$$F_i(x; \pi_i, \sigma_i) = H\left(\frac{x - \pi_i}{\sigma_i}; 0, 1\right) \qquad \text{and} \qquad F_j(x; \pi_j, \sigma_j) = H\left(\frac{x - \pi_j}{\sigma_j}; 0, 1\right).$$

Then it follows that

$$F_i(x) = F_j(x) \qquad \text{for all } x \text{ with } \quad \frac{x - \pi_i}{\sigma_i} = \frac{x - \pi_j}{\sigma_j}.$$

If F_i and F_j are two-parameter distributions where the two parameters do not depend on π and σ, then $z = (x - \pi)/\sigma$ is distributed identically with mean 0 and variance 1 for both F_i and F_j.

If $\sigma_i = \sigma_j = \sigma$ and $\pi_i > \pi_j$ for all x, we have

$$\frac{x - \pi_i}{\sigma_i} < \frac{x - \pi_j}{\sigma_j}.$$

Then $F_i(x) \leq F_j(x)$ for all values of x, and there is no intersection point between the two distributions. Thus F_i dominates F_j according to the general criterion, while if $\pi_i = \pi_j$, $F_i \equiv F_j$. If on the other hand $\sigma_i \neq \sigma_j$, the two distributions will have an intersection point x_0, defined by the equation

$$\frac{x_0 - \pi_i}{\sigma_i} = \frac{x_0 - \pi_j}{\sigma_j}. \tag{1.78}$$

We shall next prove the necessity of the conditions by assuming that the thesis is violated, i.e., that $\sigma_i > \sigma_j$. Then it follows that for $x < x_0$

$$(1.79) \qquad \frac{x - \pi_i}{\sigma_j} > \frac{x - \pi_j}{\sigma_i}, \qquad F_i(x) \geq F_j(x)$$

($F_i(x) > F_j(x)$ for some x), while for $x > x_0$

$$(1.80) \qquad \frac{x - \pi_i}{\sigma_i} \leq \frac{x - \pi_j}{\sigma_j}, \qquad F_i(x) \leq F_j(x).$$

Thus the conditions of Theorem (1.70) are violated, and F_i cannot dominate F_j.

Let us next proceed with the proof of sufficiency. Assume that $\sigma_i < \sigma_j$. Then for $x < x_0$ we have

$$(1.81) \qquad \frac{x - \pi_i}{\sigma_i} < \frac{x - \pi_j}{\sigma_j} \qquad \text{and} \qquad F_i \leq F_j,$$

while for $x > x_0$

$$(1.82) \qquad \frac{x - \pi_i}{\sigma_i} > \frac{x - \pi_j}{\sigma_j} \qquad \text{and} \qquad F_i \geq F_j.$$

Since $F_i < F_j$ for some value of x, it follows from Theorem (1.70) that $f_i \gtrsim f_j$.

For the particular case of normal distributions we have

(1.83) **Corollary**

If the distributions $F_i(x)$ and $F_j(x)$ are normal, Theorem (1.77) holds even if $F_i(x)$ and $F_j(x)$ do not intersect.

However when the distributions are not normal, the intersection requirement constitutes a necessary condition for the mean variance criterion to be applicable.

Let us now discuss the conditions, if any, that must be imposed on the utility functions in order to obtain meaningful results from the mean variance criterion. In particular, if we want to compare the efficient set of the mean variance criterion with that of the second degree stochastic dominance, we must first assume that the utility function is concave. Theorem (1.77) shows that if the two-parameter cumulative distributions, where the two parameters are independent functions of μ and σ, intersect or if they are normal and the utility function is concave, then the mean variance criterion is identical to risk aversion.

This is a very useful result for understanding the exact limits and strength of the mean variance method.

We shall now investigate further conditions on the utility functions (besides concavity) which will allow a meaningful use of the mean variance criterion. We state without proof the following result:

(1.84) **Theorem**

If the decision maker has a quadratic utility function, then the mean variance criterion provides an appropriate decision rule.

This theorem gives a second sufficient condition, allowing the use of the mean variance criterion when the conditions of Theorem (1.70) are not met. In this case, however, no information can be derived regarding the relationship between the mean variance efficient set and the second degree stochastic dominance efficient set.

The use of the quadratic utility function, in spite of its analytical simplicity and formal appeal, has an essential drawback due to the fact that the first derivative of the function is not always positive for the entire range of x. This implies that for all practical purposes only a part of the utility function, and in particular the part with a positive first derivative, can be used.

Having clarified the exact power of the mean variance criterion, in the following chapters we shall investigate analytically and exhaustively the properties of the efficient set with respect to this criterion. From this investigation many general properties of the security market will be clarified.

NOTES AND REFERENCES

The applications of quantitative methods to the problem of investment decision under uncertainty must clearly be credited to Markowitz, who in his original paper published in 1952 created the very catchy subject title "portfolio selection." Markowitz proceeded very empirically and proposed a method, i.e., the mean variance approach, which remains the most popular to this day. In his later monograph (Markowitz, 1959) he expanded the subject and included some remarks about the underlying theoretical foundations of decision under uncertainty. The aim of Markowitz's work was, however, not to propose an analytic theory, but to develop a numerical method for solving portfolio problems, and indeed in his work portfolio selection is reduced to a quadratic programming problem.

In the mean variance approach the risk connected with the investment decision is measured by the dispersion of the probability distribution of the corresponding return and in particular by the variance. The bankruptcy risk, which corresponds to the risk connected with the probability of default by the borrower, is not included in this treatment. A possible formalization of this kind of risk has recently been proposed by Szegö (1978).

Utility theory and in particular the expected utility hypothesis that provides the theoretical framework for all problems of decision under uncertainty was first formulated over two centuries ago in the works of the Bernoullis and Cramer. Only recently, however, von Neumann and

Morgenstern (1944) in their justly famous treatise on "Theory of Games and Economic Behaviour" proposed an axiomatic approach to the study of utility.

Various other equivalent axiomatic systems have been proposed since then.

In this presentation we have followed the axiomatic system of Herstein and Milnor (1953). Another interesting and intuitively very axiomatic system is the one proposed by Borch (1968).

A very interesting discussion on the developments of the theory of decision under uncertainty is contained in the monograph by Arrow (1965) as well as in the book by Levy and Sarnat (1972, Chap. VI).

In this treatment when dealing with the identification of the mean variance efficient set we make the basic assumption that investors are risk averse. On this hypothesis there is no complete agreement among economists. In particular, Friedman and Savage (1948) have shown examples in which investors are not always risk averse. A detailed discussion of this problem is again to be found in the book by Levy and Sarnat (1972, Chap. VII).

The theory of stochastic dominance, which gives a rigorous theoretical foundation to the concept of the efficient set, was fully systematized in the paper by Hanoch and Levy (1969) (reprinted also in the book by Ziemba and Vickson (1975)). In this paper not only is the basic relationship between stochastic dominance and the mean variance approach clarified, but a final word is said about the discussion among Borch (1969), Tobin (1969), and Feldstein (1969) on the results presented by Tobin in his famous paper in 1958. Most of the proofs of the theorems presented in this chapter follow the techniques proposed by Hanoch and Levy (1969).

For some applications of portfolio theory to two-parameter distributions satisfying the conditions of Theorems (1.50) and (1.70) or (1.77), we can refer to Fama (1965).

In spite of the analytical superiority of the mean variance approach. Markowitz (1977) and Gavish (1977) have recently done some interesting work on numerical techniques for finding the second degree stochastic dominance efficient set. It would be crucial to compare the problem of data gathering with that of numerical complexity in order to compare from a numerical point of view the mean variance approach to stochastic dominance. Notice that the latter does not have to make too strict hypotheses on the form of the distributions or on the utility functions.

Though not fully acceptable, quadratic utility functions are very useful. It has been proved respectively by Samuelson (1970) and Ohlson (1975) that for some more general cases, i.e., for the case of compact distributions as well as for the limit case in which the investor's horizon tends to zero, quadratic utility can be used as an acceptable approximation for the case in which the distributions have more than two nonzero moments.

A very interesting comment on quadratic utility functions is made by Borch (1968) and Mossin (1973). They show that no matter what the probability assumptions on the distributions are, the mean variance approach necessarily implies a quadratic utility function.

Finally, we must note that for some cases, in spite of practical difficulties, it may be sensible to use mean semivariance instead of a mean variance criterion. Investigations of this problem were made by Hogan and Warren (1972, 1974) and Stefani and Szegö (1976). The introduction of semivariance allows a further reduction of the mean variance efficient set, but great care should be taken in the analysis of the properties of the distributions to avoid obtaining results that are questionable from the theoretical point of view.

Clearly, not all authors agree on the use of the variance, i.e., dispersion as a measure of risk. We recall, for instance, the contribution of Baumol (1963) to this problem and a recent paper by Kira and Ziemba (1977) in which the major alternative portfolio selection criteria are compared.

Some of the problems connected with the validity of the mean variance criteria are bypassed by Merton (1971). Clearly, however, some of the geometric properties that are typical of the static portfolio selection model are not observable any longer.

From the empirical point of view, we have some difficulties from the very beginning. If we consider again the basic definition (1.1), we notice that $P_{i,t}$ is a deterministic variable, while

$P_{i,t+1}$ and $I_{i,t+1}$ are not. If we consider a time series of data that enable us to compute $E(R_i)$ and $v(R_i)$, the time series needed in the computation of the fraction at the left-hand side of (1.1) is different from the one used in the expression at the right-hand side of (1.1). While the former is the time series of the ex-post returns on the n investments, the latter is the time series of the prices of the n investments. Another delicate problem is the treatment of the interest $I_{i,t+1}$. We notice first that at the instant $t + 1 + \varepsilon$ at which the interest is paid the quoted price on the investment drops by a similar amount, i.e., $P_{i,t+1-\varepsilon} = P_{i,t+1+\varepsilon} + I_{i,t+1}$. In a situation in which the lifespan of the investment and the decision interval are larger than the interest interval (for instance when the two former intervals are one year and the latter is a quarter), we must decide whether or not the flow of interest payment must be discounted. Now, a first factor to be taken into account in this decision is the length of the sampling interval. When the sampling interval is large, the flow of interest payment must be discounted, but when it is very short in comparison with the coupon interval, allowing one to take into full account the discount on the interest payment, which is already included in the investment prices, no discounting may be needed.

CHAPTER 2

PROPERTIES OF THE EFFICIENT FRONTIER: THE NONSINGULAR CASE

Consider a one-period portfolio problem in the mean variance framework. Assume that n investments are given and consider the region of admissible portfolios R^n in the plane (v, π). This region R^n is parametrically defined by the equations

$$v = x'Vx, \qquad \pi = x'r, \qquad 1 = x'e. \tag{2.1}$$

In (2.1) V denotes the variance–covariance matrix associated with the returns on the n investments. Thus $v_{ij} = \sigma_i \sigma_j \rho_{ij}$, where σ_i is the standard deviation of the return on the ith investment, $i = 1, \ldots, n$, and ρ_{ij} the correlation coefficient between the return on investment i and that on investment j, $i, j = 1, \ldots, n$. As shown in Appendix A, the matrix V satisfies some particular conditions. Again in (2.1) r denotes the expected return vector and its component r_i the expected value of the return on the ith investment. Finally, e denotes the unit vector and x the allocation vector. Hence x_i, the ith component of x, is the fraction of the available (unit) capital invested in the ith investment.

In this chapter we shall assume that the $(n \times n)$-symmetric matrix V is nonsingular. Under this assumption we shall derive the analytic expression for the boundary of the region of admissible portfolios R^n. This boundary will be derived in the plane (v, π) (and denoted by B^n) and in the n-dimensional space X spanned by the components of the allocation x (and denoted by $\mathscr{X}^n$).

The boundary of the region of admissible portfolios can be defined by the constrained minimization problem

$$\min_{x \in R^n} x'Vx \tag{2.2}$$

subject to the constraints

$$\pi = x'r \tag{2.3}$$

and

$$1 = x'e. \tag{2.4}$$

In this chapter we shall not consider the nonnegativity constraints imposed on the vector x. This case will be developed in Chapter 12.

For the problem considered in this chapter, the following result can be proved:

(2.5) **Theorem**

Let V be nonsingular and assume that the expected returns on the n investments are nonidentical, i.e., that

$$r_i \neq r_j \qquad \text{for some} \quad i, j = 1, \ldots, n. \tag{2.6}$$

Then the boundary B^n of the region of admissible portfolios in the plane (v, π) is described by the parabola

$$v = \frac{\gamma\pi^2 - 2\beta\pi + \alpha}{\alpha\gamma - \beta^2}, \tag{2.7}$$

while in the plane (σ, π) this boundary is defined by the branch of hyperbola

$$\sigma = \left[\frac{\gamma\pi^2 - 2\beta\pi + \alpha}{\alpha\gamma - \beta^2}\right]^{1/2}. \tag{2.8}$$

The boundary $\mathscr{X}^n$ in the space of the vector x, i.e., the vector x on B^n, is given by the equation

$$\begin{aligned} x = x(\pi) &= \frac{\pi\gamma - \beta}{\alpha\gamma - \beta^2} V^{-1} r + \frac{\alpha - \pi\beta}{\alpha\gamma - \beta^2} V^{-1} e \\ &= \frac{(\gamma V^{-1} r - \beta V^{-1} e)\pi + (\alpha V^{-1} e - \beta V^{-1} r)}{\alpha\gamma - \beta^2}, \end{aligned} \tag{2.9}$$

where

$$\alpha = r'V^{-1}r, \qquad \beta = r'V^{-1}e, \qquad \gamma = e'V^{-1}e. \tag{2.10}$$

Proof

Consider the Lagrangian

$$L(x, \lambda_1, \lambda_2) = x'Vx - \lambda_1(r'x - \pi) - \lambda_2(e'x - 1). \tag{2.11}$$

The critical points of (2.11) are obtained by solving the linear system of $n + 2$ equations in $n + 2$ unknowns:

(2.12) $$\frac{\partial L}{\partial x} = 2x'V - \lambda_1 r' - \lambda_2 e' = 0,$$

(2.13) $$\frac{\partial L}{\partial \lambda_1} = -r'x + \pi = 0,$$

(2.14) $$\frac{\partial L}{\partial \lambda_2} = -e'x + 1 = 0.$$

This linear system (2.12)–(2.14) has a unique solution $(x, \lambda_1, \lambda_2)$ if and only if the determinant of its coefficients is different from zero, i.e., if

(2.15) $$\begin{vmatrix} 2V & r & e \\ r' & 0 & 0 \\ e' & 0 & 0 \end{vmatrix} \neq 0.$$

It can be proved (see Appendix C) that under the assumptions made on V and r condition (2.15) is always satisfied.

Proceed next with the solution of system (2.12)–(2.14). Since V is nonsingular, we have from (2.12)

(2.16) $$x' = \tfrac{1}{2}\lambda_1 r'V^{-1} + \tfrac{1}{2}\lambda_2 e'V^{-1}.$$

By postmultiplying (2.16) by r and substituting the result into Eq. (2.13), we obtain

(2.17) $$\tfrac{1}{2}\lambda_1 r'V^{-1}r + \tfrac{1}{2}\lambda_2 e'V^{-1}r = \pi,$$

while by postmultiplying (2.16) by e and substituting the result into Eq. (2.14), we get

(2.18) $$\tfrac{1}{2}\lambda_1 r'V^{-1}e + \tfrac{1}{2}\lambda_2 e'V^{-1}e = 1.$$

Next let

(2.19) $$\alpha = r'V^{-1}r, \qquad \beta = r'V^{-1}e, \qquad \gamma = e'V^{-1}e.$$

Substituting (2.19) into (2.17) and (2.18), these become

(2.20) $$\tfrac{1}{2}\lambda_1\alpha + \tfrac{1}{2}\lambda_2\beta = \pi, \qquad \tfrac{1}{2}\lambda_1\beta + \tfrac{1}{2}\lambda_2\gamma = 1.$$

The linear system (2.20) has a solution (λ_1, λ_2) if and only if the determinant of its coefficients is different from zero, i.e., if

(2.21) $$\begin{vmatrix} \alpha & \beta \\ \beta & \gamma \end{vmatrix} = \alpha\gamma - \beta^2 \neq 0.$$

Under the assumptions made on V and r, we have

$$(2.22) \qquad \alpha = r'V^{-1}r > 0, \qquad \gamma = e'V^{-1}e > 0, \qquad \alpha\gamma - \beta^2 > 0.$$

The first two sign conditions are obvious since V^{-1} is positive definite. The last is proved in Appendix B, and it implies that system (2.20) has the unique solution

$$(2.23) \qquad \tfrac{1}{2}\lambda_1 = (\pi\gamma - \beta)/(\alpha\gamma - \beta^2), \qquad \tfrac{1}{2}\lambda_2 = (\alpha - \pi\beta)/(\alpha\gamma - \beta^2).$$

Substituting (2.23) into (2.16) and taking its transpose, we finally obtain the equation of the boundary $\mathscr{X}^n$ as a function of π:

$$(2.24) \qquad \begin{aligned} x = x(\pi) &= [(\pi\gamma - \beta)V^{-1}r + (\alpha - \pi\beta)V^{-1}e]/(\alpha\gamma - \beta^2) \\ &= [(\gamma V^{-1}r - \beta V^{-1}e)\pi + \alpha V^{-1}e - \beta V^{-1}r]/(\alpha\gamma - \beta^2). \end{aligned}$$

If we premultiply $x(\pi)$ by V, we obtain the vector

$$(2.25) \qquad Vx(\pi) = [(\pi\gamma - \beta)r + (\alpha - \pi\beta)e]/(\alpha\gamma - \beta^2).$$

Premultiplying $Vx(\pi)$ by $x'(\pi)$, we finally obtain the equation of B^n,

$$(2.26) \qquad v = x'Vx = (\gamma\pi^2 - 2\beta\pi + \alpha)/(\alpha\gamma - \beta^2),$$

which defines a parabola in the plane (v, π).

(2.27) **Remarks**

Equation (2.24) is such that each component $x_i(\pi)$ of the allocation vector x on the boundary $\mathscr{X}^n$ is a linear function of π.

The components $(Vx(\pi))_i$ of the vector $Vx(\pi)$ define the covariances of each boundary portfolio $x(\pi) \in \mathscr{X}^n$ with the ith investment. Note that $(Vx(\pi))_i$ is a linear function of r_i.

Equation (2.26) represents in the plane (v, π) a parabola with its axis parallel to the axis v. Because of the sign conditions (2.22), this parabola takes values only on the half plane $v > 0$ (Fig. 2.1). The vertex of the parabola (2.26) is the point (v_v, π_v) with coordinates

$$(2.28) \qquad v_v = \frac{1}{\gamma}, \qquad \pi_v = \frac{\beta}{\gamma},$$

while the corresponding allocation vector $x = x^v$ is

$$(2.29) \qquad x^v = \frac{V^{-1}e}{e'V^{-1}e} = \frac{V^{-1}e}{\gamma}.$$

It is worthwhile to point out that neither v_v nor x^v depend on the expected return vector r, but only on the variance–covariance matrix V. The shape of the parabola shows that through the analysis of the critical points of

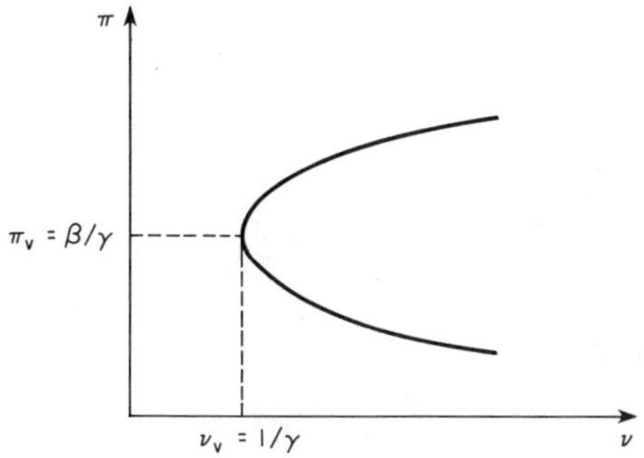

Figure 2.1

the Lagrangian (2.11) that we have performed, we have indeed identified the minimum (2.2).

For certain applications it is useful to represent the allocation vector $x = x(\pi)$ on the boundary $\mathscr{X}^n$ as a function on π_v and x^v. After some algebraic manipulations it is easy to derive the representations

(2.30) $$x(\pi) = x^v + \frac{\gamma(\pi - \pi_v)}{\alpha\gamma - \beta^2}(V^{-1}r - \pi_v V^{-1}e),$$

(2.31) $$x(\pi) = x^v + \frac{\pi - \pi_v}{\gamma\pi_v^2 - 2\beta\pi_v + \alpha}(V^{-1}r - \pi_v V^{-1}e).$$

These two forms ((2.30) and (2.31)) show that the only point of B^n at which $x(\pi)$ does not depend on r is the vertex (v_v, π_v). Other compact representations of $x(\pi)$ are given by (3.30)–(3.34) and (4.76).

Apart from the vertex (v_v, π_v), it is worthwhile to list some other remarkable points on the boundary of the region of admissible portfolios—for instance, the boundary portfolios

(2.32) $$x^r = \frac{V^{-1}r}{\beta}, \qquad \pi^r = \frac{\alpha}{\beta}, \qquad \sigma^r = \frac{\alpha}{\beta^2}$$

and

(2.33) $$x^z = \frac{\alpha V^{-1}e - \beta V^{-1}r}{\alpha\gamma - \beta^2}, \qquad \pi^z = 0, \qquad \sigma^z = \frac{\gamma}{\alpha\gamma - \beta^2}.$$

Instead of representing the boundary B^n in the plane (v, π), we can represent it in the plane (σ, π), where $\sigma = \sqrt{v}$. Clearly, from (2.26) it immediately follows that the boundary B^n in the plane (σ, π) is given by Eq. (2.8). This represents a branch of a hyperbola (Fig. 2.2) with its axis parallel to the

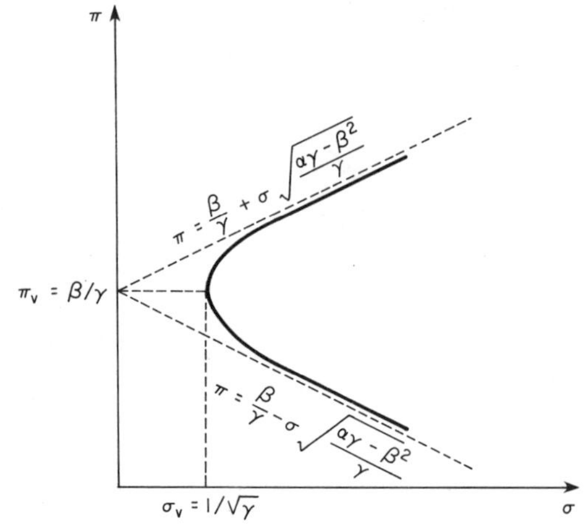

Figure 2.2

σ axis and values only on the half plane $\sigma > 0$. The vertex of this hyperbola is at the point

(2.34) $$\sigma_v = \frac{1}{\sqrt{\gamma}}, \qquad \pi_v = \frac{\beta}{\gamma},$$

and its asymptotes are given by the equation

(2.35) $$\pi = \frac{\beta}{\gamma} \pm \sigma \left[\frac{\alpha\gamma - \beta^2}{\gamma} \right]^{1/2}$$

Note that from the sign conditions (2.22) under the assumptions of Theorem (2.5), it can never occur that the minimum variance portfolio has zero variance (or standard deviation). Clearly, from (2.22) and (2.34) it follows that

(2.36) $$v_v = \frac{1}{\gamma} > 0$$

and

(2.37) $$\sigma_v = \frac{1}{\sqrt{\gamma}} > 0.$$

(2.38) **Remarks**

If we consider a risk-averse investor, he will consider as possible portfolios only those lying on the upper part of B^n, i.e., on the *efficient set*. Hence the efficient set is the part of B^n corresponding to the points $\pi \geq \pi_v = \beta/\gamma$, i.e., to values larger than or equal to the value of π_v corresponding to the "minimum variance" portfolio, i.e., the vertex of B^n.

In this chapter we have so far been concerned with the derivation of the expressions for the boundary of the region of admissible portfolios, while nothing has been said of the properties of the region itself. For that we can prove the following:

(2.39) **Theorem**

If $n = 2$, $R^2 = B^2$, i.e., the region of admissible portfolios does not have interior points. If $n > 2$ and there exists an admissible portfolio that is an interior point of R^n, then all points in the plane (v, π) or (σ, π) bounded to the left by B^n belong to R^n.

Proof

The region of admissible portfolios in this case is parametrically defined by the equations

(2.40) $$1 = x_1 + x_2,$$

(2.41) $$\pi = r_1 x_1 + r_2 x_2,$$

(2.42) $$v = x_1^2 \sigma_1^2 + x_2^2 \sigma_2^2 + 2x_1 x_2 \sigma_1 \sigma_2 \rho_{12}.$$

From (2.40) and (2.41), if

(2.43) $$r_1 \neq r_2,$$

we obtain

(2.44) $$x_1 = \frac{r_2 - \pi}{r_2 - r_1}, \qquad x_2 = \frac{\pi - r_1}{r_2 - r_1},$$

which can be substituted into (2.42), leading to

(2.45) $$v = (a_1 \pi^2 - a_2 \pi + a_3)/(r_2 - r_1)^2,$$

where

$$a_3 = r_1^2 \sigma_2^2 + r_2^2 \sigma_1^2 - 2r_1 r_2 \sigma_1 \sigma_2 \rho_{12} > 0,$$
$$a_2 = 2(r_1 + r_2)\sigma_1 \sigma_2 \rho_{12} - 2r_1 \sigma_2^2 - 2r_2 \sigma_1^2,$$
$$a_1 = \sigma_1^2 + \sigma_2^2 - 2\sigma_1 \sigma_2 \rho_{12} > 0.$$

Equation (2.45) is the equation of a parabola in the plane (v, π), which must therefore coincide with Eq. (2.8).

In the case in which condition (2.43) is not satisfied, from (2.40) and (2.39) it immediately follows that all admissible portfolios must lie on the straight line

$$\pi = r_1 = r_2, \tag{2.46}$$

and hence the region of admissible portfolios cannot have interior points.

To complete the proof of the theorem for the case $n > 2$, we note that the analysis of the critical points of the Lagrangian (2.11) leads to the identification of (2.26) as a unique boundary of the region (2.1), and this boundary turns out to be indeed a solution of the minimization problem (2.2)–(2.4). Thus if $R^n \not\equiv B^n$, i.e., if there exists an interior point of R^n, then all points of the plane (v, π) bounded to the left by B^n belong to R^n.

In Chapters 5 and 9 we shall consider again the problem of existence of interior points and derive necessary and sufficient conditions for which $R^n \equiv B^n$ for $n > 2$.

We would like, however, to stress our interest in the problem of the existence of interior points in spite of the fact that interior portfolios must be avoided by risk-averse investors and they are all "dominated" by the points on the efficient set. Our interest in the structure of the interior of the region of admissible portfolios will be evident from the following theorem:

(2.47) **Theorem**

A set of n investments can be replaced by a set of n portfolios, defined by the allocation vectors x^i $(i = 1, \ldots, n)$, all belonging to the region of admissible portfolios R^n of the original set of investments if and only if the vectors x^i are linearly independent.

Proof

Let the region of admissible portfolios of the n investments be given by the usual system

$$v = x'Vx, \qquad \pi = r'x, \qquad 1 = e'x. \tag{2.48}$$

Given n allocation vectors x^i $(i = 1, \ldots, n)$, corresponding to portfolios belonging to (2.48), we have

$$\begin{aligned} v_{ij} &= (x^i)'Vx^j, \\ \pi_i &= r'x^i, \qquad\qquad i, j = 1, \ldots, n, \\ 1 &= e'x^i. \end{aligned} \tag{2.49}$$

We shall also assume that the n allocation vectors x^i are such that

$$x^i \neq x^j \qquad \text{for all} \quad i, j = 1, \ldots, n, \quad i \neq j. \tag{2.50}$$

Next denote by y each portfolio obtained by allocation of the capital among the n portfolios x^i $(i = 1, \ldots, n)$. Thus

$$v = y'\bar{V}y, \qquad \pi = \bar{r}'y, \qquad 1 = e'y, \tag{2.51}$$

where

$$\bar{v}_{ij} = v_{ij} \tag{2.52}$$

and

$$\bar{r}_i = \pi_i, \tag{2.53}$$

where v_{ij} and π_i are given by Eqs. (2.49). Hence by substituting equations (2.49) into (2.51), written in expanded form, because of (2.52) and (2.53), we obtain

$$\begin{aligned} v &= \sum_{ij} y_i y_j (x^i)' V x^j = \sum_{ij} y_i (x^i)' V y_j x^j \\ &= \left[\sum_i y_i (x^i)'\right] V \left[\sum_i y_i (x^i)'\right], \end{aligned} \tag{2.54}$$

and

$$\pi = \sum_i y_i (r'x^i) = \sum_i r'(y_i x^i). \tag{2.55}$$

Now let

$$\sum_i y_i x^i = z. \tag{2.56}$$

Equations (2.54) and (2.55) then become

$$v = z'Vz, \qquad \pi = r'z, \tag{2.57}$$

while, because of the third equation (2.49), we have

$$e'z = \sum_j z_j = \sum_j \sum_i y_i x_j^i = \sum_i y_i \sum_j x_j^i = \sum_i y_i = 1. \tag{2.58}$$

Thus the portfolio problem defined by Eqs. (2.57) and (2.58) is equivalent to the original problem (2.48) if we set

$$z = x. \tag{2.59}$$

The new allocation vector y, which computes the allocation of x with respect to the portfolios x^i and not with respect to the original set of n investments, is then obtained by the linear system

$$\sum_i y_i x^i = x \tag{2.60}$$

obtained from (2.56) and (2.59).

The linear system (2.60) can be represented in the simpler form

(2.61) $$Ky = x,$$

where the elements k_{ij} of the $(n \times n)$ matrix K are given by

(2.62) $$k_{ij} = x^i_j,$$

i.e., K is a matrix the colums of which are the vectors x^i $(i = 1, \ldots, n)$. The linear system (2.61) has a unique solution if and only if

(2.63) $$\det K \neq 0,$$

i.e., if and only if the vectors x^i are linearly independent, i.e., if they provide a new basis for the space X spanned by the allocation vector x.

Note that substituting the set of n linearly independent portfolios for the original set of n investments is needed only when the complete identity of the regions of admissible portfolios R^n is desired. In the case in which a description of the boundary B^n is sufficient, a much smaller number of portfolios is needed, as will be shown by the next theorem.

(2.64) **Theorem**

A necessary and sufficient condition for a portfolio x to belong to $\mathscr{X}^n$ is that it be generated by a linear combination of two arbitrary portfolios x^1 and x^2, both belonging to $\mathscr{X}^n$ with $x^1 \not\equiv x^2$.

Proof

It is sufficient to prove that each vector $x(\pi)$ of the form (2.9) can be generated by a linear combination of two vectors $x(\pi_1)$ and $x(\pi_2)$, $x(\pi_1) \neq x(\pi_2)$, of the form (2.9). Hence if we use a simplified notation of the form (2.9), we have

(2.65) $$x(\pi) = a\pi + b = \eta x(\pi_1) + (1 - \eta)x(\pi_2),$$

i.e.,

(2.66) $$a\pi + b = \eta(a\pi_1 + b) + (1 - \eta)(a\pi_2 + b),$$

where the vectors a and b can easily be obtained from Eq. (2.9) as

(2.67) $$a = \frac{\gamma V^{-1}r - \beta V^{-1}e}{\alpha\gamma - \beta^2}, \qquad b = \frac{\alpha V^{-1}e - \beta V^{-1}r}{\alpha\gamma - \beta^2}.$$

From (2.66) it immediately follows that given π_1 and π_2, $\pi_1 \neq \pi_2$ (i.e., given $x(\pi_1)$ and $x(\pi_2)$), and given an arbitrary π to which there corresponds an arbitrary allocation vector $x(\pi) \in \mathscr{X}^n$, it is possible to find a real number

$$\eta = \frac{\pi - \pi_2}{\pi_1 - \pi_2}, \tag{2.68}$$

which satisfies (2.66) and proves the theorem.

Some consequences of Theorems (2.47) and (2.64) are listed in the following corollary.

(2.69) **Corollary**

The linear combination of any two boundary portfolios is a boundary portfolio; hence if the region of admissible portfolios has interior points, there does not exist any set of n linearly independent portfolios x^i $(i = 1, \ldots, n)$ belonging to $\mathscr{X}^n$.

Proof

Theorem (2.64) and in particular the relationships (2.67) and (2.68) prove the first statement. The second statement follows from the fact that if there exists a set of n linearly independent portfolios x^i $(i = 1, \ldots, n)$, all belonging to $\mathscr{X}^n$, then because of Theorem (2.47), all admissible portfolios would be representable as linear combinations of such portfolios x^i. The first statement of this theorem would then imply that all admissible portfolios belong to the boundary. This contradiction proves the second statement of the theorem.

EXAMPLES, NOTES, AND REFERENCES

The analytic approach to the determination of the boundary of the region of admissible portfolios was introduced by Lintner (1965). Lintner, however, considered only the case in which there exists a riskless investment. Indeed, he was able to derive some properties of the boundary of the region of admissible portfolios in the space $\mathscr{X}^n$.

Lintner's approach is based on the maximization of a fractional function of the type

$$\theta(x) = \frac{x'r}{x'Vx}. \tag{2.70}$$

While the first completely analytical treatment of the problem and the identification of the boundary B^n can be found in the papers by Merton (1972) and Szegö (1972a), the first analytical derivation of the boundary B^n was performed by Levin (1970).

A slightly more general approach to the analysis of the region of admissible portfolios can be performed by considering, instead of the equality constrained minimization problem (2.2)–(2.4), the inequality constrained problem

$$\{\min x'Vx \,|\, r'x \geq \pi,\ e'x = 1\}, \tag{2.71}$$

where V is positive definite. In this case it is clearly convenient to start the analysis by deriving conditions under which the linear inequality constraint $r'x \geq \pi$ is active ($r_i \neq r_j$ for some $i, j = 1, \ldots, n$). Under these conditions the inequality constrained problem (2.71) becomes

$$\{\min x'Vx \,|\, r'x = \pi,\ e'x = 1\}, \tag{2.72}$$

i.e., (2.2)–(2.4).

The results presented in this chapter provide a proof that "diversification pays." The minimum variance portfolio x^v, if it is not one of the investments, is indeed a portfolio that has a variance smaller than the smallest variance among the investments. This fact can be shown in a very impressive way by considering the following example: $n = 2$, $r_1 = r_2 = \rho$, $\sigma_1 = \sigma_2 = \sigma$. Substituting these values in Eqs. (2.40)–(2.42) and introducing (2.40) into (2.42), we obtain the equation

$$v = \sigma^2[1 - 2(1 - \rho_{12})x_1(1 - x_1)]. \tag{2.73}$$

We shall now find the value of x_1 that minimizes v. By computing dv/dx_1 and setting it equal to zero, we find that this minimizer has the value $x_1^* = \frac{1}{2}$ and that the minimum value of v is

$$v_{\min} = \tfrac{1}{2}\sigma^2(1 + \rho_{12}). \tag{2.74}$$

Thus if $\rho_{12} < 0$, $v_{\min} \leq \sigma^2$, and even if the two investments have the same expected return and the same variance, provided their correlation coefficients are negative, it pays to divide the capital between the two.

One of the basic assumptions on which the results of this chapter are based is condition (2.6) on the nonidentity of the expected returns on the n investments. It is, however, quite simple to derive the desired results for the case in which this condition is violated, i.e., when

$$\pi = r'x = \delta e'x. \tag{2.75}$$

From the last equation of system (2.1) and from (2.75), it follows that the boundary of the region of admissible portfolios B^n, and therefore the whole region R^n, must lie on the straight line

$$\pi = \delta. \tag{2.76}$$

Now in order to find which part of the straight line (2.76) defines B^n, we shall first simply find the critical points of

$$v = x'Vx \tag{2.77}$$

under the constraint

$$1 = e'x, \tag{2.78}$$

obtaining as the minimizing allocation vector

$$x = V^{-1}e/\gamma, \tag{2.79}$$

to which in the plane (v, π) there corresponds the point

$$v = 1/\gamma. \tag{2.80}$$

Thus in this case B^n is the ray on the straight line (2.76), originating at the point $v = 1/\gamma$, and with values on the half plane $v \geq 0$ (Fig. 2.3).

It is important for further applications to compute the properties of the boundary B^n when instead of definining the allocation vector x subject to the constraint

$$x'e = 1 \tag{2.81}$$

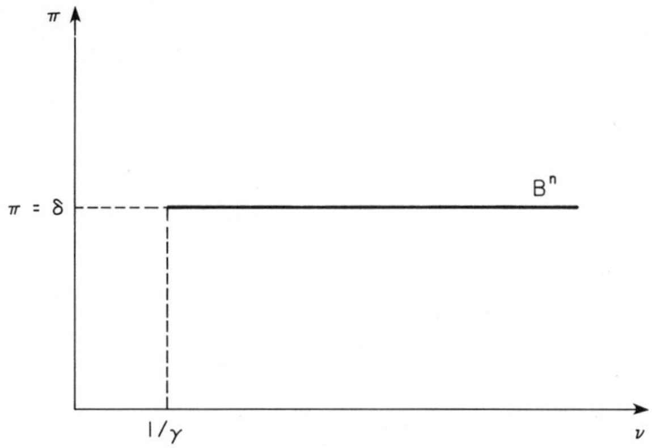

Figure 2.3

and therefore defining the ith component of x, x^i as the fraction of the total capital invested in the ith investment, we consider the initial wealth of the investor W_0 and just divide it among the different investments. This is equivalent to taking into consideration, instead of (2.1), the system.

$$v = x'Vx, \qquad \pi = x'r, \qquad W_0 = x'e. \tag{2.82}$$

The equation of the boundary of the region of admissible portfolios in the plane (v, π) takes the form

$$\sigma^2 = v = \frac{\gamma\pi^2 - 2\beta W_0 \pi + \alpha W_0^2}{\alpha\gamma - \beta^2}, \tag{2.83}$$

where the coefficients α, β, and γ are defined as before in (2.10). The equation of the allocation vector $x(\pi)$ on $\mathscr{X}^n$ becomes

$$x(\pi) = x^v + \gamma\left(\frac{\pi - \pi_v}{\alpha\gamma - \beta^2}\right)\left(V^{-1}r - \frac{\pi_v}{W_0} V^{-1}e\right), \tag{2.84}$$

while the minimum variance portfolio is given by

$$x^v = \frac{W_0}{\gamma} V^{-1}e, \qquad \pi_v = \frac{W_0\beta}{\gamma}, \qquad v_v = \frac{W_0^2}{\gamma}. \tag{2.85}$$

Since in our model there is no restriction on borrowing, we should also investigate the particular case $W_0 = 0$.

Now Eq. (2.83) simply becomes

$$\sigma^2 = v = \frac{\gamma\pi^2}{\alpha\gamma - \beta^2}, \tag{2.86}$$

while the allocation vector takes the form

$$x(\pi) = \frac{\pi(\gamma V^{-1}r - \beta V^{-1}e)}{\alpha\gamma - \beta^2}. \tag{2.87}$$

The minimum variance portfolio becomes

(2.88) $$x^v = \pi_v = v_v = 0.$$

making it clear that the minimum variance portfolio is the no-risk no-investment portfolio. Equation (2.86), defining B^n in the plane (σ, π), describes two straight lines (see Fig. 2.4) through the origin of the plane and angular coefficients

(2.89) $$\chi = \pm\sqrt{\gamma/(\alpha\gamma - \beta^2)}.$$

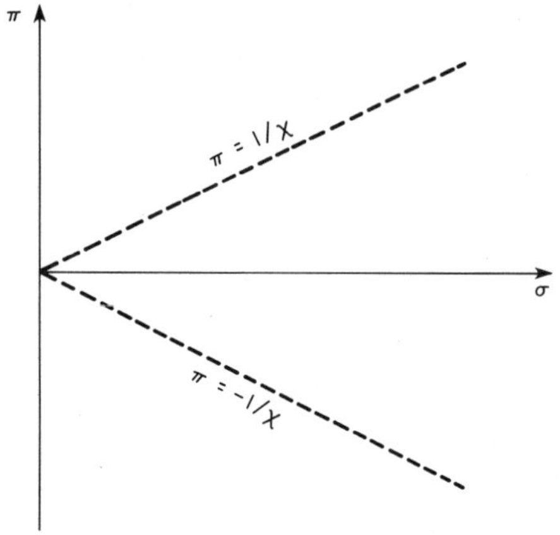

Figure 2.4

In this case while all the basic properties of B^n and $\mathscr{X}^n$, which will be investigated in the next chapter (uniqueness and linearity of $x(\pi)$), still hold, the expressions are indeed much simpler.

Equation (2.31) in which $x(\pi)$ is derived as a function of π and π_v allows to derive a similar expression for the boundary of the region of admissible portfolios in the form

(2.90) $$v = v_v + \frac{(\pi - \pi_v)^2}{\gamma\pi_v^2 - 2\beta\pi_v + \alpha}.$$

CHAPTER 3

PROPERTIES OF THE BOUNDARY PORTFOLIOS

In the preceding chapter we derived the analytic expression of the boundary of the region of admissible portfolios (2.1) both in the planes (v, π) and (σ, π) as well as in the n-dimensional space X, spanned by the components of the allocation vector x.

This chapter will be devoted to the further analysis of the properties of the boundary portfolios, i.e., the properties of the allocation vector $x(\pi)$, defined by Eq. (2.9), on the space X. In particular, we shall discuss problems connected with the sign properties of such boundary portfolios $x(\pi)$ as well as with the problems of uniqueness of the transformations between points (v, π) belonging to R^n and vectors x in X and vice versa.

Throughout this chapter the assumptions made in Theorem (2.5) on V and r are still supposed to be satisfied, i.e., V is supposed to be nonsingular, and r is supposed to have nonidentical components.

Equation (2.9), which defines the allocation vector on the boundary of the region of admissible portfolios as a function of π, has many important properties.

Note first that because of condition (2.21), for each value of π Eq. (2.9) defines a corresponding unique vector x on the boundary of the region of admissible portfolios. Indeed, (2.9) is a linear expression in π. Hence for each i $(i = 1, \ldots, n)$ the component x_i of $x(\pi)$ is represented in the plane (x_i, π) by a straight line, and the following two particular cases of (2.9) can, in theory, occur (see Fig. 3.1):

(3.1) $\quad \pi = \text{const},$

(3.2) $\quad x_i(\pi) = \chi_i = \text{const} \qquad \text{for all} \quad \pi, \ -\infty < \pi < +\infty, \quad i = 1, \ldots, n.$

These particular cases are shown in Fig. 3.1 by the vertical straight line (a) and the horizontal straight line (b), respectively. The general case is represented in Fig. 3.1 by the straight line (c).

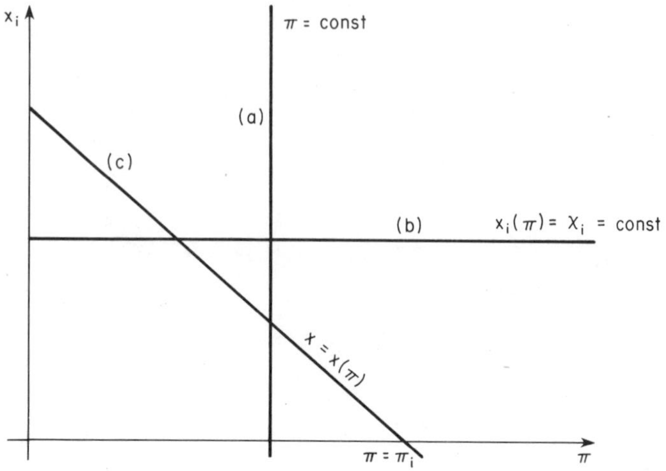

Figure 3.1

From the analysis of relationship (2.9), we deduce that case (3.1) can never occur since from (2.22) we have $\alpha\gamma - \beta^2 \neq 0$. Thus the only case in which the correspondence between π and x_i is not one to one is ruled out, and we have therefore completely proved that to each π there corresponds a unique value $x_i(\pi)$, $i = 1, \ldots, n$.

Proceeding with the discussion of the problem, from (2.9) we notice that (3.2) can take place if and only if the following two relationships simultaneously hold:

$$\gamma(V^{-1}r)_i - \beta(V^{-1}e)_i = 0, \tag{3.3}$$

$$\alpha(V^{-1}e)_i - \beta(V^{-1}r)_i = \chi_i(\alpha\gamma - \beta^2). \tag{3.4}$$

Note that while (3.3) is a truly binding condition, unless χ_i is fixed a priori, (3.4) is just a notational expression since in each case it is possible to find a real number χ_i such that (3.4) is satisfied.

From system (3.3) and (3.4) by some algebraic computation it turns out that for (3.3) and (3.4) to be satisfied we must have

$$\gamma(V^{-1}r)_i = \beta(V^{-1}e)_i = \beta\gamma\chi_i, \tag{3.5}$$

which allows an easy determination of the value χ_i.

In the important special case in which

$$\chi_i = 0, \tag{3.6}$$

it follows from (3.5) that we must have

$$(V^{-1}r)_i = (V^{-1}e)_i = 0, \tag{3.7}$$

which is a necessary and sufficient condition for

$$x_i(\pi) \equiv 0 \qquad \text{for each} \quad \pi, \; -\infty < \pi < +\infty, \quad i = 1, \ldots, n. \tag{3.8}$$

A stronger case occurs when relationship (3.3) holds for all values if $i = 1, \ldots, n$, i.e., when

$$\gamma(V^{-1}r) = \beta(V^{-1}e). \tag{3.9}$$

In this case none of the components $x_i(\pi)$ of the allocation vector on the boundary of the region of admissible portfolios depends on π. If we replace the constants γ and β by their complete expressions (2.10), Eq. (3.9) becomes

$$e'V^{-1}eV^{-1}r = r'V^{-1}eV^{-1}e, \tag{3.10}$$

which is, of course, possible if and only if there exists a real number δ with

$$r = \delta e, \tag{3.11}$$

which is the case in which the "constraint" (2.3) is not active in the minimization problems (2.2)–(2.4). Of course, case (3.11) is ruled out by assumption (2.6).

We shall summarize the preceding results in the following:

(3.12) **Theorem**

If V is nonsingular and the expected returns on the n investments are nonidentical, then Eq. (3.7) gives a necessary and sufficient condition for the identity (3.9) to be satisfied by the ith investment, while identity (3.5) is the necessary and sufficient condition for (3.2) to be satisfied by the ith investment when $\chi_i \neq 0$. Each time condition (3.5) is satisfied, the ith investment is held in a constant amount in each boundary portfolio.

If we consider now the general case represented by the straight line (c) of Fig. 3.1, we find that there exists one and only one value of π, say, π_i such that $x_i(\pi_i) = 0$, i.e., from (3.6), such that

$$\pi_i[\gamma(V^{-1}r)_i - \beta(V^{-1}e)_i] = \beta(V^{-1}r)_i - \alpha(V^{-1}e)_i. \tag{3.13}$$

From this equation it is immediate to compute the value π_i at which $x_i(\pi)$ changes its sign (vanishes):

$$\pi_i = \frac{\beta(V^{-1}r)_i - \alpha(V^{-1}e)_i}{\gamma(V^{-1}r)_i - \beta(V^{-1}e)_i}. \tag{3.14}$$

The preceding results can be summarized by the following:

(3.15) **Theorem (nonindifference theorem)**

If V is nonsingular, the expected returns on the n investments are not identical, and equality (3.7) is not satisfied by any i, $i = 1, \ldots, n$, then with the exception of the n points π_i (3.14), $i = 1, \ldots, n$, the investor holds each available investment in each boundary portfolio either in positive or in negative amounts regardless of r_i, σ_i, and ρ_{ij}. Thus under the assumptions made, the investor is never indifferent with respect to any investment opportunity.

We shall next use expression (3.14) to derive conditions under which at a certain point of the efficient frontier more than one component of the vector x simultaneously vanish. Indeed, in order that

$$x_i(\pi) = x_j(\pi) = 0 \qquad i \neq j, \quad i, j = 1, \ldots, n, \tag{3.16}$$

from (3.14) the following equality must be satisfied:

$$\frac{\beta(V^{-1}r)_i - \alpha(V^{-1}e)_i}{\gamma(V^{-1}r)_i - \beta(V^{-1}e)_i} = \frac{\beta(V^{-1}r)_j - \alpha(V^{-1}e)_j}{\gamma(V^{-1}r)_j - \beta(V^{-1}e)_j} \qquad i, j = 1, \ldots, n, \quad i \neq j. \tag{3.17}$$

From relationship (3.17), since $\alpha\gamma - \beta^2 \neq 0$, after some algebraic computation we derive the condition

$$(V^{-1}e)_i(V^{-1}r)_j = (V^{-1}e)_j(V^{-1}r)_i, \qquad i \neq j, \quad i, j = 1, \ldots, n. \tag{3.18}$$

This condition can be expressed more explicitly in the form

$$\sum_{k=1}^{n} v_{ik}^* \sum_{k=1}^{n} v_{jk}^* r_k = \sum_{k=1}^{n} v_{jk}^* \sum_{k=1}^{n} v_{ik}^* r_k, \qquad i \neq j, \quad i, j = 1, \ldots, n, \tag{3.19}$$

where we have denoted by v_{ij}^{-1} the general element of the matrix V^{-1}.

Note that the obvious trivial solutions of Eq. (3.19),

$$r = \delta e \tag{3.20}$$

and

$$v_{ik}^* = \delta v_{jk}^*, \qquad i \neq j, \quad i,j = 1, \ldots, n, \tag{3.21}$$

where δ is a real number, are both ruled out since they violate the assumptions on V and r made throughout this chapter. Thus we have

(3.22) **Theorem**

Under the assumptions of Theorem (3.15) a necessary and sufficient condition for the existence of a value of π such that $x_i(\pi) = x_j(\pi) = 0$ is that condition (3.18) (or (3.19)) be satisfied.

We shall next discuss the sign properties of the vector $x(\pi)$ along the boundary B^n. We shall first consider the sign properties of a particular point of the boundary B^n, the vertex x^v. From (2.29) we have

(3.23) $$x_i^v = (V^{-1}e)_i/\gamma = (V^{-1}e)_i/e'V^{-1}e.$$

Now since $\gamma > 0$ (2.22), we have

(3.24) **Theorem**

The sign of the ith component of the vector x^v is given by the relationship

(3.25) $$\operatorname{sgn} x_i^v = \operatorname{sgn}(V^{-1}e)_i = \operatorname{sgn} \sum_{j=1}^{n} v_{ij}^*,$$

where we have again denoted by v_{ij}^* the (i,j)th element of the matrix V^{-1}.

From (3.25) it immediately follows that

(3.26) **Theorem**

If V is diagonal,

(3.27) $$x^v = V^{-1}e/\gamma > 0.$$

The proof is immediate since if V is diagonal, V^{-1} is also a positive definite diagonal matrix.

We shall next further investigate the sign properties of $x_i(\pi)$ and in particular relate the sign properties of $x_i(\pi)$ for a general value of π to those of x_i^v. For that consider expressions (2.30) and (2.31), which relate $x(\pi)$ to π, x^v, and π_v. We shall write expression (2.30) in the more compact equivalent forms

(3.28) $$x^d(\pi_d) = \frac{\gamma\pi_d}{\alpha\gamma - \beta^2} V^{-1}d = \frac{\pi_d}{v(\pi_v)} V^{-1}d = \frac{\pi_d V^{-1}d}{d'V^{-1}d},$$

where

(3.29) $$x^d(\pi_d) = x(\pi) - x^v,$$

(3.30) $$\pi_d = \pi - \pi_v,$$

and

(3.31) $$d = r - \pi_v e.$$

Expression (3.28) measures the variations of x with respect to the minimum variance portfolio x^v, the "excess return" above the minimum variance expected return π_d, and the "risk premium" d. In expression (3.28) we have denoted by d the risk premium in accordance with the notations used in Chapter 6. The same risk premium will, however, sometimes be denoted by r^d when it is important to emphasize that it measures an expected return.

Expression (3.28) allows us immediately to identify on the boundary of the region of admissible portfolios the "efficient frontier", i.e., the region corresponding to the values $\pi_d > 0$.

In the case in which V is diagonal, (3.28) allows us also to establish an immediate sign correlation between x_i^d and d_i, as shown by the following:

(3.32) **Theorem**

If V is diagonal, (3.28) takes the form

$$x_i^d(\pi_d) = \frac{\gamma\pi_d}{\alpha\gamma - \beta^2}\frac{d_i}{\sigma_i^2} = \frac{\pi_d}{v(\pi_v)}\frac{d_i}{\sigma_i^2} \qquad i = 1, \ldots, n. \tag{3.33}$$

Thus on the efficient frontier ($\pi_d > 0$)

$$\operatorname{sgn} x_i^d = \operatorname{sgn} d \qquad i = 1, \ldots, n, \tag{3.34}$$

and x_i^d is directly proportional to $\pi_d d/\sigma_i^2$.

(3.35) **Remarks**

The result (3.34) still holds when V^{-1} is not diagonal, but has a dominant diagonal.

In the case in which V^{-1} does not have a dominant diagonal, the location of the point at which $x_i(\pi)$ vanishes and of the arc of B^n on which $x_i(\pi) > 0$ depends not only on d_i but also on the relative signs of $(V^{-1}e)_i$ and $(V^{-1}d)_i$. Some simple computations show that the location of the point $\pi = \pi_i$ at which $x_i(\pi)$ changes its sign on B^n is given by the following rules:

$$\begin{array}{llll} \text{if } (V^{-1}e)_i > 0 & \text{and } (V^{-1}d)_i > 0, & \text{then} & \pi_i < \pi_v, \\ \text{if } (V^{-1}e)_i > 0 & \text{and } (V^{-1}d)_i < 0, & \text{then} & \pi_i > \pi_v, \\ \text{if } (V^{-1}e)_i < 0 & \text{and } (V^{-1}d)_i > 0, & \text{then} & \pi_i > \pi_v, \\ \text{if } (V^{-1}e)_i < 0 & \text{and } (V^{-1}d)_i < 0, & \text{then} & \pi_i < \pi_v. \end{array} \tag{3.36}$$

The location of the arc on which $x_i(\pi) > 0$ on B^n follows immediately from (3.36).

The whole problem of the sign of $x_i(\pi)$ for the case in which V^{-1} does not have a dominant diagonal depends (see (3.28)) on the identification of the sign of

$$(V^{-1}d)_i = \sum_{j=1}^{n} v_{ij}^* d_j, \tag{3.37}$$

where we have denoted by d an arbitrary vector and where V^{-1} is positive definite.

Note that the condition for the positive definiteness of V^{-1} requires only that

(3.38) $$\sum_{i=1}^{n} d_i \left(\sum_{j=1}^{n} v_{ij}^* d_j \right) > 0,$$

where d is an arbitrary vector and does not require that each summation with respect to j be positive.

The problem of the identification of the arc of B^n, if it exists, on which $x > 0$, clearly depends on the relative solution of (3.36). If such an arc exists, it will be denoted by the inequalities

(3.39) $$\pi_m \leq \pi \leq \pi_M$$

with the convention that

(3.40) $$x(\pi) > 0 \qquad \text{for} \quad \pi_m < \pi < \pi_M$$

and that when $\pi = \pi_m$ and $\pi = \pi_M$, at least one component of the vector x vanishes. As will be shown in example (3.56), such an arc does not need to exist and (see (3.57)) if it does, its position may be quite general.

We shall next discuss some additional problems connected with the fact that given π, the problem $x(\pi)$ (2.9) is uniquely defined. The following stronger result can be proved to be true.

(3.41) **Theorem**

The boundary B^n of the region of admissible portfolios is the set of all points (v, π) to each of which there corresponds a unique allocation vector x.

Proof

We shall consider the case in which V is diagonal; indeed, if V is not diagonal, we can consider a linear transformation of type (2.61)

(3.42) $$Ky = x,$$

where K is nonsingular and such that

(3.43) $$\bar{V} = K'VK$$

is diagonal. (See Appendix D for details of the existence of such transformations.)

Clearly, transformation (3.43) preserves the uniqueness properties of the allocation vector. Thus without any loss of generality we can assume that in problem (2.1) the matrix V is diagonal. We shall decompose system (2.1) in the form

$$v = \sigma_1^2 x_1^2 + \sigma_2^2 x_2^2 + \sigma_3^2 x_3^2 + \tilde{x}'\tilde{V}\tilde{x}, \tag{3.44}$$

$$\pi = r_1 x_1 + r_2 x_2 + r_3 x_3 + \tilde{r}'\tilde{x}, \tag{3.45}$$

$$1 = x_1 + x_2 + x_3 + \tilde{e}'\tilde{x}, \tag{3.46}$$

where the matrix V and the vectors r, x, and e have been decomposed as follows:

$$V = \begin{bmatrix} \sigma_1^2 & 0 & 0 & 0 \\ 0 & \sigma_2^2 & 0 & 0 \\ 0 & 0 & \sigma_3^2 & 0 \\ 0 & 0 & 0 & \tilde{V} \end{bmatrix}, \qquad r = \begin{bmatrix} r_1 \\ r_2 \\ r_3 \\ \tilde{r} \end{bmatrix}, \qquad x = \begin{bmatrix} x_1 \\ x_2 \\ x_3 \\ \tilde{x} \end{bmatrix}, \qquad e = \begin{bmatrix} 1 \\ 1 \\ 1 \\ \tilde{e} \end{bmatrix}, \tag{3.47}$$

where $\tilde{V}$, $\tilde{r}$, $\tilde{x}$, and $\tilde{e}$ denote an $(n-3) \times (n-3)$ matrix and $(n-3)$ column vectors, respectively. Eliminating x_1 and x_2 from Eqs. (3.45) and (3.46) and substituting these equations into (3.44), we obtain

$$\begin{aligned} v = \sigma_3^2 x_3^2 + \tilde{x}'\tilde{V}\tilde{x} + [&\underset{\sim}{\gamma}(\pi - r_3 x_3 - \tilde{r}'\tilde{x})^2 \\ &- 2\underset{\sim}{\beta}(\pi - r_3 x_3 - \tilde{r}'\tilde{x}) \cdot (1 - x_3 - \tilde{e}'\tilde{x}) \\ &+ \underset{\sim}{\alpha}(1 - x_3 - \tilde{e}'\tilde{x})^2]/(\underset{\sim}{\alpha}\underset{\sim}{\gamma} - \underset{\sim}{\beta}^2), \end{aligned} \tag{3.48}$$

where we have denoted by $\underset{\sim}{\alpha}$, $\underset{\sim}{\beta}$, and $\underset{\sim}{\gamma}$ the coefficients (2.10) relative to the first two investments. Now (3.48) can be regarded as a second order algebraic equation in x_3 since we are looking for the locus of points to which, given v and π, there corresponds a unique x_3. We consider the discriminant equation of (3.48) and set it equal to zero:

$$\begin{aligned} \Delta_{x_3} = &[(\underset{\sim}{\gamma} r_3 - \underset{\sim}{\beta})(\pi - \tilde{r}'\tilde{x}) - (\underset{\sim}{\beta} r_3 - \underset{\sim}{\alpha})(1 - \tilde{e}'\tilde{x})]^2 \\ &- [(\underset{\sim}{\gamma} r_3^2 - 2\underset{\sim}{\beta} r_3 + \underset{\sim}{\alpha}) + \sigma_3^2(\underset{\sim}{\alpha}\underset{\sim}{\gamma} - \underset{\sim}{\beta}^2)] \\ &[(\pi - \tilde{r}'\tilde{x})^2 - 2\underset{\sim}{\beta}(\pi - \tilde{r}'\tilde{x}) \cdot (1 - \tilde{e}'\tilde{x}) + \underset{\sim}{\alpha}(1 - \tilde{e}'\tilde{x}) \\ &+ (\underset{\sim}{\alpha}\underset{\sim}{\gamma} - \underset{\sim}{\beta}^2)(\tilde{x}'\tilde{V}\tilde{x} - v)] = 0. \end{aligned} \tag{3.49}$$

If we set $\tilde{x} = 0$, we find in the plane (v, π) the equation of a parabola that coincides (as it must) with the boundary B^n relative to the set of the first three investments.

We shall next analyze Eq. (3.49) and find conditions under which it has, in turn, a unique solution. For that we shall further decompose $\tilde{V}$, $\tilde{x}$, $\tilde{r}$, and $\tilde{e}$ as

$$\tilde{V} = \begin{bmatrix} \sigma_4^2 & 0 \\ 0 & \tilde{\tilde{V}} \end{bmatrix}, \qquad \tilde{r} = \begin{bmatrix} r_4 \\ \tilde{\tilde{r}} \end{bmatrix}, \qquad \tilde{x} = \begin{bmatrix} x_4 \\ \tilde{\tilde{x}} \end{bmatrix}, \qquad \tilde{e} = \begin{bmatrix} 1 \\ \tilde{\tilde{e}} \end{bmatrix}, \tag{3.50}$$

where $\tilde{\tilde{\tilde{V}}}$, $\tilde{\tilde{\tilde{r}}}$, $\tilde{\tilde{\tilde{x}}}$, and $\tilde{\tilde{\tilde{e}}}$ denote an $(n-4) \times (n-4)$ matrix and $(n-4)$ column vectors, respectively. Thus introducing (3.50) into the algebraic equation (3.49), we obtain an algebraic equation of second degree in the unknown x_4, which is formally identical to the equation in x_3 obtained from (3.48). The discriminant equation $\Delta_{x_4} = 0$ will then be formally identical to (3.49) and will again for $\tilde{\tilde{\tilde{x}}} = 0$ define a parabola in the plane (v, π). Hence an iteration of the procedure will always generate a parabola as the locus of points of the plane (v, π) to which there corresponds a unique vector x. Since (2.9) shows that at all points of (2.7), given (v, π), there exists a unique x, we can clearly conclude without actually iterating the procedure that the parabola obtained by iteration of the procedure outlined in this proof and (2.7) must coincide.

EXAMPLES, NOTES, AND REFERENCES

If conditions (3.7) are satisfied for some i, $i = 1, \ldots, n$, it means that the corresponding ith investment is identically zero on the boundary of the region of admissible portfolios. This property of the ith investment with respect to the remaining investments will be further investigated in Chapter 5, where an investment with such a property will be said to be dominated by the other investments.

Note that if instead of condition (3.7), condition (3.5) is satisfied with $\chi_i \neq 0$, then the ith investment will be held in each boundary portfolio in the constant amount χ_i regardless of the value of π.

The nonindifference theorem (Theorem (3.15)) proves that each investor holds all available investments. From this point of view it clearly anticipates the results of the capital asset pricing theory (Chapter 14), and it also shows one of the major practical shortcomings of the model.

Condition (3.19), which must be satisfied in order for $x_i(\pi) = x_j(\pi) = 0$, i.e., for x_i and x_j to vanish at the same boundary point, is satisfied only in pathological cases. In particular, it is rather unlikely for $n > 2$ that an investment belongs to the boundary. In order to quantify this "unlikeliness," consider Eq. (3.19). This equation is linear in r_k, $k = 1, \ldots, n$. Thus given V, if we want to identify r such that one investment belongs to the boundary of the region of admissible portfolios, we must solve a linear system with n unknowns (r_i) and $n - 2$ equations. Indeed, in order to solve this problem, $n - 1$ components of the vector x must identically vanish at the same value of π, leading to $n - 2$ equations of type (3.19). Thus as n increases, the probability that V will be such that the system has no solution also increases.

To illustrate the case, consider for instance the portfolio problem with the data

$$V^{-1} = \begin{bmatrix} 1 & 2 & 0 \\ 2 & 2 & 1 \\ 0 & 1 & 3 \end{bmatrix}, \qquad r = \begin{bmatrix} 2 \\ 1 \\ \frac{2}{3} \end{bmatrix}. \tag{3.51}$$

Indeed, in this case condition (3.19) is satisfied, and we have

$$x_1(\pi) = x_2(\pi) = 0, \tag{3.52}$$

when

$$\pi = \tfrac{2}{3}. \tag{3.53}$$

In this case indeed the solution is acceptable, i.e., the system (3.51) does not belong to the trivial cases (3.20) and (3.21).

It is important to point out that if the variance–covariance matrix V is diagonal, then Eq. (3.19) has a unique solution of a very simple form. Consider for that Eq. (3.18). If V^{-1} is diagonal, it takes the form

$$(V^{-1}e)_i(V^{-1}e)_j r_j = (V^{-1}e)_j(V^{-1}e)_i r_i, \tag{3.54}$$

which has a unique solution

$$r_i = r_j. \tag{3.55}$$

This property may indeed be another point in favor of a diagonalization of the problem through application of a linear transformation (2.61), (2.62), which is also orthonormal (see Theorem (4.83)). Clearly, this transformation will leave B^n unchanged and vary $x(\pi)$ on B^n only.

The problem of finding some meaningful condition that ensures that $x > 0$ is still basically unsolved. An attempt made by Roll (1977) to apply the Debreu–Herstein (1953) theorem on nonnegative matrices led to the statement of a false theorem as shown by Szegö (1978a). It is important to note that the case in which V^{-1} has a dominant diagonal, which is the case in which (see Theorem (3.32)) this problem has an easy solution, is less interesting from the practical point of view since it essentially describes the situation in which the correlation coefficients are so small in absolute value that diversification does not pay and the essential criterion for the choice of investments is their "excess return" r_i^d. Diversification, which implies the convenience of holding in positive amounts investments characterized by negative excess returns r_i^d, is possible (see (3.38)) only if the other elements of the summation are sufficiently large.

It is, however, easy to show that there exist cases ($n > 2$) in which on the boundary B^n there does not exist any arc in which $x > 0$, and it is also possible to construct examples in which there exists on B^n an arc on which $x > 0$, but the minimum variance portfolio is not contained in such an arc.

For instance, the portfolio problem (see Roll, 1977)

$$V = \begin{bmatrix} 2 & 2 & 2 \\ 2 & 5 & 6 \\ 2 & 6 & 10 \end{bmatrix}, \qquad r = \begin{bmatrix} 1 \\ 2 \\ 3 \end{bmatrix} \tag{3.56}$$

does not show any arc on the boundary B^n on which $x > 0$, while the portfolio problem

$$V = \begin{bmatrix} 1 & \frac{1}{2} & 1 \\ \frac{1}{2} & 1 & 1 \\ 1 & 11 & 4 \end{bmatrix}, \qquad r = \begin{bmatrix} 1 \\ 3\frac{1}{2} \\ 2 \end{bmatrix} \tag{3.57}$$

admits a maximal arc on B^n with

$$\tfrac{4}{3} < \pi < \tfrac{11}{7} \tag{3.58}$$

on which $x > 0$; however, the vertex does not belong to this interval.

The iterative proof worked out for Theorem (3.49) substitutes a more compact geometrical proof used in some earlier work by Szegö (1972a). The proof used in this chapter gives some more insight into the degree of multiplicity of the transformation $(v, \pi) \to X$ in the interior of R^n when $n > 2$.

From the technique used in the proof of Theorem (3.41) it also clearly follows that the non-uniqueness of the transformation $(v, \pi) \to X$ in the interior of R^n is not due to the existence of covariance $\rho_{ij} \neq 0$. The nonuniqueness holds even when the returns on all investments are uncorrelated. The fact that on the boundary B^n the transformation $(v, \pi) \to X$ is one-to-one originates a set of special curves within the region B^n, $n \geq 3$, i.e., the parabolas defining the boundaries of the regions of admissible portfolios $B^{n-1}, B^{n-2}, \ldots, B^2$ corresponding to the n sets of $n-1$ investments, to the $n(n-1)$ sets of $n-2$ investments, etc. obtained by successively setting equal to zero the allocation vectors corresponding to each of the n investments, then all components of pairs of the allocation vectors, etc.

It must be pointed out that on those boundaries B^i ($i = n-1, \ldots, 2$) that lie inside the region of admissible portfolios R^n the correspondence $(v, \pi) \to x$ is not one-to-one. This property follows from the proof of Theorem (3.41) and in particular from the fact that we are dealing with quadratic equations in x_i ($i = 1, \ldots, n$).

The structure of this problem can be further investigated by considering the following example:

(3.59) $$V = \begin{bmatrix} 1 & 0 & 0 \\ 0 & 2 & 0 \\ 0 & 0 & 3 \end{bmatrix}, \qquad r = \begin{bmatrix} 1 \\ 2 \\ 3 \end{bmatrix}.$$

The boundary B^3 corresponding to the data (3.59) is defined by the parabola

(3.60) $$v = 3 - 3\pi + 11\pi^2/12.$$

If we next consider the following three reduced problems obtained from (3.59) by sequentially imposing $x_1 = 0$, $x_2 = 0$, and $x_3 = 0$, we have

(3.61) $$V = \begin{bmatrix} 2 & 0 \\ 0 & 3 \end{bmatrix}, \qquad r = \begin{bmatrix} 2 \\ 3 \end{bmatrix},$$

(3.62) $$V = \begin{bmatrix} 1 & 0 \\ 0 & 3 \end{bmatrix}, \qquad r = \begin{bmatrix} 1 \\ 3 \end{bmatrix},$$

(3.63) $$V = \begin{bmatrix} 1 & 0 \\ 0 & 2 \end{bmatrix}, \qquad r = \begin{bmatrix} 1 \\ 2 \end{bmatrix},$$

and the boundaries of the regions of admissible portfolios corresponding to these three sets of two investments have the form

(3.64) $$v = 5\pi^2 - 24\pi + 30,$$

(3.65) $$v = \pi^2 - 3\pi + 3,$$

(3.66) $$v = 3\pi^2 - 8\pi + 6.$$

The relative positions of the B^3 and B^2 (3.60) and (3.64)–(3.66) are shown in Fig. 3.2.

We can, for instance, consider the structure of the portfolio on the straight line $v = 2$ with the data (3.59), i.e., the problem

(3.67) $$2 = x_1^2 + 2x_2^2 + 3x_3^2, \qquad \pi = x_1 + 2x_2 + 3x_3, \qquad 1 = x_1 + x_2 + x_3.$$

If we eliminate x_1 and x_2 from this system (3.67) by introducing the last two equations into the first one, we obtain the quadratic equation

(3.68) $$12x_3^2 + 2x_3[6 - 5\pi] + 3\pi^2 - 8\pi + 4 = 0,$$

which clearly has only two values of π to which the equation has double roots, i.e., the values of π in which the vertical straight line $v = 2$ intersects the boundary B^3 (3.60). Thus even if the straight line $v = 2$ intersects the three subboundaries (3.64)–(3.66), to these intersection points there correspond two values of x_3.

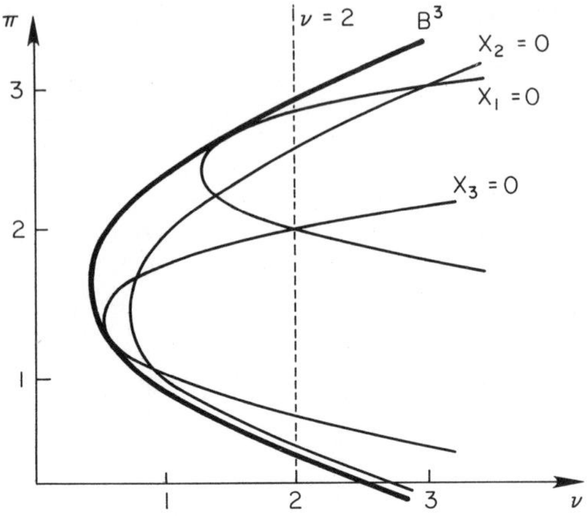

Figure 3.2

The independence of $x^v = V^{-1}e/\gamma$ from r has some deep consequences. Consider, for example, the portfolio problem defined by the data

$$V = \begin{bmatrix} 1 & 0 & 0 \\ 0 & 2 & 0 \\ 0 & 0 & 4 \end{bmatrix}, \qquad r = \begin{bmatrix} 1 \\ 2 \\ 2 \end{bmatrix}. \tag{3.69}$$

One could argue that the investment $I_3\,(v = 4, \pi = 2)$ is totally dominated by the investment $I_2\,(v = 2, \pi = 2)$ and therefore could be taken out from the given set of the three investments. On the other hand, the composition of the minimum variance portfolio of the problem (3.69) is

$$x_1^v = \tfrac{4}{7}, \qquad x_2^v = \tfrac{2}{7}, \qquad x_3^v = \tfrac{1}{7} \tag{3.70}$$

to which the minimum variance

$$v_v = \tfrac{4}{7} = \tfrac{12}{21} \tag{3.71}$$

corresponds.

By deleting the third investment from the original set of three investments and considering the problem defined by the data

$$V = \begin{bmatrix} 1 & 0 \\ 0 & 2 \end{bmatrix}, \qquad r = \begin{bmatrix} 1 \\ 2 \end{bmatrix}, \tag{3.72}$$

we obtain the minimum variance portfolio given by the relationships

$$x_1^v = \tfrac{2}{3}, \qquad x_2^v = \tfrac{1}{2} \tag{3.73}$$

to which the minimum variance

$$v_v = \tfrac{2}{3} = \tfrac{14}{21}, \tag{3.74}$$

which is larger than (3.71), corresponds. Thus the third investment contributes to reducing the variance of the portfolio.

Indeed, it can be proved that each time an uncorrelated investment is added to a set of investments, it will always be present (in a positive amount) in the minimum variance portfolio. Indeed if V_1 is nonsingular and

$$V = \begin{bmatrix} V_1 & \emptyset \\ \emptyset' & v \end{bmatrix} \tag{3.75}$$

then

$$v_v(V_1) = 1/e'V_1^{-1}e \tag{3.76}$$

and

$$v_v(V) = 1/e'V^{-1}e \tag{3.77}$$

which is always smaller than $v_v(V_1)$. Thus if all investors were total risk averters (always using the minimum variance portfolio) and all investments were uncorrelated, then the demand for each investment would coincide with the inverse of its variance regardless of its expected return.

These properties clarify some consequences of using the variance as a risk measure and throw some doubts as to the accuracy of this assumption.

CHAPTER 4

ORTHOGONAL PORTFOLIOS AND COVARIANCE AMONG BOUNDARY PORTFOLIOS

In this chapter we shall investigate the covariance properties among admissible portfolios and in particular consider the properties of orthogonal portfolios, i.e., of admissible portfolios that are uncorrelated.

Most of the results presented will be concerned with the covariance properties among boundary portfolios and between boundary portfolios and the set of n investments. Only at the end of the chapter we shall give some results on covariance properties among general admissible portfolios.

Throughout this chapter it will again be assumed that V is nonsingular and that the expected returns on the n investments are not identical.

Let us start our presentation with the following:

(4.1) **Definition**

Let x^1 and x^2 be two portfolios belonging to the region of admissible portfolios R^n (2.1). The portfolio x^1 will be said to be orthogonal to the portfolio x^2 if the covariance between them is zero, i.e., if

$$\text{cov}(x^1, x^2) = (x^1)'Vx^2 = 0, \tag{4.2}$$

i.e., if the vector x^1 is V-orthogonal to the vector x^2.

(4.3) **Theorem**

Let $x^1 = x(\pi_1)$ and $x^2 = x(\pi_2)$ be two boundary portfolios; then their covariance is given by

$$\text{cov}(x^1, x^2) = \frac{\pi_1\pi_2\gamma - \pi_1\beta - \pi_2\beta + \alpha}{\alpha\gamma - \beta^2}. \tag{4.4}$$

Hence if the portfolios defined by x^1 and x^2 lie either both in the upper or both in the lower part of B^n, their corresponding covariance is positive.

Proof

Let $x^1 = x(\pi_1)$ and $x^2 = x(\pi_2)$ be boundary portfolios, i.e.,

$$x^1 = x(\pi_1) = \frac{(\pi_1\gamma - \beta)V^{-1}r + (\alpha - \pi_1\beta)V^{-1}e}{\alpha\gamma - \beta^2} \tag{4.5}$$

and

$$x^2 = x(\pi_2) = \frac{(\pi_2\gamma - \beta)V^{-1}r + (\alpha - \pi_2\beta)V^{-1}e}{\alpha\gamma - \beta^2}. \tag{4.6}$$

If we consider the covariance between x^1 and x^2 as defined by (4.2), after some computations we obtain

$$\operatorname{cov}(x^1, x^2) = (x^1)'Vx^2 = \frac{\pi_1\pi_2\gamma - \pi_1\beta - \pi_2\beta + \alpha}{\alpha\gamma - \beta^2}. \tag{4.7}$$

To prove the second part of the theorem, assume for instance that

$$\pi_1 > \beta/\gamma \tag{4.8}$$

and

$$\pi_2 > \beta/\gamma, \tag{4.9}$$

i.e., that the boundary portfolios defined by $x(\pi_1)$ and $x(\pi_2)$ both lie in the upper part of B^n, and in addition assume that

$$\pi_1 > \pi_2 > \beta/\gamma \tag{4.10}$$

and define the new variable δ as

$$\pi_1 - \pi_2 = \delta > 0. \tag{4.11}$$

Thus dropping the index from π_2, we have

$$\pi_1 = \pi_2 + \delta = \pi + \delta \tag{4.12}$$

and from (4.10)

$$\pi > \beta/\gamma. \tag{4.13}$$

If we substitute (4.12) into relationship (4.7), we obtain

$$\operatorname{cov}(x^1, x^2) = \frac{\gamma\pi^2 - 2\beta\pi + \alpha + \pi\delta\gamma - \beta\delta}{\alpha\gamma - \beta^2}. \tag{4.14}$$

Introducing the expression for B^n (2.7) into (4.13), we obtain

(4.15) $$\operatorname{cov}(x^1, x^2) = v(\pi) + \frac{\delta(\pi - \beta/\gamma)}{\gamma(\alpha\gamma - \beta^2)}.$$

Because of the sign conditions (4.11), (4.13), and (2.22), we have from (4.15)

(4.16) $$\operatorname{cov}(x^1, x^2) > v > 0.$$

The same proof can be carried out for the case in which instead of (4.8) and (4.9) we have

(4.17) $$\pi_1 < \beta/\gamma \qquad \text{and} \qquad \pi_2 < \beta/\gamma,$$

for which it can be proved that inequality (4.16) still holds.

For the particular case in which one of the two portfolios $x(\pi_1)$, $x(\pi_2)$ considered in Eq. (4.4) is the minimum variance portfolio, we have the following important result:

(4.18) **Corollary**

The covariance between each portfolio $x(\pi) \in \mathscr{X}^n$ and the minimum variance portfolio x^v is constant and in particular

(4.19) $$\operatorname{cov}(x^v, x(\pi)) = 1/\gamma.$$

Proof

By definition

(4.20) $$\operatorname{cov}(x^v, x(\pi)) = (x^v)' V x(\pi)$$

Substituting Eqs. (2.5) and (2.29) into Eq. (4.20) we obtain (4.19).

(4.21) **Remarks**

Expression (4.4) implies that in order for two boundary portfolios to be negatively correlated, they must lie on different parts of the boundary B^n and in addition be sufficiently far apart. Theorem (4.53) will further analyze the problem of negatively correlated boundary portfolios. Clearly, the problem of negatively correlated boundary portfolios can be solved by considering first the case of two portfolios x^1 and x^2 such that

(4.22) $$\operatorname{cov}(x^1, x^2) = 0,$$

i.e., the case in which x^1 is orthogonal to x^2. If we consider expression (4.14), we notice that it is linear in δ; thus at the point δ such that (4.22) holds, $\operatorname{cov}(x^1, x^2)$ changes its sign.

Before further analyzing the problem of the covariance between boundary portfolios, we shall first conclude the discussion on orthogonal portfolios.

(4.23) **Theorem**

To each boundary portfolio $x(\pi) \in \mathscr{X}^n$, $x(\pi) \neq x^v$, there corresponds a unique orthogonal boundary portfolio $x(\pi_0)$ with

$$\pi_0 = \frac{\pi\beta - \alpha}{\pi\gamma - \beta} \tag{4.24}$$

and

$$x(\pi_0) = \frac{\pi V^{-1}e - V^{-1}r}{\pi\gamma - \beta}. \tag{4.25}$$

Proof

From (4.4) we deduce that the orthogonality condition between $x(\pi)$ and $x(\pi_0)$ has the form

$$\pi\pi_0\gamma - \pi\beta - \pi_0\beta + \alpha = 0. \tag{4.26}$$

Thus if

$$\pi \neq \beta/\gamma, \tag{4.27}$$

i.e., $x(\pi) \neq x^v$, the expected return on the portfolio that is orthogonal to $x(\pi)$ takes the form (4.24). If in expression (2.9) we let $\pi = \pi_0$ (4.24), after some computation we obtain expression (4.25).

If again we perform transformations (4.11), (4.12), and instead of the orthogonality condition (4.26) we deduce from (4.14) the orthogonality condition

$$\pi^2 - 2\beta\pi + \delta + \pi\delta\gamma - \beta\delta + \alpha = 0, \tag{4.28}$$

we obtain

(4.29) **Corollary**

The difference $\delta = \pi - \pi_0$ between the expected returns on two orthogonal portfolios is given by

$$\delta = \frac{\gamma\pi^2 - 2\pi\beta + \alpha}{\beta - \pi\gamma} = \frac{\gamma v(\alpha\gamma - \beta^2)}{(\beta/\gamma) - \pi}. \tag{4.30}$$

Again from Theorems (4.3) and (4.23) there immediately follows

(4.31) **Corollary**

Assume that $x = x(\pi)$ is V-orthogonal to $x = x(\pi_0)$. If $\pi < \beta/\gamma$, then $\pi_0 > \beta/\gamma$, while if $\pi > \beta/\gamma$, then $\pi_0 < \beta/\gamma$.

Proof

If the statement were false, then if $\pi > \beta/\gamma$, it would follow from (4.24) that

$$\frac{\pi\beta - \alpha}{\pi\gamma - \beta} > \frac{\beta}{\gamma}. \tag{4.32}$$

Since $\gamma > 0$ and $\pi\gamma - \beta > 0$, from (4.32) it follows that

$$\gamma(\pi\beta - \alpha) > \beta(\pi\gamma - \beta), \tag{4.33}$$

which implies

$$\alpha\gamma - \beta^2 < 0, \tag{4.34}$$

which contradicts (2.22) and proves the statement.

We shall next prove two theorems that allow an immediate graphical construction of the boundary portfolio orthogonal to any given boundary portfolio.

(4.35) **Theorem**

The return π_2 on the boundary portfolio orthogonal to the boundary portfolio $x(\pi_1)$ in the plane (v, π) is the ordinate of the intercept of the axis $v = 0$ with the straight line joining the point (v_1, π_1) on B^n with (v_v, π_v), while in the plane (σ, π) it is the ordinate of the intercept of the axis $\sigma = 0$ with the straight line that is tangent to B^n at the point $\pi = \pi_1$.

Proof

To prove the first statement consider the equation of the straight line joining (v_1, π_1) with (v_v, π_v):

$$\frac{v - v_1}{v_v - v_1} = \frac{\pi - \pi_1}{\pi_v - \pi_1}. \tag{4.36}$$

Its intercept with the axis $v = 0$ has the ordinate

$$\pi = \frac{\pi_1 v_v - \pi_v v_1}{v_v - v_1}. \tag{4.37}$$

Using (2.7) to compute the value v_1 and substituting the expression $v_v = 1/\gamma$, Eq. (4.37) becomes

$$\pi = \frac{\pi_1\beta - \alpha}{\pi_1\gamma - \beta}, \tag{4.38}$$

which coincides with (4.24).

To prove the second statement, consider the boundary B^n in the plane (σ, π) (2.8) and compute the equation of the tangent at the point $\pi = \pi_1$:

$$\sigma = \frac{\beta\pi_1 - \alpha - \pi(\gamma\pi_1 - \beta)}{[(\alpha\gamma - \beta^2)(\gamma\pi_1^2 - 2\beta\pi_1 + \alpha)]^{1/2}}. \tag{4.39}$$

From this expression, if we let $\sigma = 0$, we find the value of the ordinate of the intercept between (4.39) and the axis $\sigma = 0$. It can immediately be seen that this value is given by expression (4.38).

The two graphical procedures for orthogonal portfolios developed in Theorem (4.35) are shown in Fig. 4.1, parts a and b, respectively.

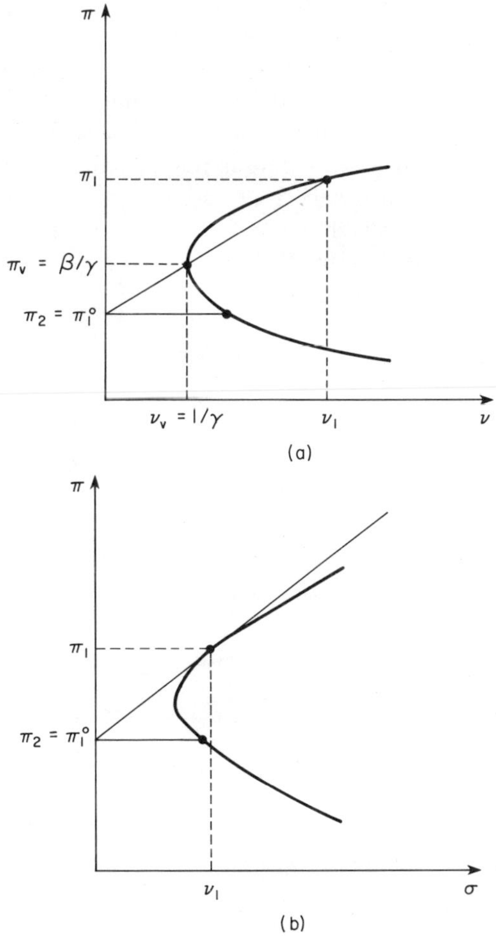

Figure 4.1

(4.40) **Remark**

It is easy to check that the two boundary portfolios x^r and x^z defined by (2.32) and (2.33), respectively, are orthogonal. Indeed, from (4.24) we have that the expected return on the boundary portfolio that is orthogonal to the boundary portfolio $\pi = 0$ (i.e., (2.33)) has the form

(4.41) $$\pi_0 = \alpha/\beta,$$

which coincides with (2.32).

(4.42) **Remark**

The graphical procedures developed in Theorem (4.33) suggest a very simple way of visualizing on B^n arcs of mutually orthogonal portfolios. Indeed, it can immediately be shown (see Fig. 4.2) that the points on the arc-segment S with one extremal on the vertex of parabola (2.7) and the other at point P are orthogonal to the points on the infinite arc A of parabola (2.7) with one extremal at point Q, or in other words, if the boundary portfolio $x(\pi)$ is such that the corresponding point $(v, \pi) \in S$, then its orthogonal boundary portfolio $x(\pi_0)$ is such that its corresponding point $(v_0, \pi_0) \in A$.

Taking the limit, we have that as $\pi \to \beta/\gamma$, $\pi_0 \to -\infty$ along A. This limit property suggests a complete investigation of the properties of the correlation coefficient of orthogonal portfolios.

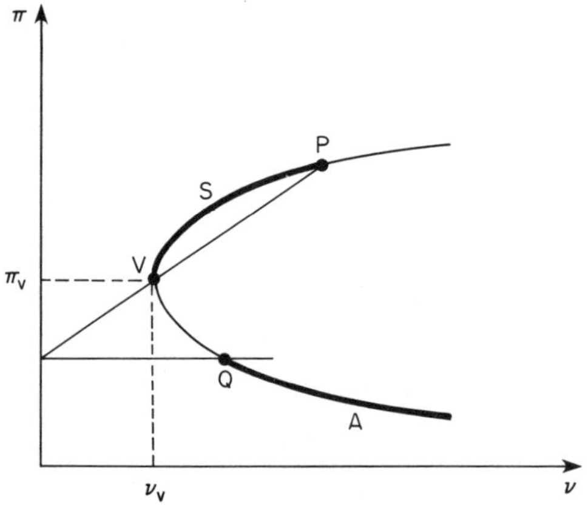

Figure 4.2

(4.43) **Theorem**

Let $x^1 = x(\pi_1)$ and $x^2 = x(\pi_2)$ be boundary portfolios. Then their correlation coefficient $\rho(\pi_1, \pi_2)$ is given by

(4.44) $$\rho(\pi_1, \pi_2) = \frac{\operatorname{cov}(x^1, x^2)}{\sigma(\pi_1)\sigma(\pi_2)} = \frac{\pi_1\pi_2\gamma - \pi_1\beta - \pi_2\beta + \alpha}{[(\gamma\pi_1^2 - 2\beta\pi_1 + \alpha)(\gamma\pi_2^2 - 2\beta\pi_2 + \alpha)]^{1/2}}.$$

Thus there does not exist any pair of perfectly negatively correlated boundary portfolios while the following asymptotic behavior holds:

$$\lim_{\pi_1 \to +\infty} \lim_{\pi_2 \to -\infty} \rho(\pi_1, \pi_2) = -1 \tag{4.45}$$

and

$$\lim_{\pi_1 \to +\infty} \lim_{\pi_2 \to \beta/\gamma} \rho(\pi_1, \pi_2) = \lim_{\pi_1 \to -\infty} \lim_{\pi_2 \to \beta/\gamma} \rho(\pi_1, \pi_2) = 0. \tag{4.46}$$

Proof

Relationship (4.44) can easily be obtained from expression (4.4), defining the covariance between two boundary portfolios and hyperbola (2.8) that defines the boundary $\sigma(\pi)$. If we let $\rho(\pi_1, \pi_2) = \pm 1$ in (4.44), we obtain the equation

$$(\pi_1 \pi_2 \gamma - \pi_1 \beta - \pi_2 \beta + \alpha)^2 = (\gamma \pi_1^2 - 2\beta \pi_1 + \alpha)(\gamma \pi_2^2 - 2\beta \pi_2 + \alpha), \tag{4.47}$$

which after some computation reduces to

$$(\pi_1 - \pi_2)^2 = 0, \tag{4.48}$$

which has a unique solution

$$\pi_1 = \pi_2 \tag{4.49}$$

to which there corresponds a correlation coefficient $\rho(\pi_1, \pi_1) = 1$. Thus no pair of boundary portfolios π_1, π_2 can be found such that $\rho(\pi_1, \pi_2) = -1$. Consider next expression (4.44) in which one of the portfolios, π_1, is kept fixed. After some computation we have

$$\lim_{\pi_2 \to -\infty} \rho(\pi_1, \pi_2) = -\frac{\pi_1 - (\beta/\gamma)}{(\gamma \pi_1^2 - 2\beta \pi_1 + \alpha)^{1/2}/\sqrt{\gamma}}. \tag{4.50}$$

Thus

$$\lim_{\pi_2 \to -\infty} \rho(\pi_1, \pi_2) > 0 \qquad \text{if} \quad \pi_1 < \beta/\gamma \tag{4.51}$$

and

$$\lim_{\pi_2 \to -\infty} \rho(\pi_1, \pi_2) < 0 \qquad \text{if} \quad \pi_1 > \beta/\gamma. \tag{4.52}$$

Finally from (4.50), taking also the $\lim_{\pi_1 \to +\infty}$, we obtain the asymptotic relation (4.45), while taking the $\lim_{\pi_2 \to \beta/\gamma}$, we have the asymptotic relation (4.46), which shows that the minimum variance portfolio is orthogonal to both "asymptotic" boundary portfolios $\pi_1 \to +\infty$ and $\pi_1 \to -\infty$.

The fact that only the asymptotic boundary portfolios are perfectly negatively correlated and that boundary portfolios lying on different branches of the boundary B^n and "sufficiently apart" are negatively correlated (see Remark (4.21)) suggests investigating the properties of the correlation coefficient of boundary portfolios characterized by the same value of the variance v. Thus

(4.53) **Theorem**

Let $x^1(v) = x(\pi_1(v))$ and $x^2(v) = x(\pi_2(v))$, $\pi_1(v) \neq \pi_2(v)$, be the two boundary portfolios characterized by the same value of v, where $(v, \pi_1(v))$ and $(v, \pi_2(v))$ denote the points on the opposite branches of parabola (2.7) corresponding to the same value of v. Then

(4.54) $$\rho(x^1(v), x^2(v)) = -1 + (2/\gamma v).$$

Proof

From the symmetry of $\pi_1(v)$ and $\pi_2(v)$ with respect to the vertex $\pi = \beta/\gamma$ of parabola (2.7) (see Fig. 4.3) we have

(4.55) $$(\beta/\gamma) - \pi_2 = \pi_1 - (\beta/\gamma),$$

from which

(4.56) $$\pi_2 = (2\beta/\gamma) - \pi_1.$$

Introducing (4.56) into (4.44), after some computation we obtain the expression

(4.57) $$\mathrm{cov}(x^1(\pi), x^2(\pi)) = -v + (2/\gamma),$$

from which

(4.58) $$\rho(x^1(v), x^2(v)) = -1 + (2/\gamma v).$$

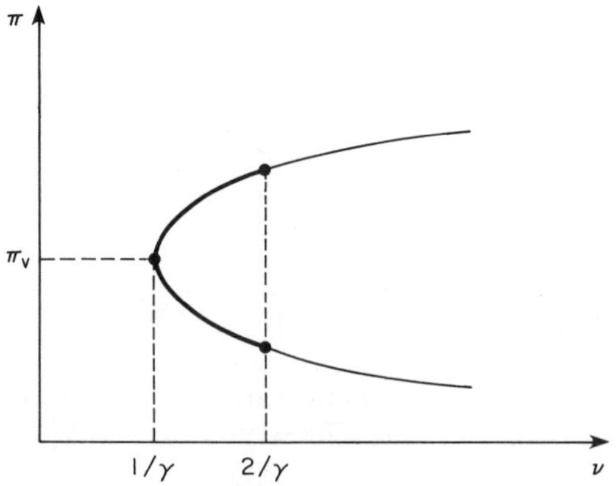

Figure 4.3

(4.59) **Remarks**

The behavior of $\rho(x^1(v), x^2(v))$ as a function of v is described as follows:

$$
\begin{aligned}
\rho(x^1(v), x^2(v)) &= 1 && \text{for} \quad v = 1/\gamma, \\
0 < \rho(x^1(v), x^2(v)) &< 1 && \text{for} \quad 1/\gamma < v < 2/\gamma, \\
\rho(x^1(v), x^2(v)) &= 0 && \text{for} \quad v = 2/\gamma, \\
\rho(x^1(v), x^2(v)) &< 0 && \text{for} \quad v > 2/\gamma, \\
\rho(x^1(v), x^2(v)) &\to -1 && \text{for} \quad v \to +\infty.
\end{aligned} \tag{4.60}
$$

In Fig. 4.3 we have, represented by a heavy line, the arc of the parabola, where the correlation coefficient among boundary portfolios with identical variance is positive. The two boundary portfolios corresponding to the value

$$v = 2/\gamma \tag{4.61}$$

are orthogonal.

The behavior of $\rho(x^1(v), x^2(v))$ as a function of v is shown in Fig. 4.4. The dotted part corresponds to the range $v < 1/\gamma$ in which ρ_{12} is not defined. The value of $\pi_1(v), \pi_2(v)$ corresponding to the value of $v = 2/\gamma$ that leads to the orthogonal portfolios are

$$\pi_{1,2} = \frac{\beta \pm \sqrt{\alpha\gamma - \beta^2}}{\gamma}. \tag{4.62}$$

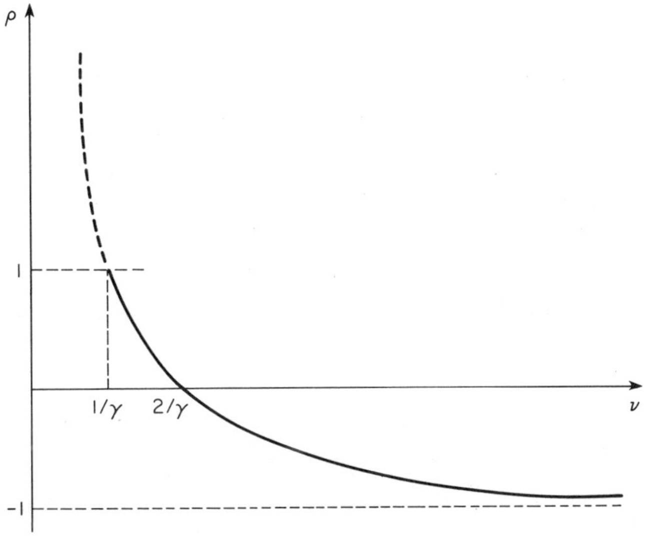

Figure 4.4

It is of interest to compute the corresponding portfolios. For that by introducing (4.62) into (2.30), we obtain

(4.63)
$$x^{1,2} = x^v \pm \frac{(V^{-1}r - (\beta/\gamma)V^{-1}e)}{\sqrt{\alpha\gamma - \beta^2}} = \frac{\pm\gamma V^{-1}r + (\alpha\gamma - \beta^2 \mp \beta)V^{-1}e}{\gamma\sqrt{\alpha\gamma - \beta^2}},$$

while in general if we let $v = \chi/\gamma$, we have

(4.64)
$$\pi_{1,2} = \frac{\beta \pm \sqrt{(\chi - 1)(\alpha\gamma - \beta^2)}}{\gamma},$$

and the corresponding values of x^1 and x^2 are

(4.65)
$$x^{1,2} = x^v \pm \sqrt{\frac{\chi - 1}{\alpha\gamma - \beta^2}}\left(V^{-1}r - \frac{\beta}{\gamma}V^{-1}e\right).$$

Let us next investigate the covariance properties, which are given by relationship (2.25), between boundary portfolios and the set of n investments. The following result can be proved:

(4.66) **Theorem**

A necessary and sufficient condition for an allocation vector x, $e'x = 1$, to belong to the boundary of the region of admissible portfolios $\mathscr{X}^n$ is that its covariance with respect to the set of n investments be a linear function of the expected return vector r.

Proof

We shall first prove necessity. For this let x^i, with

(4.67)
$$e'x^i = 1,$$

be an arbitrary admissible portfolio. Assume that its covariance with respect to the n investments has the form

(4.68)
$$Vx^i = a_i r + b_i e.$$

It must then be proved that $x^i \in \mathscr{X}^n$. For that, from (4.68) since V is nonsingular, we have

(4.69)
$$x^i = a_i V^{-1}r + b_i V^{-1}e = a_i\beta\frac{V^{-1}r}{\beta} + b_i\gamma\frac{V^{-1}e}{\gamma}.$$

Now from (2.29) and (4.25) we have that

(4.70) $$x^v = \frac{V^{-1}e}{\gamma} \quad \text{and} \quad x^r = \frac{V^{-1}r}{\beta}$$

are both boundary portfolio corresponding to the vertex and to the boundary portfolios orthogonal to $\pi = 0$, respectively. In addition,

(4.71) $$1 = e'x^i = a_i e'V^{-1}r + b_i e'V^{-1}e = a_i\beta + b_i\gamma.$$

Thus from Theorem (2.64) it follows that since x^i is represented as a convex linear combination (4.69) of two boundary portfolios it is a boundary portfolio. To prove sufficiency, it is enough to consider expression (2.25), which defines the covariance of any boundary portfolio $x(\pi)$ with respect to the set of n investments, i.e., the expression

(4.72) $$Vx(\pi) = \frac{(\pi\gamma - \beta)r + (\alpha - \pi\beta)e}{\alpha\gamma - \beta^2}.$$

Thus if $x(\pi)$ is a boundary portfolio, its covariance is a linear function of r.

(4.73) **Remark**

The linearity in r of any boundary portfolio, which has been proved in Theorem (4.66), suggests finding the vector r that satisfies Eq. (4.72) as a function of $x(\pi)$, π, and of the the expected return on the portfolio orthogonal to $x(\pi)$, π_0 (4.24). After some computation we obtain from (4.72)

(4.74) $$Vx(\pi) = \frac{v(\pi)}{\pi - \pi_0}(r - \pi_0 e),$$

from which we obtain

(4.75) $$r = \pi_0 e + (\pi - \pi_0)\frac{Vx(\pi)}{v(\pi)}$$

and

(4.76) $$x(\pi) = \frac{v(\pi)}{\pi - \pi_0} V^{-1}(r - \pi_0 e),$$

which provides yet another representation of $x(\pi)$. Relationship (4.75) will be very useful in a later chapter.

So far we have devoted ourselves to the covariance properties among boundary portfolios. We shall conclude this chapter with some remarks on the existence and properties of orthogonal admissible portfolios that may not necessarily belong to the boundary. On this subject it is important that we first make some clarifying comments on Theorem (4.23).

(4.77) **Remark**

Note that Theorem (4.23) proves only that to one boundary portfolio there corresponds a unique orthogonal boundary portfolio. Clearly, in general the set of portfolios that are orthogonal to a given boundary portfolio contains an infinite number of elements one and only one of which is a boundary portfolio. Consider for instance the boundary portfolio (2.32):

(4.78) $$x^r = V^{-1}r/\beta.$$

The admissible portfolios x^0 that are orthogonal to (4.78) are given by the relationships

(4.79) $$(x^0)'Vx^r = (x^0)'VV^{-1}r/\beta = 0$$

and

(4.80) $$e'x^0 = 1.$$

From Eq. (4.79) we obtain the simple relationship

(4.81) $$r'x^0 = 0.$$

All vectors x^0 that satisfy Eqs. (4.80) and (4.81) define admissible portfolios that are orthogonal to x^r. Clearly, if $n > 2$, in general Eqs. (4.80) and (4.81) provide a nonunique solution vector x.

An orthogonal set of n linearly independent admissible portfolios may provide a very useful basis for the representation of the region of admissible portfolios in the sense of Theorem (2.47). As shown in Appendix D, such an orthogonal set of linearly independent admissible vectors x^i $(i = 1, \ldots, n)$ (a basis) can always be found. In this case the transformed region of admissible portfolios (2.51)

(4.82) $$v = y'K'VKy = y'\bar{V}y, \qquad \pi = r'Ky, \qquad 1 = e'Ky$$

with

(4.83) $$k_{ij} = x^i_j$$

has some peculiar properties. In particular,

(4.84) **Theorem**

Consider a set of n linearly independent V-orthogonal admissible allocation vectors x^i $(i = 1, \ldots, n)$. Then the variance–covariance matrix $\bar{V} = K'VK$ of the transformed system (4.82) is diagonal.

Proof

The V-orthogonality condition of the vectors x^i implies

(4.85) $$(x^i)'Vx^j = 0 \qquad \text{for all} \quad i \neq j, \quad i,j = 1, \ldots, n.$$

Thus from (4.81) and (4.82) we have

(4.86) $$\bar{v}_{ij} = \begin{cases} (x^i)'Vx^i & i = j, \quad i,j = 1, \ldots, n, \\ 0 & i \neq j, \quad i,j = 1, \ldots, n, \end{cases}$$

which proves that $\bar{V}$ is diagonal.

From this result it follows that all previous results (3.26) and (3.32) that are concerned with the case in which V is diagonal apply to the transformed system when the basis is V-orthogonal. Thus

(4.87) **Corollary**

Under the conditions of Theorem (4.84), the transformed system is such that

(4.88) $$y^v = \frac{\bar{V}^{-1}e}{\gamma} > 0$$

and

(4.89) $$y_i^d(\pi_d) = \frac{\pi_d}{v(\pi_v)} \frac{r_i^d}{\sigma_i^2} \qquad i = 1, \ldots, n.$$

The results presented in Remark (4.73) can be expressed in a much more compact and useful form as shown in the following theorem.

(4.90) **Theorem**

The risk premium of all investments relative to an admissible portfolio $x(\pi)$ is a constant, i.e.,

(4.91) $$\frac{r_i - \pi_0}{\sigma_{i,x(\pi)}} = \frac{\pi - \pi_0}{v(\pi)} = \text{const} \qquad \text{for all} \quad i = 1, \ldots, n,$$

where π_0 is again the return on the boundary portfolio orthogonal to $x(\pi)$, and $\sigma_{i,x(\pi)}$ is the covariance between the ith investment and $x(\pi)$.

Proof

From (4.24) and (4.25) after some computations we obtain, respectively,

(4.92) $$v(\pi) = \frac{\pi - \pi_0}{\beta - \gamma\pi_0}$$

and

$$x(\pi) = \frac{V^{-1}(r - \pi_0 e)}{\beta - \gamma\pi_0}. \tag{4.93}$$

From (4.93) we have

$$(Vx(\pi))_i = \sigma_{i,x(\pi)} = \frac{r_i - \pi_0}{\beta - \gamma\pi_0}. \tag{4.94}$$

Eliminating $(\beta - \gamma\pi_0)$ from (4.94) and (4.92), we obtain

$$r_i - \pi = \frac{\sigma_{i,x(\pi)}(\pi - \pi_0)}{v(\pi)}, \tag{4.95}$$

from which (4.91) follows.

Equations (4.91) and (4.95) will be used in Chapter 14.

NOTES AND REFERENCES

The aim of the investigation performed in this chapter was to clarify the extent of the reduction of risk induced by diversification.

In particular, some asymptotic relationships have been established (see for instance (4.60)). The main result of Theorem (4.43) is of a negative nature; indeed, this theorem shows that there does not exist any boundary portfolio to which all boundary portfolios are perfectly linearly correlated.

The asymptotic expression (4.45) shows another consequence of diversification. Indeed, no matter what the original properties of the matrix V and in particular of the correlation coefficients ρ_{ij} may be, diversification has an important effect on the correlation coefficients of boundary portfolios by ensuring that there will always exist some boundary portfolios x^i, x^j that are connected by a negative correlation coefficient $\rho(x^j, x^j)$.

Some of the results presented in this chapter are contained in a paper by Roll (1977).

CHAPTER 5

ENLARGING THE SET OF INVESTMENTS: PROPERTIES OF EQUIVALENCE AND DOMINANCE

This chapter, as well as the next four chapters, will be devoted to the study of the different situations that may occur when we add an $(n + 1)$th investment to a set of n investments which satisfy the conditions on V and r that are assumed to be satisfied in Chapters 2–4. For the reader's convenience we recall that this implies that the variance-covariance matrix V and the expected return vector r, relative to the set of the first n investments, are such that rank $V = n$ and that the expected returns r_i $(i = 1, \ldots, n)$, relative to the n investments, are not the same for all i, $i = 1, \ldots, n$.

The results presented in this chapter, as well as in Chapters 6–9, can easily be generalized to the case in which we add m new investments to the original set of n investments as well as to the case in which the original set of n investments is either such that condition (2.10) is not satisfied by all investments or such that V is singular.

Throughout this chapter we shall denote by $\tilde{V}$, $\tilde{x}$, $\tilde{r}$, and $\tilde{e}$, respectively, the $(n + 1) \times (n + 1)$ variance–covariance matrix, the $(n + 1)$-dimensional expected return vector, and the $(n + 1)$-dimensional unit vector associated with the augmented set of $n + 1$ investments.

For simplicity, we shall introduce the following simplified notation:

$$(5.1)\qquad \tilde{V} = \begin{bmatrix} V & b \\ b' & \varepsilon \end{bmatrix}, \qquad \tilde{r} = \begin{bmatrix} r \\ \rho \end{bmatrix}, \qquad \tilde{e} = \begin{bmatrix} e \\ 1 \end{bmatrix}, \qquad \tilde{x} = \begin{bmatrix} x \\ \tilde{x}_{n+1} \end{bmatrix},$$

where

$$(5.2)\qquad b_i = \sigma_i \sigma_{n+1} \rho_{i,n+1}, \qquad \varepsilon = \sigma_{n+1}^2, \qquad \rho = \tilde{r}_{n+1}.$$

When the $(n + 1)$th investment is added to the original set of n investments, we are led to consider an augmented region of admissible portfolios described by the system

$$v = \tilde{x}'\tilde{V}\tilde{x}, \qquad \pi = \tilde{x}'\tilde{r}, \qquad 1 = \tilde{x}'\tilde{e}. \tag{5.3}$$

Of the crucial conditions derived in Chapter 2, i.e., the nonsingularity of the variance–covariance matrix and condition (2.6), only (2.6), if satisfied by the set of n investments, will be automatically satisfied by the augmented set of $n + 1$ investments. According to which of the other two conditions are satisfied, the following four different significant situations may arise:

(5.4) the augmented set of $n + 1$ investments satisfies all regularity conditions, i.e., $\tilde{V}$ is nonsingular, and the $(n + 1)$th investment does not satisfy Eq. (3.7);

(5.5) the augmented set of $n + 1$ investments is such that $\tilde{V}$ is nonsingular while the $(n + 1)$th investment satisfies Eq. (3.7);

(5.6) the $(n + 1)$th investment does not satisfy Eq. (3.7), but it is such that $\sigma_{n+1} = 0$; thus the variance–covariance matrix relative to the augmented set of $n + 1$ investments $\tilde{V}$ is singular;

(5.7) the $(n + 1)$th investment does not satisfy Eq. (3.7), $\sigma_{n+1} \neq 0$, but the variance–covariance matrix relative to the augmented set of $n + 1$ investments $\tilde{V}$ is singular.

Let us start our analysis with the first case listed (5.4). All results derived in Chapters 2, 3, and 4 relative to the set of n investments apply to the augmented set of $n + 1$ investments. Since $\tilde{V}$ is nonsingular, we can introduce the scalars

$$\tilde{\alpha} = \tilde{r}'\tilde{V}^{-1}\tilde{r}, \qquad \tilde{\beta} = \tilde{r}'\tilde{V}^{-1}\tilde{e}, \qquad \tilde{\gamma} = \tilde{e}'\tilde{V}^{-1}\tilde{e}. \tag{5.8}$$

All results of the previous chapter can be applied to this case by formally replacing α, β, and γ with $\tilde{\alpha}$, $\tilde{\beta}$, and $\tilde{\gamma}$. In particular, the nonindifference Theorem (3.15) applies.

Thus if the $(n + 1)$th investment does not satisfy Eq. (3.7), which in this case takes the form

$$(\tilde{V}^{-1}\tilde{r})_{n+1} = (\tilde{V}^{-1}\tilde{e})_{n+1} = 0 \tag{5.9}$$

then the $(n + 1)$th investment will be held in each boundary portfolio with the possible exception of the boundary portfolio corresponding to the value $\pi = \pi_{n+1}$ (3.14). On the other hand, if

$$(\tilde{V}^{-1}\tilde{r})_{n+1} = (\tilde{V}^{-1}\tilde{e})_{n+1} = 0 \tag{5.10}$$

(see (3.5)), then the $(n + 1)$th investment will not be present in any boundary portfolio.

Because of theorem (3.41) on the uniqueness properties of the vector $\tilde{x}(\pi)$, it must follow that in case (5.4), $R^n \subset R^{n+1}$ and that B^{n+1} may have at the most one point in common with B^n, the point corresponding to the value $\pi = \pi_{n+1}$ (3.14), provided of course that equality (5.10) does not hold.

Consider next the second alternative (5.5). Now the $(n+1)$th investment satisfies Eq. (5.9). Thus from Theorem (3.12) we have

(5.11) $$x_i(\pi) = 0 \qquad -\infty < \pi < +\infty, i = 1, \ldots, n.$$

We shall devote the rest of this chapter to the study of this case while the other cases (5.6) and (5.7) will be the subject of the next three chapters.

We shall begin our analysis from the following;

(5.12) **Definition**

The $(n+1)$th investment is said to be dominated by the set of n investments if

$$\tilde{x}_{n+1}(\pi) = 0 \qquad -\infty < \pi < +\infty.$$

(5.13) **Definition**

The original set of n investments is said to be *equivalent* to the augmented set of $n+1$ investments if $B^n = B^{n+1}$.

On these problems the following main theorem can be proved:

(5.14) **Theorem**

The following four statements are equivalent:

(5.15) the $(n+1)$th investment is dominated by the n investments;

(5.16) the set of n investments is equivalent to the set of $n+1$ investments;

(5.17) the first n components of $\tilde{x}$ are equal to the n components of x;

(5.18) $\rho = r'V^{-1}b$ and $1 = e'V^{-1}b$.

Proof

The proof of this theorem is based on the following formulas for computing the inverse of $\tilde{V}$ as a function of V^{-1}, the detailed proof of which is given in Appendix E:

(5.19) $$\tilde{V}^{-1} = \begin{bmatrix} W & c \\ c' & \delta \end{bmatrix},$$

where

$$W = V^{-1} + V^{-1}bb'V^{-1}/D, \tag{5.20}$$

$$c = -V^{-1}b/D, \tag{5.21}$$

$$\delta = 1/D, \tag{5.22}$$

in which

$$D = \det \tilde{V}/\det V = \varepsilon - b'V^{-1}b. \tag{5.23}$$

In (5.20)–(5.23) we assume that partition (5.1) holds. We shall begin the proof of the theorem by recalling that condition (5.9) is a necessary and sufficient condition for (5.15) to be true, and it is therefore equivalent to the occurrence of (5.15).

As a first step, we shall prove that (5.15) is equivalent to (5.18). Indeed, from (5.10) using formulas (5.19)–(5.23) and after some algebraic manipulation, we derive conditions (5.18).

We shall next prove that (5.18) implies (5.16), i.e., that $B^{n+1} = B^n$. We shall first prove that $B^{n+1} = B^n$ if and only if

$$\tilde{\alpha} = \alpha, \qquad \tilde{\beta} = \beta, \qquad \tilde{\gamma} = \gamma. \tag{5.24}$$

Indeed, by comparing the equations of parabolas (2.7) in the case of n investments as well as in the augmented case of $n + 1$ investments, we have $B^{n+1} = B^n$ if and only if the following three equations are satisfied:

$$\tilde{\alpha}/(\tilde{\alpha}\tilde{\gamma} - \tilde{\beta}^2) = \alpha/(\alpha\gamma - \beta^2), \tag{5.25}$$

$$\tilde{\beta}/(\tilde{\alpha}\tilde{\gamma} - \tilde{\beta}^2) = \beta/(\alpha\gamma - \beta^2), \tag{5.26}$$

$$\tilde{\gamma}/(\tilde{\alpha}\tilde{\gamma} - \tilde{\beta}^2) = \gamma/(\alpha\gamma - \beta^2). \tag{5.27}$$

We shall consider the three relationships (5.25)–(5.27) as a system of nonlinear algebraic equations in which $\tilde{\alpha}, \tilde{\beta}$, and $\tilde{\gamma}$ are given and α, β, and γ are unknown.

It is immediately seen by means of some simple algebraic computation that system (5.25)–(5.27) has a unique solution (5.24).

Using again formulas (5.19)–(5.23), we can express $\tilde{\alpha}, \tilde{\beta}$, and $\tilde{\gamma}$ as functions of α, β, γ, and of the elements of partitions (5.1) as follows:

$$\tilde{\alpha} = \alpha + \{(r'V^{-1}b)^2 - 2r'V^{-1}b + \rho^2\}/D, \tag{5.28}$$

$$\tilde{\beta} = \beta + \{(r'V^{-1}b - \rho)(e'V^{-1}b - 1)\}/D, \tag{5.29}$$

$$\tilde{\gamma} = \gamma + \{(e'V^{-1}b)^2 - 2e'V^{-1}b + 1\}/D. \tag{5.30}$$

If we substitute into (5.28)–(5.30) conditions (5.18), we obtain (5.24), which proves that (5.18) implies (5.16). In order to prove the inverse statement, i.e., that equivalence implies condition (5.18), we notice that for (5.24) to hold, from (5.28)–(5.30) it must follow that

$$(r'V^{-1}b - \rho)^2 = 0 \tag{5.31}$$

and

$$(e'V^{-1}b - 1)^2 = 0, \tag{5.32}$$

which imply (5.18).

Finally, in order to prove that conditions (5.18) imply the identity (5.17), we consider the expression that gives the allocation vector $\tilde{x}$ on B^{n-1}:

$$\tilde{x}' = \frac{(\pi\tilde{\gamma} - \tilde{\beta})\tilde{r}'\tilde{V}^{-1} + (\tilde{\alpha} - \pi\tilde{\beta})\tilde{e}'\tilde{V}^{-1}}{\tilde{\alpha}\tilde{\gamma} - \tilde{\beta}^2}. \tag{5.33}$$

Using again formulas (5.19)–(5.23) that give V^{-1} as a function of the elements of partitions (5.1), we can compute the vectors $\tilde{r}'\tilde{V}^{-1}$ and $\tilde{e}'\tilde{V}^{-1}$ as functions of the elements of partition (5.19) as follows:

$$\tilde{r}'\tilde{V}^{-1} = \left[r'V^{-1} + \frac{(r'V^{-1}b - \rho)b'V^{-1}}{D}, \rho - r'V^{-1}b\right] \tag{5.34}$$

and

$$\tilde{e}'\tilde{V}^{-1} = \left[e'V^{-1} + \frac{(e'V^{-1}b - 1)b'V^{-1}}{D}, 1 - e'V^{-1}b\right]. \tag{5.35}$$

In this representation of the row vectors $r'\tilde{V}^{-1}$ and $e'\tilde{V}^{-1}$, the comma separates the first n components from the $(n+1)$th component.

Because of (5.18), expressions (5.34) and (5.35) become

$$\tilde{r}'\tilde{V}^{-1} = [r'V^{-1}, 0] \tag{5.36}$$

and

$$\tilde{e}'\tilde{V}^{-1} = [e'V^{-1}, 0], \tag{5.37}$$

which shows that if the $(n+1)$th investment is dominated by the previous n investments, then

$$\tilde{x}_i(\pi) = x_i(\pi), \qquad i = 1, \ldots, n, \qquad -\infty < \pi < +\infty \tag{5.38}$$

and

$$x_{n+1}(\pi) = 0 \qquad -\infty < \pi < +\infty. \tag{5.39}$$

Since the converse, which states that (5.17) implies (5.15), immediately follows from the definition of dominance, this completes the proof of the theorem.

Problems of dominance and equivalence will be discussed again in a slightly more general form in Chapter 11.

EXAMPLES, NOTES, AND REFERENCES

The problems of dominance and equivalence were first investigated by Szegö (1972b) and by Rusconi (1975). This analysis was suggested by the need to investigate in a more complete form the case in which the "no-indifference" theorem is not satisfied, i.e., the case in which one investor does not keep in his boundary portfolio one given investment. This problem will be fully solved only in Chapter 7, but it must be clear that if V is nonsingular, an investment is either dropped by all investors (the case of Theorem (5.14)) or contained in all boundary portfolios. Thus we can reach the conclusion that when V is nonsingular, the investor does not have the option of deciding whether or not to keep a given investment in his boundary portfolio (see also Zambruno (1975)).

It goes without saying that the results obtained in this chapter can provide conditions under which in the original set of n investments the ith investment is dominated by the remaining $(n-1)$. In this case Theorem (5.14) will still hold, rephrased accordingly. The problem of dominance and equivalence will again be discussed in Chapters 7, 9, and 11.

The notion of equivalence and dominance as emphasized in Theorem (5.14) (property (5.17)) does not imply that the $(n+1)$th investment can be deleted, but only that it does not show in any boundary portfolio.

In order to stress this point, consider the following portfolio problem:

(5.40)
$$\tilde{V} = \begin{bmatrix} 1 & 1 & 1 \\ 1 & 4 & 6 \\ 1 & 6 & 16 \end{bmatrix}, \qquad \tilde{r} = \begin{bmatrix} 1 \\ 2 \\ \frac{8}{3} \end{bmatrix}.$$

We have that for this problem the third investment is dominated by the first two. Indeed, condition (5.18) is satisfied since

(5.41)
$$\frac{1}{3}[1,2]\begin{bmatrix} 4 & -1 \\ -1 & 1 \end{bmatrix}\begin{bmatrix} 1 \\ 6 \end{bmatrix} - \frac{8}{3} \quad \text{and} \quad \frac{1}{3}[1,1]\begin{bmatrix} 4 & -1 \\ -1 & 1 \end{bmatrix}\begin{bmatrix} 1 \\ 6 \end{bmatrix} = 1$$

Now the inverse of the matrix $\tilde{V}$ is given by

(5.42)
$$\tilde{V}^{-1} = \frac{1}{20}\begin{bmatrix} 28 & -10 & 2 \\ -10 & 15 & -5 \\ 2 & -5 & 3 \end{bmatrix},$$

and it is immediately verifiable that

(5.43)
$$(\tilde{V}^{-1}\tilde{e})_3 = (\tilde{V}^{-1}\tilde{r})_3 = 0.$$

It follows that for the given problem

(5.44)
$$\tilde{\gamma} = 1 \quad \text{and} \quad \tilde{\beta} = 1.$$

Thus the coordinates of the vertex of the parabola B^{n+1} in the plane (v, π) are

(5.45)
$$\pi_v = \tilde{\beta}/\tilde{\gamma} = 1. \qquad v_v = 1/\tilde{\gamma} = 1.$$

Now any point corresponding to $\pi = 1$ and $v > 1$ will be located in the interior of the region of admissible portfolios.

If we consider the allocation vector

(5.46) $$x_1 = \tfrac{4}{3}, \qquad x_2 = \tfrac{5}{6}, \qquad x_3 = \tfrac{1}{2},$$

it can immediately be seen that to this allocation vector there corresponds in the plane (v, π) the point

(5.47) $$\pi = 1, \qquad v = \tfrac{8}{3} > 1,$$

which is well inside the region of admissible portfolios. It can also be seen that to the point (5.47) there does not correspond an allocation vector with $x_3 = 0$.

Note that the variance–covariance matrix $\tilde{V}$ (5.40) is not singular; thus the case of dominance and equivalence must indeed be considered in a class different from the cases in which the augmented matrix $\tilde{V}$ is singular.

The situation is, however, completely different in the case $n = 2$. In this case represented as

(5.48) $$\tilde{V} = \begin{bmatrix} v_{11} & v_{12} \\ v_{12} & v_{22} \end{bmatrix}, \qquad \tilde{r} = \begin{bmatrix} r_1 \\ r_2 \end{bmatrix},$$

conditions (5.18) simply become

(5.49) $$r_2 = r_1 v_{12}/v_{11}, \qquad \text{and} \qquad 1 = v_{12}/v_{11}$$

since

$$\rho = r_2, \; V^{-1} = 1/v_{11}, \qquad \text{and} \qquad b = v_{12}.$$

From (5.49) it follows that

(5.50) $$v_{11} = v_{12}$$

and

(5.51) $$r_1 = r_2.$$

This last equality shows that condition (2.6) is not satisfied, while from condition (5.50) we have that the augmented variance–covariance matrix V has the form

(5.52) $$\tilde{V} = \begin{bmatrix} v_{11} & v_{11} \\ v_{11} & v_{22} \end{bmatrix}.$$

However, if we expand equality (5.50), we have

(5.53) $$v_{11} = \sigma_1^2 = \sigma_1 \sigma_2 \rho_{12} = v_{12},$$

from which

(5.54) $$\sigma_2 = \sigma_1/\rho_{12}.$$

If we substitute (5.54) into (5.52), it becomes

(5.55) $$\tilde{V} = \begin{bmatrix} \sigma_1^2 & \sigma_1^2/\rho_{12} \\ \sigma_1^2/\rho_{12} & \sigma_1^2/\rho_{12}^2 \end{bmatrix}$$

Thus

(5.56) $$\det \tilde{V} = 0,$$

which shows that $\tilde{V}$ (5.52) is singular.

In this chapter the emphasis has been on dominance and equivalence properties. However, a similar set of results can also be proved for the case of *semidominance*, i.e., for the case in which, instead of condition (3.7), condition (3.5) is satisfied, i.e., there exists at least one $i = 1, \ldots, n$ with

$$\tilde{\gamma}(\tilde{V}^{-1}\tilde{r})_i = \tilde{\beta}(\tilde{V}^{-1}\tilde{e})_i. \tag{5.57}$$

From this it follows that

$$x_i(\pi) = (\tilde{V}^{-1}\tilde{e})/\tilde{\gamma} \qquad \text{for all} \quad \pi, \quad -\infty < \pi < +\infty. \tag{5.58}$$

The concept of semidominance implies that each investor, regardless of his propensity to risk, will hold in his portfolio the fixed amount x_i of semidominated investment i. This, in turn, implies that each investor keeps in his optimal portfolio a fixed fraction of his wealth invested in semidominated securities.

The idea of dominance and semidominance, which seems perhaps of only theoretical interest, has in fact found its application. In a recent study of the optimal ex-post minimum variance portfolio for the Italian market by Szegö and Rusconi (1980), when instead of the nominal returns one takes into account the real returns, it turns out that some investments are dominated. In particular, the analysis has proved that the stock market as a whole is dominated and the real estate market is semidominated by a combination of the bond and commodity markets.

CHAPTER 6

ENLARGING THE SET OF INVESTMENTS WITH A RISKLESS ASSET

The aim of this chapter is the complete analysis of the properties of case (5.6) in which the enlarged matrix $\tilde{V}$ is singular and in addition the $(n+1)$th investment added has zero standard deviation, i.e., $\sigma_{n+1} = 0$; or in other words, the $(n+1)$th investment is "riskless."

For simplicity of notation we shall again use partitions of type (5.1), which in this case take the form

$$\tilde{V} = \begin{bmatrix} V & \emptyset \\ \emptyset' & 0 \end{bmatrix}, \quad \tilde{r} = \begin{bmatrix} r \\ \rho \end{bmatrix}, \quad \tilde{e} = \begin{bmatrix} e \\ 1 \end{bmatrix}, \quad \tilde{x} = \begin{bmatrix} x \\ x_\rho \end{bmatrix}. \tag{6.1}$$

Throughout this chapter it will again be assumed that

$$\det V \neq 0 \qquad \text{and} \qquad r_i \neq r_j \qquad \text{for some} \quad i, j = 1, \ldots, n. \tag{6.2}$$

We shall compute the boundaries B^{n+1} and $\mathscr{X}^{n+1}$ of the region of admissible portfolios (5.1) in the space (v, π) and in the space X, respectively. Again these boundaries can be defined by the following constrained minimization problem:

$$\min_{\tilde{x} \in R^{n+1}} \tilde{x}'\tilde{V}\tilde{x} \tag{6.3}$$

subject to

$$\pi = \tilde{x}'\tilde{r} \tag{6.4}$$

and

$$1 = \tilde{x}'\tilde{e}, \tag{6.5}$$

where the elements of the problem are defined in (6.1). Then the following theorem can be proved:

(6.6) **Theorem**

Let V be nonsingular and the expected returns not identical for all investments. Then the boundary B^{n+1} of the region of admissible portfolios (5.3) relative to problem (6.1) in the plane (v, π) is given by the parabola

(6.7) $$v = \frac{(\pi - \rho)^2}{\gamma\rho^2 - 2\beta\rho + \alpha},$$

while in the plane (σ, π) it is given by the two half straight lines

(6.8) $$\pi = \rho \pm \sigma[\gamma\rho^2 - 2\beta\rho + \alpha]^{1/2},$$

in which

(6.9) $$\sigma > 0.$$

The boundary $\mathscr{X}^{n+1}$ of the region of admissible portfolios (5.3) in the $(n + 1)$ dimensional space X is given by the expressions

(6.10) $$x(\pi) = \frac{\pi - \rho}{\gamma\rho^2 - 2\beta\rho + \alpha} V^{-1}(r - \rho e)$$

and

(6.11) $$x_\rho(\pi) = \frac{\pi(\gamma\rho - \beta) + \alpha - \beta\rho}{\gamma\rho^2 - 2\beta\rho + \alpha}.$$

Proof

Consider the Lagrangian

(6.12) $$L(\tilde{x}, \lambda_1, \lambda_2) = \tilde{x}'\tilde{V}\tilde{x} - \lambda_1(\tilde{x}'\tilde{r} - \pi) - \lambda_2(\tilde{x}\tilde{e} - 1).$$

The critical points of (6.12) are obtained by solving the following linear system of $n + 3$ equations and $n + 3$ unknowns:

(6.13) $$\frac{\partial L}{\partial x} = 2x'V - \lambda_1 r' - \lambda_2 e' = 0,$$

(6.14) $$\frac{\partial L}{\partial x_\rho} = -\lambda_1\rho - \lambda_2 = 0,$$

(6.15) $$\frac{\partial L}{\partial \lambda_1} = -x'r - \rho x_\rho + \pi = 0,$$

(6.16) $$\frac{\partial L}{\partial \lambda_2} = -x'e - x_\rho + 1 = 0.$$

The linear system (6.13)–(6.16) has a unique solution $(x, x_\rho, \lambda_1, \lambda_2)$ if and only if the determinant of its coefficients is different from zero, i.e., if and only if

(6.17)
$$\begin{vmatrix} 2V & \emptyset & r & e \\ \emptyset' & 0 & \rho & 1 \\ r' & \rho & 0 & 0 \\ e' & 1 & 0 & 0 \end{vmatrix} \neq 0.$$

It can be proved (see Appendix F) that under the assumption made on V and r condition (6.17) is satisfied. We can then proceed with the solution of system (6.15)–(6.16).

From (6.13) we have

(6.18)
$$x' = \tfrac{1}{2}\lambda_1 r' V^{-1} + \tfrac{1}{2}\lambda_2 e' V^{-1}.$$

Multiplying (6.18) on the right by r and e, respectively, substituting the resulting expressions into (6.15) and (6.16), and taking into account (6.14), we obtain the linear system

(6.19)
$$\begin{aligned} \tfrac{1}{2}\lambda_1\alpha + \tfrac{1}{2}\lambda_2\beta + \rho x_\rho &= \pi, \\ \tfrac{1}{2}\lambda_1\beta + \tfrac{1}{2}\lambda_2\gamma + x_\rho &= 1, \\ \lambda_1\rho + \lambda_2 &= 0, \end{aligned}$$

which has a unique solution if and only if the determinant of its coefficients is different from zero, i.e., if and only if

(6.20)
$$\begin{vmatrix} \alpha & \beta & \rho \\ \beta & \gamma & 1 \\ \rho & 1 & 0 \end{vmatrix} = -\gamma\rho^2 + 2\beta\rho - \alpha \neq 0.$$

Note that determinant (6.20) is exactly the numerator of parabola (2.7) at the point $\pi = \rho$, taken with negative sign. Thus if we apply the results obtained in Chapter 2 relative to the sign of this expression, and in particular conditions (2.22) and (2.36), it follows that determinant (6.20) is always negative.

We can then proceed to the solution of system (6.19) and introduce its solution $(x_\rho, \lambda_1, \lambda_2)$ into expression (6.18). After some computation we obtain the boundary of the region of admissible portfolios in the space X, defined by the following two expressions for $x(\pi)$ and $x_\rho(\pi)$:

(6.21)
$$x(\pi) = \frac{\pi - \rho}{\gamma\rho^2 - 2\beta\rho + \alpha} V^{-1}(r - \rho e)$$

and

(6.22)
$$x_\rho(\pi) = \frac{\pi(\gamma\rho - \beta) + \alpha - \beta\rho}{\gamma\rho^2 - 2\beta\rho + \alpha}.$$

Substituting (6.21) and (6.22) into the first equation of (5.3) and remembering partition (6.1) of the vector $\tilde{x}$, after some computation we obtain the boundary B^{n+1} of the region of admissible portfolios in the plane (v, π), which is represented by the parabola

(6.23) $$v = (\pi - \rho)^2/(\gamma\rho^2 - 2\beta p + \alpha),$$

while in the plane (σ, π) the boundary B^{n+1} is given by the equation

(6.24) $$\sigma = \pm(\pi - \rho)/(\gamma\rho^2 - 2\beta\rho + \alpha)^{1/2},$$

which represents two half lines with equation

(6.25) $$\pi = \rho \pm \sigma\chi \qquad \sigma > 0,$$

where χ is the absolute value of their angular coefficients, i.e.,

(6.26) $$\chi = (\gamma\rho^2 - 2\beta\rho + \alpha)^{1/2}.$$

Note that since the quantity under the square root is always positive, being the value of the numerator of parabola (2.27) evaluated at the point $\pi = \rho$, the square root does always exist.

(6.27) **Remarks**

The vertex of parabola (6.23) (see Fig. 6.1) is at the point (v_v, π_v) with coordinates

(6.28) $$v_v = 0, \qquad \pi_v = \rho.$$

Thus in this case the minimum variance portfolio has zero variance.

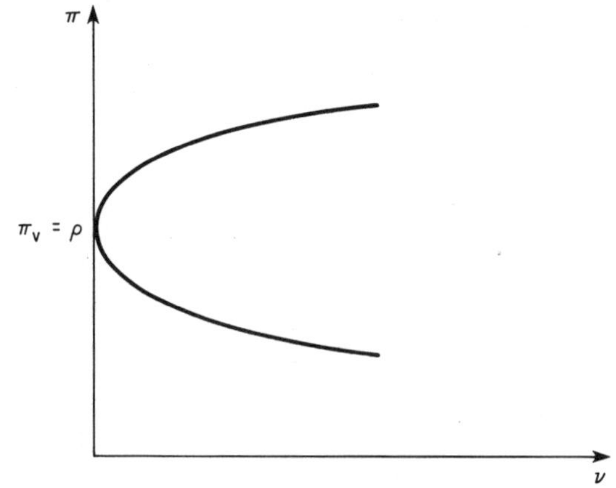

Figure 6.1

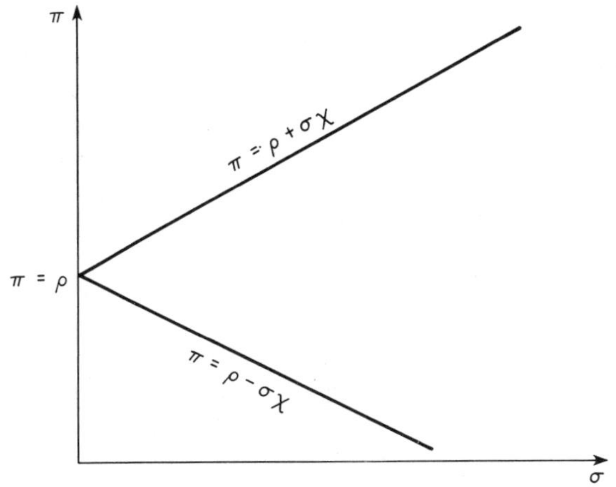

Figure 6.2

The two straight lines (6.25) (see Fig. 6.2) that are the boundary of the region of admissible portfolios in the plane (σ, π) originate at the point $\pi = \rho$. The zero-variance allocation vector then becomes

(6.29) $$x^v = 0, \qquad x_\rho^v = 1.$$

(6.30) **Remarks**

If we introduce again notations (3.32) and (3.33), keeping in mind that in this case expressions (6.28) and (6.29) hold, we have

(6.31) $$\pi_d = \pi - \rho,$$

(6.32) $$d = r - \rho e,$$

(6.33) $$x^d(\pi_d) = x(\pi_d).$$

Hence (6.21) becomes

(6.34) $$x(\pi_d) = \frac{\pi_d}{v(\rho)} V^{-1} d = \frac{\pi_d}{d'V^{-1}d} V^{-1} d,$$

while (6.22) becomes

(6.35) $$x_\rho(\pi) = \frac{(r - \pi e)'V^{-1}d}{d'V^{-1}d}.$$

Note that expression (6.34), which gives the behavior of the first n (risky) components of the vector $\tilde{x}(\pi)$ along B^{n+1}, is exactly the same as (3.28).

Expressions (6.34) and (6.35) clearly show that in this case also for each given π (or π_d) there exists a unique vector $\tilde{x}$. Using the same technique developed in Chapter 3 (Theorem (3.44)), one can also show that in the case considered in this chapter all points in the interior of the region of admissible portfolios do not have uniqueness of the mapping $(v, \pi) \to \tilde{x}$.

In expressions (6.21)–(6.24), which provide a solution to our problems, the only coefficients that appear are α, β, and γ, which are the coefficients associated with the first n (risky) investments. It is therefore quite sensible to investigate the relationship between the boundary B^{n+1} of the region of admissible portfolios on the enlarged set of $n+1$ investments and the boundary B^n of the region of admissible portfolios of the original set of n investments.

On this problem we shall prove the following:

(6.36) **Theorem**

Under assumptions (6.1) and (6.2) all the admissible portfolios (5.3) associated with the enlarged set of $n+1$ investments can be generated by linear combinations of the $(n+1)$th (riskless) investment and any admissible portfolio generated by the original set of n investments.

Proof

Consider an admissible portfolio generated by the set of the first n investments and defined by the following equations (see (2.1)):

(6.37) $$x'Vx = v_r, \qquad x'r = \pi_r, \qquad x'e = 1.$$

Next combine linearly the portfolio (6.33) with the $(n+1)$th "riskless" asset and let η be the fraction of the capital invested in the portfolio (6.37). Thus we obtain the portfolios (see (5.3) and (6.1))

(6.38) $$1 = \eta + x_\rho = \eta x'e + x_\rho,$$

(6.39) $$\pi = \eta\pi_r + x_\rho\rho = \eta x'r + x_\rho\rho,$$

(6.40) $$v = \eta^2 v_r.$$

Finally, if we let

(6.41) $$\tilde{x}_i = \eta x_i, \qquad \tilde{x}_{n+1} = x_\rho, \qquad i = 1, \ldots, n,$$

from (6.38) and (6.1) we obtain the equations

(6.42) $$1 = \tilde{x}'\tilde{e}, \qquad \pi = \tilde{x}'\tilde{r}, \qquad v = \tilde{x}'\tilde{V}\tilde{x},$$

which coincide with Eqs. (5.3) and prove the theorem.

From Eqs. (6.38)–(6.40), which define an arbitrary admissible portfolio of the set of $n+1$ investments as a linear combination of an admissible portfolio of the set of n investments and of the $(n+1)$th investment, we can also deduce a stronger result on the geometric properties in the plane (σ, π) of the locus defined by (6.38)–(6.40) and parameterized by η.

(6.43) **Theorem**

Assume again that conditions (6.1) and (6.2) are satisfied and consider the point (σ_r, π_r) that belongs to the region of admissible portfolios of the set of n investments (2.1) in the plane (σ, π). Then each linear combination (6.38)–(6.40) with $\eta > 0$ of (σ_r, π_r) with $(0, \rho)$ lies in the plane (σ, π) on the straight line

(6.44) $$\pi = \rho + \frac{(\pi_r - \rho)\sigma}{\sigma_r}, \qquad \sigma > 0,$$

that joins the points (σ_r, π_r) and $(0, \rho)$. In addition, the straight line

(6.45) $$\pi = \rho - \frac{(\pi_r - \rho)\sigma}{\sigma_r}, \qquad \sigma > 0,$$

that joins the point $(0, \rho)$ with the point

(6.46) $$\sigma = \sigma_r, \qquad \pi = 2\rho - \pi_r$$

is also completely contained in the region of admissible portfolios of the $n+1$ investments and corresponds to a linear combination (6.38)–(6.40) with $\eta < 0$.

Proof

Let

(6.47) $$\sigma^2 = v \qquad \text{and} \qquad \sigma_r^2 = v_r.$$

Then from (6.40) we have

(6.48) $$\eta = \pm\sigma/\sigma_r.$$

Substituting (6.48) into (6.38) and (6.39) and eliminating x from the two resulting equations, we obtain

(6.49) $$\pi = \rho \pm (\pi_r - \rho)\sigma/\sigma_r,$$

from which (6.44) and (6.45) follow.

(6.50) **Remark**

The ordinate of the point (6.46) $\pi = 2\rho - \pi_r$ has the same distance from $\pi = \rho$ as from $\pi = \pi_r$. Indeed, we have

(6.51) $$2\rho - \pi_r = \rho - (\pi_r - \rho).$$

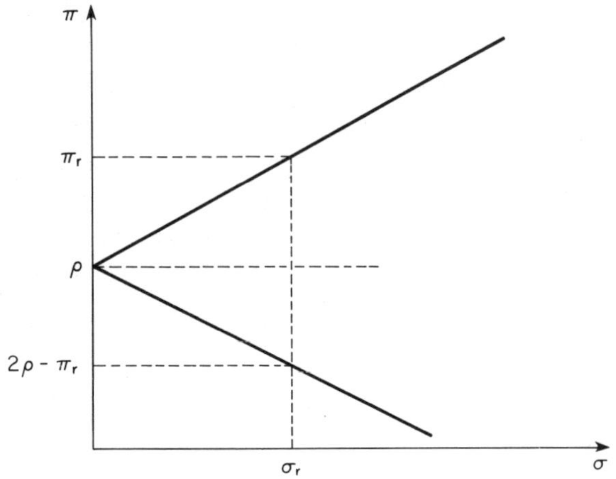

Figure 6.3

The relationship between the point (σ_r, π_r) and its mirror image with respect to $\pi = \rho$, i.e., the point $(\sigma_r, 2\rho - \pi_r)$, is shown in Fig. 6.3.

It is rather interesting to compute the allocation vector $x(\pi)$ corresponding to the point $(\sigma_r, 2\rho - \pi_r)$. If we assume that the allocation vector x, corresponding to the point (σ_r, π_r), satisfies the partitioning between the first n investments and the $(n + 1)$th investment represented by

(6.52) $$x'e = \eta, \qquad x_\rho = 1 - \eta$$

then the point (σ_r, π_r) satisfies the partitioning

(6.53) $$x'e = -\eta, \qquad x_\rho = 1 + \eta.$$

From Theorems (6.36) and (6.43) we shall next prove the following:

(6.54) **Theorem**

Assume that conditions (6.1) and (6.2) are satisfied. Then in the plane (σ, π), if $\rho = \beta/\gamma$, the straight lines B^{n+1} (6.25) are the asymptotes of the branch of hyperbola B^n (2.8); if $\rho \neq \beta/\gamma$, one of the straight lines (6.25) has one tangency point (σ^*, π^*) with the branch of hyperbola (2.8). In particular, if $\rho > \beta/\gamma$, then $\pi^* < \beta/\gamma$, while if $\rho < \beta/\gamma$, then $\pi^* > \beta/\gamma$, where

(6.55) $$\pi^* = \frac{\beta\rho - \alpha}{\gamma\rho - \beta} = \frac{r'V^{-1}d}{e'V^{-1}d},$$

(6.56) $$\sigma^* = \frac{[\gamma\rho^2 - 2\beta\rho + \alpha]^{1/2}}{\gamma\rho - \beta} \qquad \text{if} \quad \rho > \beta/\gamma,$$

(6.57) $$\sigma^* = -\frac{[\gamma\rho^2 - 2\beta\rho + \alpha]^{1/2}}{\gamma\rho - \beta} \quad \text{if} \quad \rho < \beta/\gamma,$$

(6.58) $$x^* = \frac{V^{-1}(r - \rho e)}{\beta - \gamma\rho} = \frac{V^{-1}d}{e'V^{-1}d},$$

(6.59) $$x_\rho^* = 0.$$

Proof

By comparing the equations of the straight lines (6.8) and (6.48), we can identify at least one point $(\sigma_r, \pi_r) \in B^n$ such that the corresponding straight line (6.49) coincides with (6.8). Since both straight lines have in common the point $\pi = \rho$, they coincide if their angular coefficients are the same, i.e., if i.e., if

(6.60) $$(\pi_r - \rho)/\sigma_r = \pm(\gamma\rho^2 - 2\beta\rho + \alpha)^{1/2},$$

which gives the equation

(6.61) $$\pi_r = \rho \pm \sigma_r[\gamma\rho^2 - 2\beta\rho + \alpha]^{1/2},$$

which is exactly Eq. (6.8) evaluated at the point (σ_r, π_r). Hence Eq. (6.61) states that the point (σ_r, π_r), which was assumed (see Theorem (6.43)) to be an admissible portfolio generated by the original set of n investments, must also belong to B^{n+1}, which is the boundary of the region of admissible portfolios of the enlarged set of $n + 1$ investments (6.1). Because of the uniqueness of the vector x on B^{n+1} and on B^n, this can happen only at a point π_r in which x_ρ (6.11) identically vanishes. Thus from (6.11) we must have

(6.62) $$\pi_r(\gamma\rho - \beta) + \alpha - \beta\rho = 0,$$

from which if $\gamma\rho - \beta \neq 0$, i.e., if $\rho \neq \beta/\gamma$, it follows that

(6.63) $$\pi_r = \frac{\beta\rho - \alpha}{\gamma\rho - \beta}.$$

Since this point is a unique contact point between the straight line B^{n+1} (6.62) and the hyperbola B^n, clearly in this case it must be a tangency point in the plane (σ, π) between B^{n+1} and B^n. We shall denote this point by by (σ^*, π^*) and its allocation vector by x^*. Thus

(6.64) $$\pi^* = \frac{\beta\rho - \alpha}{\gamma\rho - \beta} = \frac{\beta}{\gamma} - \frac{\alpha\gamma - \beta^2}{\gamma^2(\rho - \beta/\gamma)} = \frac{r'V^{-1}d}{e'V^{-1}d},$$

$$\sigma^* = \frac{[\gamma\rho^2 - 2\beta\rho + \alpha]^{1/2}}{\gamma\rho - \beta} \qquad \text{if} \quad \rho > \beta/\gamma, \tag{6.65}$$

$$\sigma^* = \frac{[\gamma\rho^2 - 2\beta\rho + \alpha]^{1/2}}{\beta - \gamma\rho} \qquad \text{if} \quad \rho < \beta/\gamma, \tag{6.66}$$

$$x^* = \frac{V^{-1}(r - \rho e)}{\beta - \gamma\rho} = \frac{V^{-1}d}{\gamma(\beta/\gamma - \rho)}, \qquad x^*_\rho = 0, \tag{6.67}$$

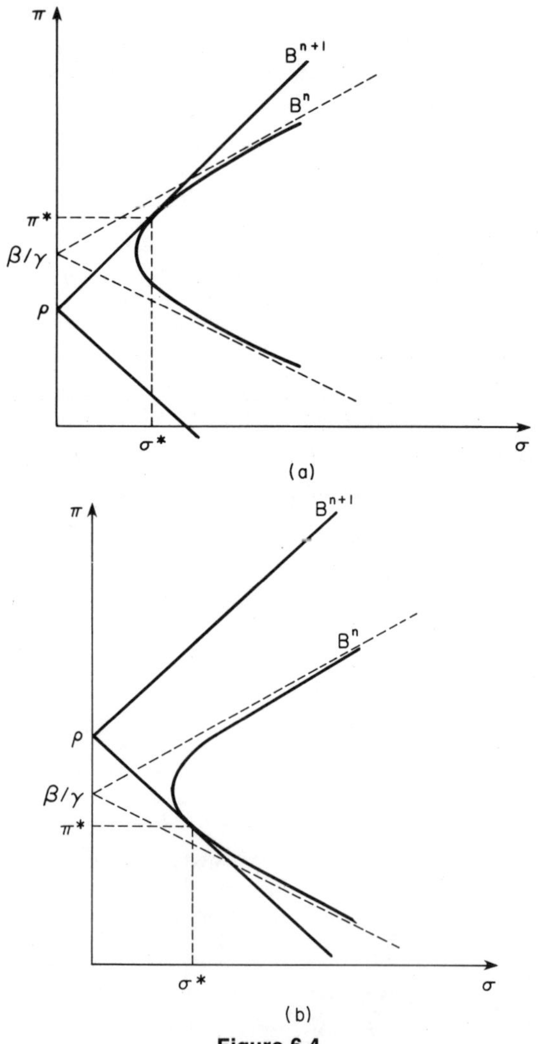

Figure 6.4

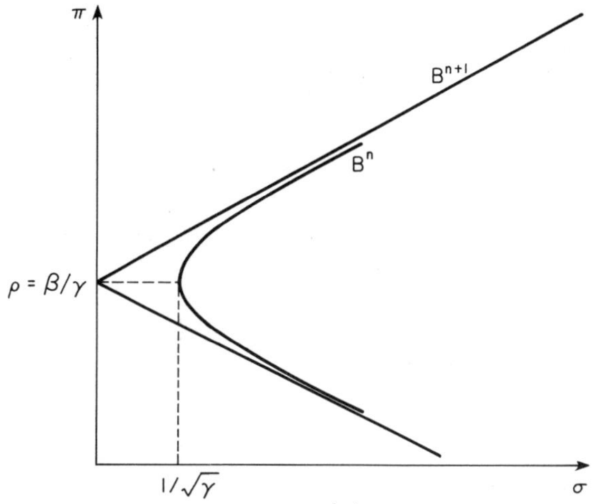

Figure 6.4 (*Continued*)

where the vector d is defined by Eq. (6.32). It is immediate to check that

(6.68) $$\pi^* > \beta/\gamma \qquad \text{if} \quad \rho < \beta/\gamma \quad \text{(Fig. 6.4a)}$$

and that

(6.69) $$\pi^* < \beta/\gamma \qquad \text{if} \quad \rho > \beta/\gamma \quad \text{(Fig. 6.4b)}.$$

When $\rho = \beta/\gamma$, Eq. (6.59) simply becomes

(6.70) $$\pi = \beta/\gamma \pm \sigma[(\alpha\gamma - \beta^2)/\gamma]^{1/2},$$

which are the two asymptotes (2.35) of the hyperbola (2.8) that is the boundary B^n in the plane (σ, π) (Fig. 6.4c).

The various alternatives discussed in this theorem are represented in Fig. 6.4a, b, c.

(6.71) **Remark**

The equation of the efficient frontier is given by the half line

(6.72) $$\pi = \rho + \sigma(\gamma\rho^2 - 2\beta\rho + \alpha)^{1/2}, \qquad \sigma > 0.$$

It is important to point out that the tangency point (σ^*, π^*) belongs to the efficient frontier if and only if $\rho < \beta/\gamma$, which is equivalent to $e'V^{-1}d > 0$.

The portfolio x^* will be called the *optimal portfolio of risky assets*, and it will be of great importance in Chapter 14.

Note that very important expressions (6.55), (6.56), and (6.58) are particular cases of the more general results (4.24), (4.92), and (4.93). This is evident since the riskless investment x_ρ is orthogonal to x^* (see also Theorem (4.35)).

EXAMPLES, NOTES, AND REFERENCES

When one riskless asset is added to the original set of n "risky" investments, then the boundary of the region of admissible portfolios becomes linear. This result is implicit in the paper by Tobin (1958) and is explicitly stated in the paper by Lintner (1965) as well as in the paper by Sharpe (1964). However, neither paper proved Theorem (6.54) in a complete form nor, in particular, realized the mutually exclusive cases (6.68)–(6.70) on the location of the tangency point (if it exists). Note that the proof given by Sharpe (1964) applies only to the case in which non-negativity constraints $x \geq 0$ are taken into account, a case in which, as will be shown in Chapter 12, there almost always exists only a tangency point of the type considered by Sharpe. Again the proof of all the statements of Theorem (6.54) can be found in the papers by Merton (1972) and Szegö (1972a).

It is interesting to recall a theorem of Stone (1970, p. 72) in which it is proved that if the risk is measured by a differentiable function $R(x)$ and if there exists one riskless asset, then in the plane $(R^{1/k}, \pi)$ the boundary of the region of admissible portfolios becomes a straight line if and only if $R(x)$ is a homogeneous function of degree k.

Many other proofs of Theorem (6.54) are available (see, for instance, Buser (1972)). All results that have been proved in this chapter are true under the basic assumption (2.6) that implies the nonidentity of the expected returns on the n investments.

If condition (2.6) is violated and instead there exists a real number δ with

$$r = \delta e, \tag{6.73}$$

then most of the results obtained in this chapter are still valid, and in particular Eq. (6.8), defining the boundary of the region of admissible portfolios B^{n+1}, holds and because of (6.73) takes the form

$$\pi = \rho \pm \sigma(\delta - \rho)\sqrt{\gamma}, \tag{6.74}$$

while the allocation vector $\tilde{x}(\pi)$ is defined by

$$x(\pi) = \frac{\pi - \rho}{\gamma} V^{-1} e, \tag{6.75}$$

$$x_\rho(\pi) = \frac{\delta - \pi}{\delta - \rho}. \tag{6.76}$$

In this case, however, since the boundary B^n (in the plane (σ, π)) is defined not by a branch of a hyperbola but by the ray originating in the point $\sigma = 1/\gamma$, $\pi = \delta$ and lying on the straight line $\pi = \delta$ (see (2.76)), the results of Theorem (6.54) do not apply, even if the origin of B^n indeed belongs to one of the straight lines (6.72).

The situation has a further degeneracy in the case in which

$$\delta = \rho, \tag{6.77}$$

in which case the boundary B^{n+1} becomes the half line

$$\pi = \delta = \rho, \qquad \sigma \geq 0. \tag{6.78}$$

It is interesting again to investigate the behavior of the region of admissible portfolios in the case in which this region is parametrically defined by system (2.82), i.e., when the investor must allocate a general initial capital W_0.

In this particular case, when a riskless asset is added to the original set of n risky assets, the boundary B^{n+1} in the plane (σ, π) takes the form

$$\sigma = \pm(\pi - \rho W_0)/(\gamma\rho^2 - 2\beta\rho + \alpha)^{1/2}, \tag{6.79}$$

which are two straight lines through the point $(0, \rho W_0)$.

The equations defining the allocation vector $\tilde{x}(\pi)$ become

$$x(\pi) = (\pi - \rho W_0)(V^{-1}r - V^{-1}\rho e)/(\gamma\rho^2 - 2\beta\rho + \alpha) \tag{6.80}$$

and

$$x_\rho(\pi) = [\pi(\gamma\rho - \beta) + W_0\alpha - W_0\beta\rho]/(\gamma\rho^2 - 2\beta\rho + \alpha). \tag{6.81}$$

Again usually one of the two straight lines (6.79) is tangent in the plane (σ, π) to the hyperbola derived from (2.82), defining the boundary B^n of the n risky investments. The tangency point is given by

$$\pi^* = \frac{W_0(\beta\rho - \alpha)}{\alpha\gamma - \beta}, \qquad x^* = \frac{W_0 V^{-1}(r - \rho e)}{\beta - \gamma\rho}. \tag{6.82}$$

Note that in the particular case in which $W_0 = 0$, the only solution is $x^* = 0$. In order to fully understand the implications of this result, we must compare (6.79) with (2.85) in which formally there exists a riskless asset $\pi = v = x = 0$. Hence in this case there cannot exist an optimal combination of risky assets with the usual properties.

CHAPTER 7

PROPERTIES OF THE EFFICIENT FRONTIER WITH ONE RISKLESS ASSET

In the preceding chapter we derived the analytic expression (6.8) for the boundary of the region of admissible portfolios in the plane (σ, π) as well as in the space X.

This chapter will be devoted to a further analysis of the properties of boundary portfolios and in particular of efficient portfolios, i.e., of boundary portfolios corresponding to the upper branch of B^{n+1}. Thus the properties of the allocation vector $\tilde{x}(\pi)$ on the space X, which is defined by Eqs. (6.10) and (6.11), will be investigated. In this analysis we shall take into particular account the peculiar properties of this case, and in particular the properties proved in Theorems (6.36), (6.43), and (6.54).

Throughout this chapter it will be assumed that the hypotheses (6.1) and (6.2) are still satisfied.

Consider then the expressions for the allocation vector $\tilde{x}(\pi)$ on the boundary of the region of admissible portfolios, which in view of the decomposition (6.1) will be split into two parts: $x(\pi)$ relative to the first (risky) components of the vector $\tilde{x}$, and $x_\rho(\pi)$ relative to the $(n+1)$th (riskless) asset.

We shall represent such an allocation vector $\tilde{x}(\pi)$ in its form (6.34), (6.35), which we shall rewrite in the following slightly modified form:

$$x(\pi) = \frac{(\pi - \rho)V^{-1}d}{d'V^{-1}d}, \tag{7.1}$$

$$x_\rho(\pi) = \frac{(r - \pi e)'V^{-1}d}{d'V^{-1}d}, \tag{7.2}$$

where

$$d = r - \rho e \tag{7.3}$$

and ρ is again the return on the $(n+1)$th (riskless) asset.

We note first that expressions (7.1) and (7.2) are linear in π and therefore to each π on B^{n+1} there corresponds a unique $\tilde{x}(\pi)$.

We shall begin our analysis with a discussion of the sign properties of $\tilde{x}(\pi)$ on the boundary of the region of admissible portfolios. From (7.1) and (7.2) it follows that at the point $(0, \rho)$, corresponding to the riskless investment, the allocation vector $\tilde{x}(\pi)$ has the form

$$x(\rho) = \emptyset, \tag{7.4}$$

$$x_\rho(\rho) = 1. \tag{7.5}$$

Note that all components of the vector $x(\pi)$ vanish for $\pi = \rho$ because of the linearity of $x(\pi)$ as a function of π. It then follows that at the point $\pi = \rho$ all components of $x(\pi)$ change their sign and that there does not exist any other point $\pi = \pi_i \neq \rho$ such that $x_i(\pi_i) = 0$. This behavior of $x(\pi)$ is also quite clear from (7.1) since V^{-1} is positive definite.

In the case in which

$$\rho \neq \beta/\gamma, \qquad \text{i.e.,} \quad e'V^{-1}d \neq 0, \tag{7.6}$$

the boundary B^{n+1} is tangent to the boundary B^n relative to the original set of (risky) investments at the point π^* (6.55) to which corresponds an allocation vector $\tilde{x}(\pi^*)$ ((6.58), (6.59)) with the form

$$x^* = x(\pi^*) = \frac{V^{-1}(r - \rho e)}{\beta - \gamma\rho} = \frac{V^{-1}d}{e'V^{-1}d}, \tag{7.7}$$

$$x_\rho^* = x_\rho(\pi^*) = 0. \tag{7.8}$$

Because of the linearity of $x_\rho(\pi)$ as a function of π (see (7.2)), it then follows that in the plane (σ, π) on the subset of the boundary B^{n+1} that corresponds to the ray originating at the point (σ^*, π^*) (see Fig. 7.1), we have

$$x_\rho(\pi) < 0, \tag{7.9}$$

while on the open segment of B^{n+1} with extremals at the points (σ^*, π^*) and $(0, \rho)$ we have

$$0 < x_\rho(\pi) < 1. \tag{7.10}$$

Finally, on the subset of the boundary B^{n+1} corresponding to the ray originating at the point $(0, \rho)$ and not including the tangency point (σ^*, π^*) we have

$$x_\rho(\pi) > 1. \tag{7.11}$$

This last statement is clearly in agreement with the partitioning (6.53). On this ray the first n components of the allocation vector $\tilde{x}$, corresponding

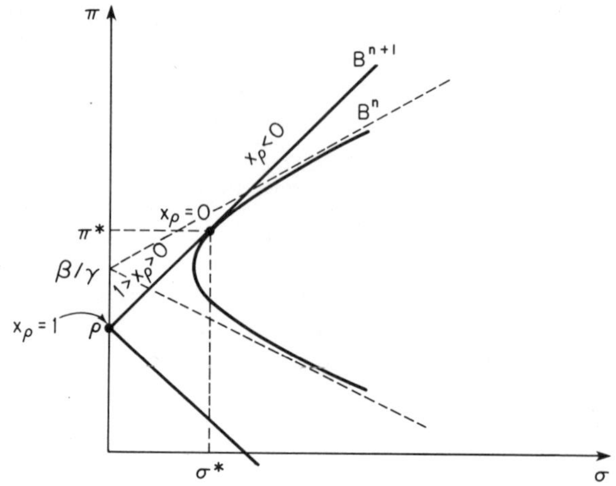

(a)

Figure 7.1

to the n "risky" investments, are such that

(7.12) $$e'x(\pi) < 0, \qquad -\infty < \pi < +\infty.$$

Consider next the particular case in which

(7.13) $$\rho = \beta/\gamma,$$

and therefore (see Theorem (6.54)) in the plane (σ, π) the boundary B^{n+1} coincides with the asymptotes of B^n and the tangency point (σ^*, π^*) between B^{n+1} and B^n does not exist. It follows that the vector $\tilde{x}(\pi)$ on the whole boundary B^{n+1} is defined as

(7.14) $$x(\pi) = \frac{\gamma(\pi - \rho)}{\alpha\gamma - \beta^2} V^{-1}(r - \rho), \qquad \rho = \beta/\gamma, \quad -\infty < \pi < +\infty.$$

(7.15) $$x_\rho(\pi) = 1, \qquad -\infty < \pi < +\infty.$$

From (7.14) it follows that in this particular case

(7.16) $$e'x(\pi) = 0, \qquad -\infty < \pi < +\infty$$

for each allocation vector $x(\pi)$ on B^{n+1}. Clearly, in this case in partition (6.53) we have $\eta \equiv 0$. Note that expression (7.14) is still formally identical to (7.1), which coincides with (2.9) written in the form (3.31). All the results obtained in Chapter 3 on the sign properties of (7.1), and in particular Theorem (3.32) and formulas (3.36), clearly apply if we replace π_v by ρ. This formal identity allows us to conclude that Theorem (3.41) on the uniqueness properties of the transformation $(\sigma, \pi) \to x$ applies fully to the case of the boundary B^{n+1} of the region of admissible portfolios relative to the enlarged set of $n + 1$ investments.

Theorem (2.39) applies in its present form. Thus under the assumptions made on V and r and because of Theorem (6.43) and of remarks (5.48)–(5.56), it follows that if $\rho \neq \beta/\gamma$ even without additional assumptions on V and r, if $n > 2$ (i.e., if $n + 1 > 3$), the region of admissible portfolios R^{n+1} has interior points, i.e., all points in the half plane $\sigma > 0$ lying between the two straight lines (6.24).

It is possible to show (see the notes and references for this chapter) that in general if $n > 2$, R^{n+1} has interior points also in the case in which $\rho = \beta/\gamma$. In this case, because of (7.15), the situation is quite similar to some cases investigated in the previous chapter.

The particular properties of B^{n+1} and of $\tilde{x}(\pi)$ on B^{n+1} in the case in which the $n + 1$ investments satisfy conditions (6.1) and (6.2) lead to the formulation of the following general theorem which summarizes all the properties of the particular portfolio problem:

(7.17) **Theorem**

Consider the portfolio problem relative to the set of $n + 1$ investments that satisfy conditions (6.1) and (6.2), i.e., such that V is nonsingular, the expected returns are not the same for all investments, and $\sigma_{n+1} = 0$; then the following properties hold:

(7.18) In the plane (σ, π) the efficient frontier is a straight line (linearity property).

(7.19) If $\rho \neq \beta/\gamma$, the efficient frontier can be generated by scaling the optimal portfolio in risky assets (return to scale property).

(7.20) If $\rho \neq \beta/\gamma$, the set of $(n + 1)$ investments is equivalent to two nonintersecting portfolios: the riskless asset (7.4), (7.5) and the optimal portfolio of risky asset $\tilde{x}^*$ ((7.7), (7.8)). By nonintersecting portfolios we mean portfolios such that the investments which are contained in one are not contained in the other (separation property).

(7.21) If $\rho \neq \beta/\gamma$, all portfolios of B^{n+1} except x_ρ are perfectly positively correlated among themselves (perfect correlation property).

(7.22) The riskless asset x_ρ is orthogonal to all portfolios.

Proof

Statement (7.18), which stresses the geometric properties of the efficient frontier, is proved in Theorem (6.6). Statement (7.19) follows from the proof of Theorem (6.54). Notice that the portfolio in risky assets is unique, and it is characterized by relationships (6.55)–(6.59). The rules that apply to the scaling relation are identical to the ones given by Eqs. (6.38)–(6.40), i.e.,

$$1 = \eta + x_\rho, \qquad \pi = \eta\pi^* + \rho x_\rho, \qquad \sigma = \eta\sigma^*, \tag{7.23}$$

where again η denotes the fraction of the unit capital invested in the risky portfolio x, while x_ρ is the amount invested in the riskless asset.

From (7.23) by eliminating x_ρ we can derive the following useful equations:

$$\pi = \eta(\pi^* - \rho) + \rho, \qquad \sigma = \eta\sigma^*, \tag{7.24}$$

which provides the scaling relationship.

The proof of statement (7.20) follows immediately from the particular form ((7.4), (7.5) and (7.7), (7.8)) of the two portfolios x_ρ and x between which our capital is divided according to system (7.23).

In order to prove statement (7.21), we shall first consider the covariance between a general portfolio on B^{n+1}, $\tilde{x}(\pi)$, and $\tilde{x}^*$, which is given by the expression

$$\operatorname{cov}(\tilde{x}(\pi), \tilde{x}^*) = \tilde{x}'(\pi)\tilde{V}\tilde{x}^* = [x'(\pi), x_\rho(\pi)]\,\tilde{V}\begin{bmatrix} x^* \\ 0 \end{bmatrix}, \tag{7.25}$$

where $x(\pi)$ and $x_\rho(\pi)$ are given by (7.1) and (7.2), respectively; $\tilde{V}$ is defined by (6.1) and x^* by (7.7). By making the necessary substitutions, after some computation we have

$$\operatorname{cov}(\tilde{x}(\pi), \tilde{x}^*) = \rho(\tilde{x}(\pi), \tilde{x}^*)\sigma_{\tilde{x}(\pi)}\sigma_{\tilde{x}^*} = \frac{\rho - \pi}{\gamma\rho - \beta}. \tag{7.26}$$

Now from (6.8) we have

$$\sigma_{\tilde{x}(\pi)} = \frac{\pi - \rho}{[\gamma\rho^2 - 2\beta\rho + \alpha]^{1/2}}, \tag{7.27}$$

while from (6.65) and (6.66) we obtain

$$\sigma_{\tilde{x}^*} = \frac{[\gamma\rho^2 - 2\beta\rho + \alpha]^{1/2}}{\beta - \gamma\rho}. \tag{7.28}$$

Finally, from (7.26)–(7.28) we obtain

$$\rho(\tilde{x}(\pi), \tilde{x}(\pi^*)) = 1, \qquad \pi \neq \rho, \tag{7.29}$$

for each $\tilde{x}(\pi)$ on the boundary B^{n+1}. Now since all portfolios on B^{n+1} are a linear combination (see (7.23)) of $\tilde{x}_\rho$ and $\tilde{x}^*$, from (7.29) it immediately follows that

$$\rho(\tilde{x}(\pi_1), \tilde{x}(\pi_2)) = 1, \qquad \pi_1, \pi_2 \neq \rho, \tag{7.30}$$

for each $\tilde{x}(\pi_1)$ and $\tilde{x}(\pi_2)$ belonging to B^{n+1}.

The final statement (7.22) is obvious since $\sigma_{n+1} = 0$. This statement is also confirmed by Theorem (4.35).

(7.31) **Remarks**

Equations (7.23) can be used in three different ways. Given π, we may find η and σ; given σ, we may find η and π; or given η, we may find π and σ. In particular, in the first utilization of this equation for each value π we identify the corresponding point on the boundary B^{n+1} (through the identification of σ) and the composition of the corresponding portfolio ηx^*, $(1-\eta)x_\rho$. The explicit solution σ, η of (7.24) is

(7.32) $$\eta = \frac{\pi - \rho}{\pi^* - \rho}, \qquad \sigma = \frac{\sigma^*(\pi - \rho)}{\pi^* - \rho}.$$

This type of relation will be quite important in a later chapter. We shall conclude this chapter with the following:

(7.33) **Theorem**

If we consider the covariance between each investment and the optimal risky portfolio σ_{ix^*} and the variance of the optimal risky portfolio v^*, they are related by the equation

(7.34) $$r_i - \rho = \frac{\sigma_{ix^*}}{v^*}(\pi^* - \rho).$$

Proof

Rewrite Eq. (6.23) in the form

(7.35) $$v = \frac{(\pi - \rho)(\pi - \rho)}{\gamma\rho^2 - 2\beta\rho + \alpha}.$$

Evaluating it at the point $\pi = \pi^*$ and substituting for one of the variables π in Eq. (7.35) the value (6.55), we obtain

(7.36) $$v^* = (\pi^* - \rho)\left(\frac{\beta\rho - \alpha}{\gamma\rho - \beta} - \rho\right)\Big/(\gamma\rho^2 - 2\beta\rho + \alpha),$$

which after some computation takes the form

(7.37) $$v^* = \frac{\pi^* - \rho}{\beta - \gamma\rho}.$$

On the other hand, by definition we have from (6.58)

$$\sigma_{ix^*} = (Vx^*)_i = \frac{r_i - \rho}{\beta - \gamma\rho}. \tag{7.38}$$

Combining (7.38) and (7.39), we obtain (7.34).

(7.39) **Remarks**

Equation (7.34) relates the risk premium of the investment to the risk premium of the optimal risky portfolio and can be written as

$$d_i = \frac{\sigma_{ix^*}}{v^*} d^*. \tag{7.40}$$

or as

$$\frac{d_i}{\sigma_{ix^*}} = \frac{r_i - \rho}{\sigma_{ix^*}} = \text{const.} \qquad \text{for all} \quad i = 1, \ldots, n, \tag{7.40a}$$

which is true for the return r_i and risk σ_{ix^*} of all investments as well as for all portfolios. Note that expressions (7.40a) and (7.34) are familiar cases of the more general expressions (4.91) and (4.95). Equations (7.40) and (7.40a) will be very useful in Chapter 14.

EXAMPLES, NOTES, AND REFERENCES

The main consequence of the main theorem (Theorem (7.17)) is that all rational investors will use the same optimal portfolio of risky assets x^*. The risk level suited to individual needs will be achieved by choosing η and therefore the related risk level σ (see (7.32)).

The parameter η will define that fraction of the capital which will be invested in x^* by the investor.

This result has some far-reaching effects under the assumption that all investors are risk averse and have the same probability beliefs. These effects will be discussed in Chapter 14.

It is important to point out that one of the peculiarities of the particular case investigated in this chapter is the simultaneous coexistence of properties (7.18)–(7.22). In Chapter 10 it will be shown that some of properties (7.18)–(7.20) may be found separately in some other problems, while (7.21) seems to be possible only in the case that we have now investigated.

We shall next present an example from which follows the existence of interior points (without uniqueness of the mapping $(\sigma, \pi) \to x$) even in the case $n = 2$, $\rho = \beta/\gamma$.

Consider the portfolio problem relative to the case (6.1), where

$$V = \begin{bmatrix} 1 & 0 \\ 0 & 4 \end{bmatrix}, \qquad \tilde{r} = \begin{bmatrix} 1 \\ 2 \\ \frac{6}{5} \end{bmatrix}, \tag{7.41}$$

for which,

$$\beta = \tfrac{3}{2}, \qquad \gamma = \tfrac{5}{4}, \qquad \rho = \beta/\gamma = \tfrac{6}{5}, \tag{7.42}$$

and the portfolio problem (6.1) takes the form

$$v = x_1^2 + 4x_2^2, \qquad \pi = x_1 + 2x_2 + \tfrac{6}{5}x_3, \quad 1 = x_1 + x_2 + x_3. \tag{7.43}$$

It is easy to check that the portfolios

$$x_1 = \frac{2}{\pm\sqrt{5}}, \qquad x_2 = \frac{1}{\pm 2\sqrt{5}}, \qquad x_3 = \frac{2 \pm \sqrt{5}}{2} \tag{7.44}$$

define the point $v = 1$, $\pi = \frac{6}{5}$, which clearly is lying between the two straight lines that define the boundary of the region of admissible portfolios of our problem.

One further consequence of Theorem (7.17) and in particular of the separation property is that the solution to the general portfolio problem could be reached in two steps: first the identification of (σ^*, π^*) and the construction of the ray $B^{n=1}$, then along this ray the identification of η, which maximizes the utility function of the investor.

Clearly, all results related to the existence of an optimal combination of risky assets x^* that we have derived in this and the previous chapters hold only if ρ, the riskless rate, applies both to borrowing and to lending. The more realistic case in which there exists a borrowing rate that is different from the lending rate will be investigated in Chapter 16.

The main result obtained in this chapter, which is one of the major results of portfolio theory, i.e., the existence of a unique optimal combination of risky assets, as well as the consequences of the nonindifference Theorem (3.15), is clearly contradicted by investment practice. The reasons for this contradiction may be many, and they are all related to the relative simplicity of the model. In particular, the lack of consideration of transaction costs, bookkeeping costs, and the assumption on the infinite divisibility of assets may indeed affect the practical applicability of the model. One difference between theory and practice can at first glance be attributed to the fact that in our model short sales are allowed; but in practice not many investors are willing to use this form of investment. This fact will however be clarified in Chapter 14 where it will be proved that if all investors are risk-averters, have the same probability beliefs, and have the same information, it must follow that the optimal combination of risky assets has all positive components.

It remains to be seen under what circumstances, even within the framework of our model, the optimal combination of risky assets is not unique—this will be done in Chapter 11.

Expression (7.7) defines the optimal combination of risky assets and therefore the demand of each risky asset in the case of system (6.1)–(6.2). In this case Eq. (7.7) allows us to analyze the structure of $x_i(\pi)$ much better than the general expression (3.28). By applying formula (A.9), we shall rewrite the expression of the components of x^* (7.7) in the form

$$x^* = \frac{(V^{-1}d)_i}{\sum(V^{-1}d)_i} = \frac{(V^1 C^A V d)_i}{e V^1 C^A V d}, \tag{7.45}$$

where C^A denotes the adjoint of the matrix C (A.5), i.e., the matrix the elements of which are the algebraic complements of the elements of C. In the fraction at the right-hand side of (7.45) we have eliminated both from the numerator and the denominator the determinant of the matrix C. The fraction at the left-hand side of (7.45) shows an interesting property of the sign of x_i^*. Recalling that

$$e'V^{-1}d = \sum(V^{-1}d)_i = \beta - \rho\gamma, \tag{7.46}$$

it follows that if

$$(V^{-1}d)_i > 0 \qquad \text{for all} \quad i = 1, \ldots, n_1 \tag{7.47}$$

then

$$e'V^{-1}d = \beta - \rho\gamma > 0, \tag{7.48}$$

which implies that (see Remark (6.71)) if condition (7.47) is satisfied, x^* belongs to the efficient set ($\pi^* > \beta/\gamma$). Going back to expression (7.45) we see that

$$\text{sgn}\, x_i = \text{sgn}(C^A P)_i = \text{sgn} \sum_{j=1}^{n} (-1)^{i+j} \rho_{ij} d_j/\sigma_j, \qquad i = 1, \ldots, n_1 \tag{7.49}$$

where

$$p_j = (Vd)_j = d_j/\sigma_j = (r_j - \rho)\sigma_j, \qquad i = 1, \ldots, n. \tag{7.50}$$

Thus it is not necessarily true that

$$\text{sgn}\, x_i = \text{sgn}\, d_i, \tag{7.51}$$

and since $\sigma_i > 0$ for all i, $i = 1, \ldots, n$, the correlation coefficients ρ_{ij} are essential in the determination of $\text{sgn}\, x_i^*$.

In the particular case in which V is diagonal and $\rho_{ij} = 0$ for all $i \neq j$, $i, j = 1, \ldots, n$, (4.75) then takes the form

$$x_i^* = \frac{(V^1 Vd)_i}{eV^1 Vd} = \frac{d_j/\sigma_i}{\sum d_j/\sigma_j}. \tag{7.52}$$

Hence, if V is diagonal, it follows that

$$\text{sgn}\, x_i^* = \text{sgn}\, d_i. \tag{7.53}$$

The relationship (7.52), as compared with (7.45) allows the empirical testing of one of the main practical questions of portfolio theory, i.e., it allows us to test whether the investors do indeed make use of the information on the correlation coefficients ρ_{ij} ($i \neq j$) or whether they on the contrary make their investment decisions only on estimates of r_i and v_i. In the case in which the former hypothesis holds, there could indeed exist on the market investments characterized by negative excess returns d_i. This fact could not take place when the investors disregard the correlation coefficients.

We would next like to verify in a particular case the possibility that (7.51) is indeed violated when V is not diagonal.

For instance, in the case $n = 2$, from (7.49) in order that $x_1^*, x_2^* > 0$, we must have

$$p_1 - p_2\rho_{12} > 0, \qquad -p_1\rho_{12} + p_2 > 0. \tag{7.54}$$

These inequalities can be satisfied when

$$p_1 > 0, \qquad p_2 > 0, \qquad \rho_{12} \leq 0 \tag{7.55}$$

or also when

$$p_i < 0, \qquad p_j > 0, \qquad i,j = 1, 2, \qquad \rho_{12} < 0 \tag{7.56}$$

with

$$p_j > |p_i| \tag{7.57}$$

and

$$|p_i|/p_j < |\rho_{12}| < p_j/|p_i|. \tag{7.58}$$

Keeping in mind that $|\rho_{12}| < 1$, all other situations must be ruled out.

CHAPTER 8

ENLARGING THE SET OF INVESTMENTS: THE GENERAL SINGULAR CASE

In this chapter we shall investigate the properties of the region of admissible portfolios when to the original set of n investments that satisfy the usual regularity conditions we add an $(n + 1)$th investment such that V (5.1) is singular, but $\sigma_{n+1} \neq 0$. This is the case labeled as case (5.7) in our previous classification.

We shall approach this case by reducing it by a suitable transformation to the singular case investigated in Chapter 6. This transformation, however, will not always be possible and the general singular case investigated in this chapter will be divided into three subcases.

Throughout this chapter it will again be assumed that the $(n + 1)$ investments portfolio problem can be decomposed in the form (5.1), i.e.,

$$(8.1) \qquad \tilde{V} = \begin{bmatrix} V & b \\ b' & \varepsilon \end{bmatrix}, \qquad \tilde{r} = \begin{bmatrix} r \\ r_{n+1} \end{bmatrix}, \qquad \tilde{e} = \begin{bmatrix} e \\ 1 \end{bmatrix}, \qquad \tilde{x} = \begin{bmatrix} x \\ x_\rho \end{bmatrix}$$

and that

$$(8.2) \qquad \det V \neq 0 \qquad \text{and} \qquad r_i \neq r_j \qquad \text{for some} \quad i, j = 1, \ldots, n.$$

Before computing the boundary of the region of admissible portfolios and investigating its properties in the various cases, we must recall the following known theorem from the theory of determinants:

(8.3) **Lemma**

If V is nonsingular, then a necessary and sufficient condition for the enlarged $(n + 1) \times (n + 1)$ variance–covariance matrix $\tilde{V}$(8.1) to be singular is the existence of an n-dimensional vector a such that

$$(8.4) \qquad b = Va$$

and

$$\varepsilon = a'Va, \tag{8.5}$$

or in other words, a necessary and sufficient condition for $\tilde{V}$ to be singular is that the elements of the $(n + 1)$th row (column) are linear combinations of the elements of the first n columns.

In order to solve the portfolio problem relative to the enlarged set of $n + 1$ investments, i.e., to identify and analyze analytically the properties of the boundary of the region of admissible portfolios of the problem

$$v = \tilde{x}'\tilde{V}\tilde{x}, \qquad \pi = \tilde{x}'\tilde{r}, \qquad 1 = \tilde{x}'\tilde{e}, \tag{8.6}$$

we must consider the following three different cases according to the relative properties of the vector a defining the linear combinations (8.4) and of the augmented expected return vector r:

$$e'a \neq 1, \tag{8.7}$$

$$e'a = 1 \qquad \text{and} \qquad r_{n+1} = r'a, \tag{8.8}$$

$$e'a = 1 \qquad \text{and} \qquad r_{n+1} \neq r'a. \tag{8.9}$$

The first alternative (8.7) arises when the vector a is not an allocation vector. This implies that the covariance b_i, $i = 1, \ldots, n$, defined by each component of vector (8.4), does not coincide with the covariance of any portfolio in the region of admissible portfolios relative to the original set of n investments (V, r, e) defined by Eq. (2.1).

The second case (8.8) is concerned with that in which the $(n + 1)$th investment completely concides with one of the admissible portfolios generated by the original set of n investments.

The third and last alternative (8.9) describes a situation in which among the portfolios relative to the set of the original n investments (V, r, e) it is possible to find one portfolio such that its covariance is identical to that of the $(n + 1)$th investment; but, on the other hand, the $(n + 1)$th investment, because of the second condition (8.9), does not belong to the region of admissible portfolios (2.1) of the original set of n investments.

If we substitute expressions (8.4) and (8.5) into (8.1), the following theorem can be proved:

(8.10) **Theorem**

Consider the region of admissible portfolios (8.6) relative to the problem (8.1), where

$$\tilde{V} = \begin{bmatrix} V & Va \\ a'V & a'Va \end{bmatrix}. \tag{8.11}$$

If

$$e'a \neq 1, \tag{8.12}$$

then the boundary B^{n+1} of the region of admissible portfolios in the plane (σ, π) is given by the straight lines

$$\pi = \bar{\rho} \pm \sigma[\gamma\bar{\rho}^2 - 2\beta\bar{\rho} + \alpha]^{1/2}, \tag{8.13}$$

where

$$\bar{\rho} = \frac{r_{n+1} - r'a}{1 - e'a}. \tag{8.14}$$

All results derived in Chapter 6 can in the particular case $\sigma_{n+1} = 0$ apply to this case if ρ is replaced by $\bar{\rho}$.

If

$$e'a = 1 \qquad \text{and} \qquad r_{n+1} = r'a, \tag{8.15}$$

then the boundary B^{n+1} of the region of admissible portfolios coincides with the boundary B^n relative to the set of n original investments (V, r, e). In this case however, given π, there no longer exists a unique vector $x(\pi)$ on B^{n+1}. Finally, if

$$e'a = 1 \qquad \text{and} \qquad r_{n+1} \neq r'a, \tag{8.16}$$

the boundary B^{n+1} of the region of admissible portfolios in the plane (v, π) is given by the vertical straight line

$$v = 1/\gamma. \tag{8.17}$$

This straight line is tangent to the parabola B^n (2.7) at its vertex (2.28).

In the first case (8.12) the scalar $\bar{\rho}$ (8.14) will be called the equivalent riskless asset.

Proof

If condition (8.16) is satisfied, we shall search for a nonsingular linear transformation

$$\tilde{x} = \tilde{K}\tilde{y} \tag{8.18}$$

such that the matrix $\tilde{V}$ (8.11) in problem (8.6) relative to the allocation vector $\tilde{x}$ will be transformed into a matrix $\bar{V}$ relative to the allocation vector $\tilde{y}$ that is identical to the matrix $\tilde{V}$ defined by (6.1). Thus the portfolio problem (8.6) will be reduced to the one already solved in Chapter 6.

Consider to this end the nonsingular matrix

$$\tilde{K} = \begin{bmatrix} I & -\xi a \\ \emptyset' & \xi \end{bmatrix}, \tag{8.19}$$

where I denotes the $(n \times n)$ unit matrix, a is the vector defined in Lemma (8.3), and $\xi \neq 0$ is an arbitrary constant. The derivation of the matrix $\tilde{K}$ (8.19) is presented in Appendix G. Consider then the nonsingular transformation (8.18) where $\tilde{K}$ is given by (8.19).

Applying transformation (8.18) to Eqs. (8.6), which define our region of admissible portfolios, we obtain the equations

$$v = \tilde{y}'\tilde{K}'\tilde{V}\tilde{K}\tilde{y}, \qquad \pi = \tilde{r}'\tilde{K}\tilde{y}, \qquad 1 = \tilde{e}'\tilde{K}\tilde{y}. \tag{8.20}$$

We shall next introduce the $(n + 1) \times (n + 1)$ transformed matrix $\overline{V}$ defined as

$$\overline{V} = \tilde{K}'\tilde{V}\tilde{K}. \tag{8.21}$$

If we introduce in (8.21) the variance–covariance matrix $\tilde{V}$ (8.11) and the nonsingular transformation matrix $\tilde{K}$ (8.19), after some simple computation we get

$$\overline{V} = \begin{bmatrix} I & \emptyset \\ -\xi a' & \xi \end{bmatrix} \begin{bmatrix} V & Va \\ a'V & a'Va \end{bmatrix} \begin{bmatrix} I & -\xi a \\ \emptyset' & \xi \end{bmatrix} = \begin{bmatrix} V & \emptyset \\ \emptyset' & 0 \end{bmatrix}, \tag{8.22}$$

which shows that indeed the transformation (8.18) transforms the matrix $\tilde{V}$ (8.11) into the particular form (6.1).

In order to proceed with the solution of the problem, we must apply the transformation (8.18) to the expected return vector $\tilde{r}$ and to the unit vector $\tilde{e}$. The transformed vector, which will be denoted by $\overline{r}$, has the form

$$\begin{aligned} \overline{r}' = \tilde{r}'\tilde{K} &= (r', r_{n+1}) \begin{bmatrix} I & -\xi a \\ \emptyset' & \xi \end{bmatrix} \\ &= (r', -\xi r'a + \xi r_{n+1}) = (r', \overline{r}_{n+1}), \end{aligned} \tag{8.23}$$

which shows that the transformation (8.18) acts only on the $(n + 1)$th component of $\tilde{r}$, transforming $\tilde{r}_{n+1}$ into $\overline{r}_{n+1}$ as shown by (8.23).

Consider next the transform of the vector $\tilde{e}$ which will be denoted by $\overline{e}$. We have

$$\overline{e}' = \tilde{e}'\tilde{K} = (e', 1) \begin{bmatrix} I & -\xi a \\ \emptyset' & \xi \end{bmatrix} = (e', -\xi e'a + \xi) = (e', \overline{e}_{n+1}). \tag{8.24}$$

In the new notation, the transformed problem (8.20) takes the form

$$v = \tilde{y}'\overline{V}\tilde{y}, \qquad \pi = \overline{r}'\tilde{y}, \qquad 1 = \overline{e}'\tilde{y}, \tag{8.25}$$

where $\overline{V}, \overline{r}$, and $\overline{e}$ are given by (8.22), (8.23), and (8.24), respectively.

Now, in order that $\tilde{y}$ be considered an allocation vector, we must have

$$\overline{e} = \tilde{e}, \tag{8.26}$$

i.e., e must be the $(n + 1)$-dimensional unit vector. If we consider expression (8.24), we see that this is possible if and only if $\bar{e}_{n+1} = 1$, i.e.,

$$\xi(1 - e'a) = 1. \tag{8.27}$$

From condition (8.12) we have that we can always find a real number ξ which satisfies Eq. (8.27), i.e., such that

$$\xi = 1/(1 - e'a). \tag{8.28}$$

With this choice of the constant ξ, the transformation matrix $\tilde{K}$ (8.19) is completely defined, and problem (8.25) is indeed an allocation problem with the following data:

$$\bar{V} = \begin{bmatrix} V & \emptyset \\ \emptyset' & 0 \end{bmatrix}, \qquad \bar{r} = \begin{bmatrix} r \\ \bar{\rho} \end{bmatrix}, \qquad \bar{e} = \begin{bmatrix} e \\ 1 \end{bmatrix}, \qquad \tilde{y} = \begin{bmatrix} y \\ y_{\bar{\rho}} \end{bmatrix}. \tag{8.29}$$

In the representation of the vector $\bar{r}$, its $(n + 1)$th component, which we have denoted by $\bar{\rho}$, by substituting (8.28) into (8.23), has the form

$$\bar{\rho} = \frac{r_{n+1} - r'a}{1 - e'a} \tag{8.30}$$

and will be called return on the equivalent riskless asset, since it is formally equivalent to the return on the riskless asset considered in the problem (6.1).

Problem (8.25) with the data of (8.29)–(8.30) is now formally identical to problem (6.1), and therefore all results obtained in Chapter 6 on the boundary of the region of admissible portfolios can be applied.

The boundary B^{n+1} of the region of admissible portfolios in the plane (σ, π) of problem (8.25) is therefore described by the following two straight lines (Fig. 8.1):

$$\pi = \bar{\rho} \pm \sigma(\gamma\bar{\rho}^2 - 2\beta\bar{\rho} + \alpha)^{1/2}, \tag{8.31}$$

while on B^{n+1} the allocation vector $\tilde{y}(\pi)$ takes the form (see (6.34) and 6.35))

$$\begin{aligned} y(\pi) &= (\pi - \bar{\rho})V^{-1}\bar{d}/\bar{\delta}, \\ y_\rho(\pi) &= (r - \pi e)'V^{-1}\bar{d}/\bar{\delta}, \end{aligned} \tag{8.32}$$

where

$$\bar{d} = r - \bar{\rho}e, \qquad \bar{\delta} = \bar{d}'V^{-1}\bar{d}, \tag{8.33}$$

and $\bar{\rho}$ is given by (8.30).

While (8.31) provides the actual equation for the boundary of the original problem (8.6), formulas (8.32) give the expression of the auxiliary vector $\tilde{y}$ on such a boundary, an auxiliary vector that in general will not coincide with the original allocation vector $\tilde{x}$ of problem (8.6). In order to find the equation

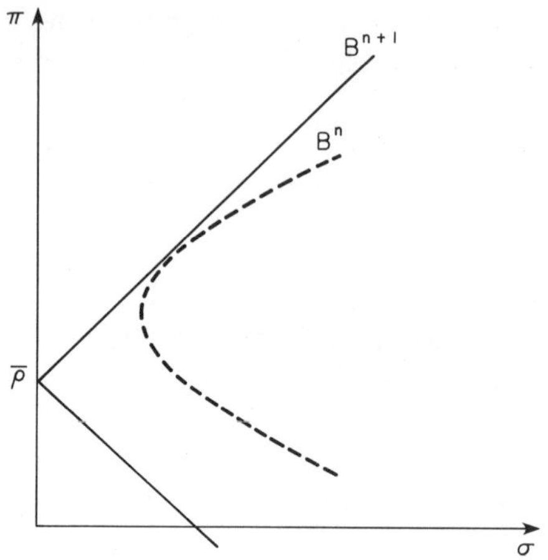

Figure 8.1

for $\tilde{x}(\pi)$, which defines $\tilde{x}$ on B^{n+1}, we must apply the transformation (8.18) to the vector $\tilde{y}(\pi)$ defined by (8.32). Thus

$$\tilde{x}(\pi) = \tilde{K}\tilde{y}(\pi) = \begin{bmatrix} I & -\xi a \\ \emptyset' & \xi \end{bmatrix}\begin{bmatrix} y(\pi) \\ y_{\bar{\rho}}(\pi) \end{bmatrix} = \begin{bmatrix} y(\pi) - ay_{\bar{\rho}}(\pi)/(1-e'a) \\ y_{\bar{\rho}}(\pi)/(1-e'a) \end{bmatrix}, \tag{8.34}$$

where we have introduced in place of the constant ξ its expression (8.28).

Theorems (6.36), (6.43), and (6.54) still apply if we replace ρ by $\bar{\rho}$. In particular, expressions (6.55)–(6.58) still hold if we replace ρ by $\bar{\rho}$ (8.30).

Consider next the case in which condition (8.15) holds. In this case if we introduce the two equalities (8.15) into expressions (8.23) and (8.24), we see that the transformed problem (8.25) has the following data:

$$\bar{V} = \begin{bmatrix} V & \emptyset \\ \emptyset' & 0 \end{bmatrix}, \qquad \bar{r} = \begin{bmatrix} r \\ 0 \end{bmatrix}, \qquad \bar{e} = \begin{bmatrix} e \\ 0 \end{bmatrix}. \tag{8.35}$$

In order to stress the difference between this case and the previous one, we shall represent the transformed allocation vector $\tilde{y}$ in the form

$$\tilde{y} = \begin{bmatrix} y \\ \tilde{y}_{n+1} \end{bmatrix}. \tag{8.36}$$

The transformed allocation problem (8.25) then becomes

$$v = y'Vy, \qquad \pi = r'y, \qquad 1 = e'y, \tag{8.37}$$

which is identical to the original nonsingular portfolio selection problem associated with the original set of n risky investments and solved in Chapter 2.

Thus the results of these two problems must coincide, and the boundary B^{n+1} of the region of admissible portfolios of problem (8.6) must coincide with the boundary B^n of the problem (2.1), namely, in the plane (σ, π) with the branch of hyperbola (2.8). Considering the problem of the identification of the allocation vector $\tilde{x}(\pi)$ on the boundary B^{n+1} of the problem (8.6), we shall first consider the composition of the auxiliary allocation vector $\tilde{y}(\pi)$ on B^{n+1}. Taking again into account the data (8.35) and the corresponding form of problems (8.25), (8.37), we see that the first n components of the vector $\tilde{y}(\pi)$ on B^{n+1} must coincide with those of the vector $y(\pi)$ on the boundary B^n of the region of admissible portfolios of the nonsingular problem (8.37). Thus from (2.9)

(8.38)
$$y(\pi) = \frac{(\pi\gamma - \beta)V^{-1}r + (\alpha - \pi\beta)V^{-1}e}{\alpha\gamma - \beta^2}.$$

We must now compute the allocation vector $\tilde{x}(\pi)$ of problem (8.6) on B^{n+1}. For that we shall proceed as in the previous case and apply the transformation (8.18) to the vector $\tilde{y}(\pi)$. Note that the constant in the transformation matrix (8.19) is still completely arbitrary and the last component $\tilde{y}_{n+1}(\pi)$ of the allocation vector $\tilde{y}(\pi)$ on B^{n+1} is still to be identified.

By applying the transformation (8.18) to the vector $\tilde{y}(\pi)$ ((8.36) and (8.38)), we obtain

(8.39)
$$\tilde{x}(\pi) = \tilde{K}\tilde{y}(\pi) = \begin{bmatrix} I & -\xi a \\ \emptyset' & \xi \end{bmatrix} \begin{bmatrix} y(\pi) \\ \tilde{y}_{n+1}(\pi) \end{bmatrix} = \begin{bmatrix} y(\pi) - \xi a \tilde{y}_{n+1}(\pi) \\ \xi \tilde{y}_{n+1}(\pi) \end{bmatrix}.$$

Next let

(8.40)
$$\xi \tilde{y}_{n+1}(\pi) = -\varphi,$$

where φ is an arbitrary real number. Then

(8.41)
$$\tilde{x}(\pi) = \begin{bmatrix} y(\pi) + \varphi a \\ -\varphi \end{bmatrix},$$

where $y(\pi)$ is given by (8.38). Now since φ is arbitrary, it follows that the allocation vector $x(\pi)$ of problem (8.6) under hypothesis (8.15) is defined by a family of linear functions of π. Clearly, the correspondence between points (v, π) on B^{n+1} and $\tilde{x}(\pi)$ is no longer unique, but rather there exists a simple infinity of linear correspondences.

As a further check on the validity of the solution (8.41), we shall compute the last equation of system (8.6) for the case in which $\tilde{x}(\pi)$ is given by (8.41). We obtain

(8.42)
$$1 = e'y(\pi) + \varphi e'a - \varphi.$$

Now since a satisfies the first equation of hypothesis (8.15), it follows that indeed (8.42) is satisfied whatever value is chosen for φ.

Finally, consider the case in which condition (8.16) is satisfied. In this case if we introduce the two relationships (8.16) into Eqs. (8.23) and (8.24), we see that the data $\bar{V}, \bar{r}$, and $\bar{e}$ relative to the transformed allocation problem (8.25) take the form

$$\bar{V} = \begin{bmatrix} V & \emptyset \\ \emptyset' & 0 \end{bmatrix}, \qquad \bar{r} = \begin{bmatrix} r \\ \bar{r}_{n+1} \end{bmatrix}, \qquad \bar{e} = \begin{bmatrix} e \\ 0 \end{bmatrix}, \tag{8.43}$$

where $\bar{r}_{n+1}$ is given by (8.23). Again representing the transformed allocation vector $\tilde{y}$ in the form (8.36), the transformed allocation problem (8.25) becomes

$$v = y'Vy, \qquad \pi = r'y + \bar{r}_{n+1}\tilde{y}_{n+1}, \qquad 1 = e'y. \tag{8.44}$$

This transformed problem in which the component $\tilde{y}_{n+1}$ of the transformed allocation vector $\tilde{y}$ appears only in the second equation does not seem to coincide with any of the previously considered cases. We shall then identify the boundary B^{n+1} and the allocation vector $\tilde{y}(\pi)$ on B^{n+1} relative to the region of admissible portfolios (8.44) by considering the constrained minimization problem

$$\min y'Vy \tag{8.45}$$

subject to equations

$$\pi = r'y + \bar{r}_{n+1}\tilde{y}_{n+1}, \qquad 1 = e'y, \tag{8.46}$$

where $\bar{r}_{n+1}$ is given by (8.23). We shall solve the minimization problem (8.45), (8.46) by considering the Lagrangian function

$$L(y, \tilde{y}_{n+1}, \lambda_1, \lambda_2) = y'Vy - \lambda_1(r'y + \bar{r}_{n+1}\tilde{y}_{n+1} - \pi) - \lambda_2(e'y - 1). \tag{8.47}$$

The critical points of (8.44) are obtained by solving the following linear system of $n + 3$ equations in $n + 3$ unknowns, obtained by equating to zero the $n + 3$ partial derivatives of $L(y, \tilde{y}_{n+1}, \lambda_1, \lambda_2)$ with respect to their arguments:

$$\begin{aligned} \frac{\partial L}{\partial y} &= 2y'V - \lambda_1 r' - \lambda_2 e' = 0, \\ \frac{\partial L}{\partial \tilde{y}_{n+1}} &= -\lambda_1 \bar{r}_{n+1} = 0, \\ \frac{\partial L}{\partial \lambda_1} &= -r'y - \bar{r}_{n+1}\tilde{y}_{n+1} + \pi = 0, \\ \frac{\partial L}{\partial \lambda_2} &= -e'y + 1 = 0. \end{aligned} \tag{8.48}$$

The linear system has a unique solution if and only if the determinant of its coefficients is different from zero, i.e., if

$$\det L = \begin{vmatrix} 2V & \emptyset & r & e \\ \emptyset' & 0 & \overline{r}_{n+1} & 0 \\ r' & \overline{r}_{n+1} & 0 & 0 \\ e' & 0 & 0 & 0 \end{vmatrix} \neq 0. \tag{8.49}$$

We can show (Appendix H) that if assumptions (8.2) and (8.16) are satisfied, then condition (8.49) always holds. After some algebraic computation we can show that the solution to system (8.48), i.e., the value of the transformed allocation vector $\tilde{y}(\pi)$ on B^{n+1}, is

$$\tilde{y}(\pi) = \begin{bmatrix} V^{-1}e/\gamma \\ \dfrac{\gamma\pi - \beta}{\overline{r}_{n+1}\gamma} \end{bmatrix} = \begin{bmatrix} x^v \\ \dfrac{\gamma\pi - \beta}{\overline{r}_{n+1}\gamma} \end{bmatrix}, \tag{8.50}$$

where we have again denoted by x^v the allocation vector on the vertex of the parabola (2.7) (see (2.29)) and $\overline{r}_{n+1}$ is again given by (8.23). From (8.50) we can easily compute the equation of the boundary B^{n+1} of the region of admissible portfolios in the plane (v, π), which has the form

$$v = y'Vy = \frac{e'V^{-1}}{\gamma} V \frac{V^{-1}e}{\gamma} = \frac{1}{\gamma} = v_v, \tag{8.51}$$

which in the plane (v, π) is the equation of a vertical straight line through the point $v = 1/\gamma$, the abscissa of the vertex of parabola (2.7) (Fig. 8.2). This vertical straight line is therefore tangent to parabola (2.7) at its vertex.

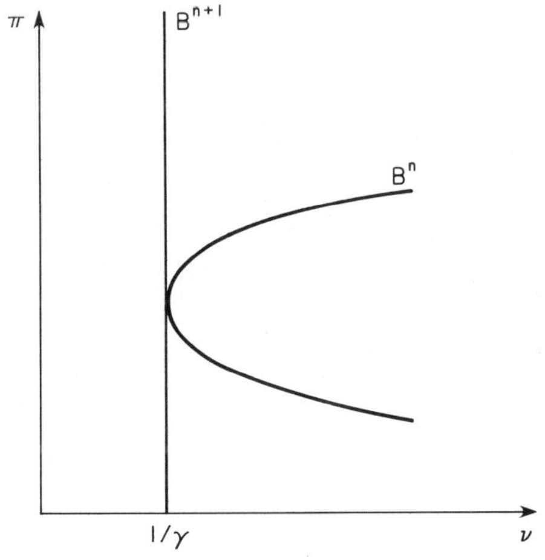

Figure 8.2

We can now compute the equation of the admissible portfolio $x(\pi)$ on the boundary B^{n+1} relative to problem (8.6) under assumption (8.16). In order to obtain such a vector, we shall again apply transformation (8.18) to result (8.51). After some computation we obtain

$$x(\pi) = \begin{bmatrix} I & -\xi a \\ \emptyset' & \xi \end{bmatrix} \begin{bmatrix} x^v \\ \dfrac{\gamma\pi - \beta}{\bar{r}_{n+1}\gamma} \end{bmatrix} = \begin{bmatrix} x^v - \dfrac{(\gamma\pi - \beta)a}{\gamma(r_{n+1} - r'a)} \\ \dfrac{\gamma\pi - \beta}{(r_{n+1} - r'a)} \end{bmatrix}, \tag{8.52}$$

which is independent of ξ and is a linear expression in π. In this case, given π, there exists a unique value of $\tilde{x}(\pi)$ on the boundary B^{n+1}.

It is important to note that in the case in which condition (8.12) holds, in spite of the geometrical coincidence with the situation analyzed in Chapters 6 and 7, there is a major difference in the sign behavior of the allocation vector x on B^{n+1}. Indeed, while the minimum variance portfolio $x = 0$, $x_{n+1} = \rho$ of Chapter 6 always satisfies the nonnegativity condition $x \geq 0$, in the case of condition (8.12) the minimum variance portfolio becomes

$$x(\bar{\rho}) = \frac{-a}{1 - e'a}, \qquad x_\rho(\bar{\rho}) = \frac{1}{1 - e'a}. \tag{8.53}$$

This portfolio, on the other hand, does not always necessarily satisfy the condition $x \geq 0$.

EXAMPLES, NOTES, AND REFERENCES

The variety of alternative situations that may arise in the general singular case investigated in this chapter makes its analysis very cumbersome and involved. On the other hand, some incomplete analysis (Roll, 1977) led to wrong results, i.e., to the disregard of the two situations characterized by conditions (8.8) and (8.9). The technique used in the proof of Theorem (8.10) is clearly not the only one possible. In particular, the theorem can be proved by a straightforward Lagrangian method. The reader can, however, easily see that the Lagrangian method leads to much more complicated computations than does that of the technique adopted in this chapter.

In Chapter 11 we shall investigate the case in which the given matrix V has rank $m < n$, and corresponding reference will be made to the results proven in Theorem (8.10).

The results obtained in this chapter hold completely only in the case in which the nondegeneracy condition on the vector r (2.6) holds; when instead of (2.6) we have

$$r = \delta e, \tag{8.54}$$

some of the results obtained are no longer true. In the case in which condition (8.12) holds, the results obtained in Chapter 6 (e.g., (6.72)–(6.76)) still apply when we replace ρ by $\bar{\rho}$ (8.14).

In the case in which condition (8.15) holds in conjunction with equality (8.54), $B^{n+1} = B^n$, and the boundary is given by the ray defined by Eqs. (2.76) and (2.80), while again the transformation $(v, \pi) \rightarrow \dot{x}$ is no longer one-to-one. Note that in this case

$$r_{n+1} = r'a = \delta e'a = \delta. \tag{8.55}$$

Finally, when condition (8.16) holds, B^{n+1} is still defined by (8.17), and the origin ($v = 1/\gamma$) of the ray on the straight line $\pi = \delta$ defining B^n clearly belongs to (8.17).

CHAPTER 9

PROPERTIES OF THE EFFICIENT FRONTIER IN THE GENERAL SINGULAR CASE

In the preceding chapter we derived the analytic expression for the boundary of the region of admissible portfolios in the plane (σ, π) as well as in the space X for the case in which the variance–covariance matrix of the augmented problem $\tilde{V}$ is singular, but the $(n+1)$th investment has a nonzero standard deviation. The problem was analyzed under three different assumptions, (8.7)–(8.9), leading in the plane (σ, π) to the boundaries (8.13), (2.8), and (8.17), respectively.

In the space X the boundaries of the region of admissible portfolios are given by Eqs. (8.34), (8.41), and (8.52), respectively.

This chapter is devoted to a further analysis of the properties of boundary portfolios and in particular of efficient portfolios.

In order to do this, we shall again make a detailed investigation of the properties of allocation vector $\tilde{x}(\pi)$ on X, and we shall discuss whether and how some of the properties of Theorem (7.17) that are proved for the case $\sigma_{n+1} = 0$ are still valid in the general singular case.

Because of the great differences in the behavior of the three special cases (8.7)–(8.9), which we singled out in the previous chapter, we shall discuss each particular case separately.

We shall begin our analysis by assuming that

$$e'a \neq 1, \tag{9.1}$$

i.e., that condition (8.7) is verified. In this case, as shown in Theorem (8.10), the behavior of the boundary of the region of admissible portfolios in the plane (σ, π) as well as in the space X is identical to that of the case in which the $(n+1)$th asset is riskless $(\sigma_{n+1} = 0)$, which was fully investigated in Chapters 6 and 7. Indeed, when assumptions (8.2) and (8.11), together with condition (9.1) hold, then Theorem (7.17) is still true if we replace the return from the riskless asset ρ by the return from the equivalent riskless asset $\bar{\rho}$, defined by

$$\bar{\rho} = \frac{r_{n+1} - r'a}{1 - e'a}. \tag{9.2}$$

In particular, if

$$\bar{\rho} \neq \beta/\gamma, \tag{9.3}$$

then the set of $n + 1$ investments is equivalent to two nonintersecting portfolios, i.e., the equivalent riskless asset $(0, \bar{\rho})$ and the optimal portfolios of risky assets defined by the tangency point between the straight lines (8.13) (B^{n+1}) and hyperbola (2.8) (B^n).

The composition of this tangency portfolio in the auxiliary allocation vector y is formally identical to the result obtained in Chapter 6 if in expression (6.67) we replace ρ by $\bar{\rho}$. Thus $\tilde{y}^*$ is given by

$$y^* = \frac{V^{-1}(r - \bar{\rho}e)}{\beta - \gamma\bar{\rho}}, \qquad y^*_{\bar{\rho}} = 0, \tag{9.4}$$

where $\bar{\rho}$ is defined by Eq. (8.29). The location of the tangency point is given by replacing ρ by $\bar{\rho}$ in expressions (6.61)–(6.66). Thus if we denote again by (σ^*, π^*) the point at which B^{n+1} is tangent to B^n, we have

$$\pi^* = \frac{\beta\bar{\rho} - \alpha}{\gamma\bar{\rho} - \beta}, \tag{9.5}$$

$$\sigma^* = \frac{[\gamma\bar{\rho}^2 - 2\beta\bar{\rho} + \alpha]^{1/2}}{\gamma\bar{\rho} - \beta} \qquad \text{if} \quad \bar{\rho} > \frac{\beta}{\gamma}, \tag{9.6}$$

$$\sigma^* = \frac{[\gamma\rho^2 - 2\beta\bar{\rho} + \alpha]^{1/2}}{\beta - \gamma\bar{\rho}} \qquad \text{if} \quad \bar{\rho} < \frac{\beta}{\gamma}. \tag{9.7}$$

We must finally compute the composition of the tangency portfolio, i.e., the optimal combination of risky investments in the original allocation vector x. Applying transformation (8.18) to the vector $\tilde{y}^*$ (9.4), we obtain the expression for $\tilde{x}^*$.

$$\tilde{x}^* = \begin{bmatrix} I & -\xi a \\ \emptyset' & \xi \end{bmatrix} \cdot \begin{bmatrix} y^* \\ 0 \end{bmatrix} = \begin{bmatrix} y^* \\ 0 \end{bmatrix}, \tag{9.8}$$

i.e., $\tilde{x}^*$ is given by the relationships

$$x^* = \frac{V^{-1}(r - \bar{\rho}e)}{\beta - \gamma\bar{\rho}}, \qquad x^*_{n+1} = 0. \tag{9.9}$$

We then conclude that

$$\tilde{x}^* = \tilde{y}^*. \tag{9.10}$$

It is evident from the analysis of the transformation that the vector $\tilde{y}^*$ is the only allocation vector that is invariant with respect to transformation (8.18). Indeed, since $\xi \neq 0$ by assumption, the identity

$$\tilde{x} = \tilde{K}\tilde{y} = \tilde{y} \tag{9.11}$$

can hold if and only if

$$\tilde{y}_{n+1} = 0, \tag{9.12}$$

i.e., only when $\tilde{y} = \tilde{y}^*$.

Consider now the composition of the equivalent riskless asset. We must point out that while in Chapter 6, in the case $\sigma_{n+1} = 0$, the riskless asset $(0, \rho)$ was the particular investment defined by the vector

$$\tilde{x}_\rho = \begin{bmatrix} \emptyset \\ 1 \end{bmatrix}, \tag{9.13}$$

in the case that we are now discussing, while we have

$$\tilde{y}_\rho = \begin{bmatrix} \emptyset \\ 1 \end{bmatrix}, \tag{9.14}$$

the allocation vector $\tilde{x}(\pi)$ at the point $\pi = \bar{\rho}$ has the form

$$\tilde{x}(\bar{\rho}) = \frac{1}{e'a - 1} \begin{bmatrix} a \\ -1 \end{bmatrix}. \tag{9.15}$$

Thus contrary to the case $\sigma_{n+1} = 0$, the equivalent riskless asset is not one of the n investments, but is a combination of investments, a portfolio. Comparing then the composition of $x(\pi)$ with that of x^*, we must conclude that if $a \neq 0$, then $x(\bar{\rho}) \neq 0$, and therefore some components of $x(\pi)$ that have nonzero values at $\pi = \pi^*$ have nonzero values at $\pi = \bar{\rho}$. Thus the separation property (7.20) discussed in Theorem (7.17) does not hold in this case.

We shall next investigate the covariance properties among boundary portfolios. We have

$$\operatorname{cov}(\tilde{x}(\pi_1), \tilde{x}(\pi_2)) = (\tilde{x}(\pi_1))'\tilde{V}\tilde{x}(\pi_2) = (\tilde{y}^1)'\tilde{K}'\tilde{V}\tilde{K}(\tilde{y}^2), \tag{9.16}$$

where $(\tilde{y}^1\tilde{K})'$ and $\tilde{K}\tilde{y}^2$ can easily be computed from transformation (8.18) for the particular value (8.28), as shown in expression (8.34).

After some computation we obtain

$$\operatorname{cov}(\tilde{x}(\pi_1), \tilde{x}(\pi_2)) = \operatorname{cov}(\tilde{y}^1, \tilde{y}^2), \tag{9.17}$$

where the auxiliary allocation vectors $\tilde{y}^1$ and $\tilde{y}^2$ belong to the boundary B^{n+1}. We can then apply the results of Chapter 7 (property (7.21)) proved in (7.25)–(7.30). It also follows immediately that for the case we are discussing, i.e., when condition (9.1) is satisfied, we have

$$\rho(\tilde{x}(\pi_1), \tilde{x}(\pi_2)) = 1 \tag{9.18}$$

for all $\tilde{x}(\pi_1)$, $\tilde{x}(\pi_2)$ belonging to B^{n+1} with $\pi_1, \pi_2 \neq \bar{\rho}$. On the other hand, applying again the results of Chapter 7 (property (7.22)) to the auxiliary allocation vector $\tilde{y}$ and then using relationship (9.17), we have that all boundary portfolios are orthogonal to the equivalent riskless asset $(0, \bar{\rho})$.

(9.19) **Theorem**

If condition (9.1) is satisfied, then Theorem (7.17) also holds partially for the problem (8.1), (8.2). In particular, if we replace ρ by $\bar{\rho}$, properties (7.18)–(7.22) are still true, with the exception of property (7.20) which does not hold.

We shall next consider the case for which

$$e'a = 1 \qquad \text{and} \qquad r_{n+1} = r'a. \tag{9.20}$$

This is the only case encountered so far in which, given a point on the boundary of the region of admissible portfolios, there does not exist a corresponding unique allocation vector x. Indeed, we can prove the following

(9.21) **Theorem**

If $B^n = B^{n+1}$, i.e., if the set of n investments is equivalent to the enlarged set of $n + 1$ investments, a necessary and sufficient condition for the non-uniqueness of the correspondence $(\pi, v) \to x$ is that the $(n + 1)$th investment be an admissible portfolio generated by the original set of n investments.

Proof

We have assumed that the region of admissible portfolios defined by the system

$$v = \tilde{x}'\tilde{V}\tilde{x}, \qquad \pi = \tilde{x}'\tilde{r}, \qquad 1 = \tilde{x}'\tilde{e} \tag{9.22}$$

is equivalent to the region of admissible portfolios defined by the system

$$v = x'Vx, \qquad \pi = x'r, \qquad 1 = x'e, \tag{9.23}$$

where $\tilde{V}$, $\tilde{r}$, $\tilde{e}$, and $\tilde{x}$ are defined by (8.1). In addition, from the assumptions of the theorem we have

$$\det \tilde{V} = 0, \qquad \det V \neq 0. \tag{9.24}$$

Thus from the results of Chapter 8 we can assume that (8.4) and (8.5) hold, i.e., that the enlarged matrix $\tilde{V}$ has the form (8.11).

We must show that the nonuniqueness of the mapping is equivalent to the condition

$$r_{n+1} = r'a. \tag{9.25}$$

From the equivalence of the two systems (9.22) and (9.23), it follows from Theorem (5.14) that the allocation vector $\tilde{x}(\pi)$ on the boundary of the region of admissible portfolios B^{n+1} relative to the enlarged problem (9.22) must have the form

$$\tilde{x}(\pi) = \begin{bmatrix} x(\pi) \\ 0 \end{bmatrix} \tag{9.26}$$

with

$$\tilde{e}'\tilde{x} = e'x = 1. \tag{9.27}$$

From our assumptions however this solution is not unique. Thus the general solution of the problem has the form

$$\tilde{x}(\pi) = \begin{bmatrix} x(\pi) + b \\ \varepsilon \end{bmatrix}, \tag{9.28}$$

where b and ε are again defined by (8.1) and must be such that

$$\tilde{e}'\tilde{x} = e'(x + b) + \varepsilon = 1, \tag{9.29}$$

from which since

$$e'x = 1, \tag{9.30}$$

we have

$$\varepsilon = -e'b. \tag{9.31}$$

Thus the general solution of problem (9.22) has the form

$$\tilde{x}(\pi) = \begin{bmatrix} x(\pi) + b \\ -e'b \end{bmatrix}. \tag{9.32}$$

We shall next identify the vector b, which guarantees that (9.22) is equivalent to (9.23). If we introduce the expression for $\tilde{x}(\pi)$ into the first of Eqs. (9.22), after some computation we obtain

$$\tilde{x}'\tilde{V}\tilde{x} = [(x + b)' - (e'b)a']V[(x + b) - (e'b)a], \tag{9.33}$$

Now since (9.22) and (9.23) must be equivalent, their respective first equations must coincide, i.e.,

$$x'Vx = [(x + b)' - (e'b)a']V[(x + b) - (e'b)a] \tag{9.34}$$

for each $x = x(\pi)$ on the common boundaries of the region of admissible portfolios of the two problems. If we expand Eq. (9.34), after some computation we see that it can be true for each $x = x(\pi)$ if and only if

$$a' = b'/e'b. \tag{9.35}$$

Now since the second equations of (9.22) and (9.23) must also be identical, we have

$$r'x = r'x + r'b - \rho e'b, \tag{9.36}$$

from which it follows that

$$\rho = r'a, \tag{9.37}$$

which proves the theorem.

We shall finally consider the case in which

$$e'a = 1 \qquad \text{and} \qquad r_{n+1} \neq r'a. \tag{9.38}$$

In this case, as shown by Eq. (8.51), the boundary of the region of admissible portfolios becomes a vertical straight line. This implies that by taking the risk $v = 1/\gamma$ the investor can achieve an infinite expected return. This property is due to the fact that the $(n + 1)$th investment has variance–covariance properties equal to those of an admissible portfolio P generated by the original set of n investments, while its expected return is different. To fix these ideas, assume that $\pi(P) < r_{n+1}$. Then by selling P short and investing in the $(n + 1)$th investment, one can indeed obtain an infinite expected return. The strategy would be inverted if it were instead $r_{n+1} < \pi(P)$.

In the three cases into which our problem has been split, we have found only one case in which the minimum variance portfolio has zero variance, i.e., the first case, for which condition (9.6) holds.

Since our analysis has been exhaustive, i.e., we have taken into account all possible cases, we have

(9.39) **Theorem**

If condition (8.2) is satisfied, then a necessary and sufficient condition for the minimum variance portfolio to have zero variance is that

$$\det \tilde{V} = 0 \tag{9.40}$$

and

$$e'a \neq 1. \tag{9.41}$$

Clearly, the case investigated in Chapters 6 and 7 satisfies condition (9.41).

EXAMPLES, NOTES, AND REFERENCES

The most characteristic of the three cases that we have listed is the second, for which condition (9.20) holds, since in this case we do not have the uniqueness of the transformation $(v, \pi) \to x$. We shall return to the analysis of this problem in Chapter 11 and prove that a statement slightly stronger than that of Theorem (9.39) can be made.

The nonuniqueness of the correspondence $(v, \pi) \to x$ in these circumstances implies that any investment to which there corresponds a nonzero value of the weight vector a can be deleted from the set of n investments and replaced by x_{n+1} or alternatively that the $(n + 1)$th investment can be dropped. This property is clearly shown by the particular form of allocation vector (8.41), which contains an arbitrary parameter φ.

This situation can be thoroughly illustrated by the example

(9.42) $$\tilde{V} = \begin{bmatrix} 1 & \frac{1}{2} & \frac{1}{4} \\ \frac{1}{2} & 4 & \frac{23}{4} \\ \frac{1}{4} & \frac{23}{4} & \frac{17}{2} \end{bmatrix}, \qquad \tilde{r} = \begin{bmatrix} 1 \\ 2 \\ \frac{5}{2} \end{bmatrix}.$$

Note that the last row (column) of the matrix V is a linear combination of the first two with the weight vector

(9.43) $$a = \begin{bmatrix} -\frac{1}{2} \\ \frac{3}{2} \end{bmatrix}.$$

It is easy to check that

$$r_3 = r'a = \tfrac{5}{2} \qquad \text{and} \qquad e'a = 1.$$

Applying the transformation matrix $\tilde{K}$ (8.19) to our problem, it will take the form

(9.44) $$\bar{V} = \begin{bmatrix} V & \emptyset \\ \emptyset' & 0 \end{bmatrix}, \qquad \bar{r} = \begin{bmatrix} r \\ 0 \end{bmatrix}, \qquad \bar{e} = \begin{bmatrix} e \\ 0 \end{bmatrix}, \qquad \tilde{y} = \begin{bmatrix} y \\ y_3 \end{bmatrix},$$

where

(9.45) $$V = \begin{bmatrix} 1 & \frac{1}{2} \\ \frac{1}{2} & 4 \end{bmatrix}, \qquad r = \begin{bmatrix} 1 \\ 2 \end{bmatrix}, \qquad e = \begin{bmatrix} 1 \\ 1 \end{bmatrix}.$$

The transformation matrix $\tilde{K}$ in our case takes the form

(9.46) $$\tilde{K} = \begin{bmatrix} 1 & 0 & \frac{1}{2}\xi \\ 0 & 1 & -\frac{3}{2}\xi \\ 0 & 0 & \xi \end{bmatrix},$$

where ξ is an arbitrary real number. If we proceed with the solution of the problem through the auxiliary system (8.37) with the data of (9.45), we have

(9.47) $$V^{-1} = \begin{bmatrix} \frac{16}{15} & -\frac{2}{15} \\ -\frac{2}{15} & \frac{4}{15} \end{bmatrix}.$$

Thus

(9.48) $$\alpha = \tfrac{8}{5}, \qquad \beta = \tfrac{6}{5}, \qquad \gamma = \tfrac{16}{15}, \qquad \alpha\gamma - \beta^2 = \tfrac{4}{15},$$

and therefore the boundary $B^3 = B^2$ of the region of admissible portfolios in the plane (v, π) is given by the parabola

(9.49) $$v = 4\pi^2 - 9\pi + 6.$$

The auxiliary allocation vector $y(\pi)$ on the boundary of the region of admissible portfolios has the form

$$y(\pi) = \begin{bmatrix} -\pi + 2 \\ \pi - 1 \end{bmatrix}, \tag{9.50}$$

while the allocation vector $\tilde{x}(\pi)$ (8.41) becomes

$$\tilde{x}(\pi) = \begin{bmatrix} -\pi + 2 - \frac{1}{2}\varphi \\ \pi - 1 + \frac{3}{2}\varphi \\ -\varphi \end{bmatrix}, \tag{9.51}$$

where φ is arbitrary. Note that

$$\tilde{e}'\tilde{x}(\pi) = -\pi + 2 - \tfrac{1}{2}\varphi + \pi - 1 + \tfrac{3}{2}\varphi - \varphi = 1 \tag{9.52}$$

and

$$\tilde{r}'\tilde{x}(\pi) = -\pi + 2 - \tfrac{1}{2}\varphi + 2\pi - 2 + 3\varphi - \tfrac{5}{2}\varphi = \pi \tag{9.53}$$

regardless of the value given to φ. Now if we choose $\varphi = 0$, then the third investment will be identically zero on the boundary $B^3 = B^2$, i.e., will be dominated by the two original investments. On the other hand, if we choose

$$\varphi = 4 - 2\pi, \tag{9.54}$$

the allocation vector $\tilde{x}(\pi)$ takes the form

$$\tilde{x}(\pi) = \begin{bmatrix} 0 \\ 5 - 2\pi \\ -4 + 2\pi \end{bmatrix}, \tag{9.55}$$

and the first investment is dominated by the second and third, while if we let

$$\varphi = \tfrac{2}{3}(1 - \pi), \tag{9.56}$$

the allocation vector becomes

$$\tilde{x}(\pi) = \begin{bmatrix} \frac{1}{3}(1 - 2\pi) \\ 0 \\ \frac{2}{3}(\pi - 1) \end{bmatrix}, \tag{9.57}$$

and now it is the turn of the second investment to be dominated by the first and third.

In Chapter 14 we shall discuss some further consequences of this case.

It is worthwhile to point out that the situation arising from assumption (9.20), which was described in the previous example, even if it allows that one component of the allocation vector be taken identically zero on the boundary B^n, is quite different from the case of dominance in which one component of the allocation vector must identically vanish on the boundary B^n. This diversity has, among others, been pointed out by Zambruno (1973).

For the first case that we analyzed, i.e., the case for which condition (9.1) is satisfied, we recall that the remark made at the end of Chapter 7 about the possibility of dividing the portfolio selection problem into two steps still applies.

CHAPTER 10

MUTUAL FUNDS AND GENERALIZED SEPARATION

One of the most important results achieved so far is Theorem (7.17) in which we summarized the properties of the boundary of the region of admissible portfolios in the plane (σ, π) as well as in the space X for the case in which the $(n + 1)$th investment is riskless. For a certain period in the literature on portfolios the main properties listed there (linearity, return to scale, separation, and perfect correlation) were considered as one property since the only case investigated was indeed the case that we analyzed in Chapters 6 and 7, the case in which all these properties coexist.

However, in Chapter 8 we discovered one case for which condition (8.12) holds, that in which all properties focused in Theorem (7.17) still hold with the exception of property (7.20) (separation). Indeed, as we pointed out in the previous chapter, by comparing the composition of the equivalent optimal combination of risky assets $\tilde{x}^*$ (9.9) with the composition of the equivalent riskless asset $\tilde{x}(\bar{\rho})$ (9.15), the separation property does not hold in this case.

The aim of this chapter is therefore to prove that on the other hand a separation property in the sense of (7.20) can indeed hold independently from the other properties listed in Theorem (7.17). This form of separation will be called generalized separation.

We shall begin our investigation by proving the weak form of the separation property under which the boundary of the region of admissible portfolios B^n can be uniquely identified by two portfolios on it, which can therefore replace the whole market. From the practical point of view, we can regard these portfolios as mutual funds that are indeed proxies of the set of investments, and for this reason the following theorem, which is a slight generalization of Theorem (2.64), will be called the *mutual fund theorem.*

(10.1) **Theorem**

Assume that the vector $x(\pi)$, which defines the boundary of the region of admissible portfolios in the space π, is a linear function of X

$$x(\pi) = a\pi + b, \tag{10.2}$$

where a and b are n-dimensional column vectors; then each pair of non-identical portfolios that belong to such a boundary fully defines it, i.e., for the definition of B^n the original set of n investments can be fully replaced by two arbitrary portfolios $x(\pi_1)$ and $x(\pi_2)$ lying on B^n.

Proof

It is enough to prove that given $\pi_1, \pi_2, \pi_1 \neq \pi_2$, the linear combination of $x(\pi_1)$ and $x(\pi_2)$ will describe each $x(\pi)$. Indeed

$$x(\pi) = a\pi + b = \eta x(\pi_1) + (1 - \eta)x(\pi_2). \tag{10.3}$$

It is enough to show that for each π there exists an η that satisfies (10.3). Substituting (10.2) into (10.3), we have

$$a\pi + b = \eta(a\pi_1 + b) + (1 - \eta)(a\pi_2 + b), \tag{10.4}$$

for which

$$\eta = \frac{\pi - \pi_2}{\pi_1 - \pi_2}, \tag{10.5}$$

which is uniquely defined for each π and for each pair $\pi_1, \pi_2, \pi_1 \neq \pi_2$.

Note that in each case that we have investigated so far, the allocation vector $x(\pi)$ has always had the linear structure (10.2). This is shown, for instance, by (2.24), (6.23), (8.34), (8.41), and (8.50). This is indeed a special case of a general result.

(10.6) **Theorem**

The boundary $\mathscr{X}^n$ of the region of admissible portfolios in the space X, parametrically defined by the equations

$$v = x'Vx, \qquad \pi = x'r, \qquad 1 = x'e, \tag{10.7}$$

where V is an $(n \times n)$ positive semidefinite symmetric matrix, is a linear function of π.

Proof

We shall outline a proof by contradiction by pointing out that a linear relationship of type (10.2) is the only polynomial relationship for which each component $x_i(\pi)$ of the allocation vector changes its sign at most once on B^n. If it were a polynomial of higher degree, then there could exist a problem in which the same allocation vector would correspond to more than one point on the boundary of admissible portfolios, i.e., to the same $x(\pi)$ there would correspond more than one point (v, π) on B^n. Clearly, this contradicts the basic equation (2.1) that defines the region of admissible portfolios.

This theorem enables us to conclude that

(10.8) **Theorem (generalized mutual fund theorem)**

Each pair of nonidentical portolios belonging to the boundary B^n of the region of admissible portfolios completely characterizes the boundary.

(10.9) **Remarks**

We must immediately point out the differences between Theorems (10.1) and (10.8). Theorem (10.1) applies to the case in which the allocation vector $x(\pi)$ on the boundary of the region of admissible portfolios is a linear function of π, but since we have proved (Theorem 10.6), that regardless of the properties of V and r, $x(\pi)$ is always linear, we can state the stronger result (10.8), which is then applicable in all cases. In the next chapter we shall again discuss the result presented in Theorem (10.6), but from a different viewpoint. We shall next clarify a few basic points. First, Theorem (10.1) and, therefore, Theorem (10.8) consider the boundary of the region of admissible portfolios in the space X through Eqs. (10.3) and (10.5). Clearly, from (10.5) and (10.3), by considering the usual equation

$$v = x'Vx, \tag{10.10}$$

it is possible to derive an equation for the boundary B^n in the plane (v, π).

The application of Theorem (10.8) is completely straightforward in all particular cases that have so far been analyzed with the possible exception of the singular case analyzed in Chapter 8 under condition (8.15). Now in this case the allocation vector $\tilde{x}(\pi)$ (8.40) is not defined by a unique linear form (10.2), but instead by a family of linear forms whose coefficients depend on an arbitrary parameter φ. In this case, given only π_1, π_2, and π, if we take into account (10.4) and (10.5), we will note that even if the vectors a and b are not constant but depend on the arbitrary parameter φ as was detailed in Eq. (8.41), the parameter η will still be given by Eq. (10.5) and will not depend on φ, and the same will apply to the boundary B^n in the plane (v, π), defined Eq. (10.10).

We shall next present a few results of generalized separation, i.e., the case in which on the boundary of the region of admissible portfolios there exist two portfolios with an empty intersection, i.e., portfolios such that the investments which appear in one do not appear in the other. This situation clearly arises if and only if the set of n investments can be divided into three subsets I_1, I_2, and I_3, wherein the investments of subset I_1 are such that there exists π_1 such that on the boundary of the region of admissible portfolios B^n we have

(10.11) $$x_i(\pi_1) = 0, \qquad i \in I_1,$$

the investments in subset I_2 are such that there exists π_2 with $\pi_1 \neq \pi_2$ such that on B^n

(10.12) $$x_i(\pi_2) = 0, \qquad i \in I_2,$$

while the investments in subset I_3 are such that on B^n

(10.13) $$x_i(\pi) = 0, \qquad i \in I_3, \quad -\infty < \pi < +\infty.$$

In Theorem (7.17) we had $\pi_1 = \rho, I_1 = 1, \ldots, n, \pi_2 = \pi^*, I_2 = n + 1, I_3 = \emptyset$. A similar situation arose in Theorem (8.10) with condition (8.12). In general, separation may occur also in the nonsingular case of Theorem (2.5), and we have the following generalized separation theorem:

(10.14) **Theorem**

Assume that the conditions of Theorem (2.5) are satisfied. Then a necessary and sufficient condition for the existence of two boundary portfolios with empty intersection, i.e., up to a reordering of the components of the vector x such that

(10.15) $$\begin{aligned} x_i(\pi_1) &= 0, \qquad i = 1, \ldots, m, \\ x_i(\pi_1) &\neq 0, \qquad i = m + 1, \ldots, n, \\ x_i(\pi_2) &\neq 0, \qquad i = 1, \ldots, m, \\ x_i(\pi_2) &= 0, \qquad i = m + 1, \ldots, n, \end{aligned}$$

is that

$$\sum_{k=1}^{n} v_{ik}^* \sum_{k=1}^{n} v_{jk}^* r_k = \sum_{k=1}^{n} v_{jk}^* \sum_{k=1}^{n} v_{ik}^* r_k \qquad \text{for all} \quad i, j = 1, \ldots, m, \quad i \neq j,$$

(10.16)

$$\sum_{k=1}^{n} v_{ik}^* \sum_{k=1}^{n} v_{jk}^* r_k = \sum_{k=1}^{n} v_{jk}^* \sum_{k=1}^{n} v_{ik}^* r_k \qquad \text{for all} \quad i, j = m + 1, \ldots, n, \quad i \neq j,$$

where we have denoted by v_{ik}^* the elements of the matrix V^{-1}.

Proof

Applying formulas (3.22) to the specific problem (10.15), we immediately find conditions (10.16). Clearly, $\pi_1 \neq \pi_2$ since if not, there would exist a point $\pi_1 = \pi_2$ on the boundary B^n such that

$$x_i(\pi_1) = 0, \qquad i = 1, \ldots, n, \tag{10.17}$$

which is clearly impossible since the last equation that defines the region of admissible portfolios,

$$e'x(\pi_1) = 1, \tag{10.18}$$

would be contradicted.

(10.19) **Remarks**

We recall from Chapter 3 that the trivial solutions (3.23) and (3.24) of system (10.16) are both ruled out since they violate the assumptions of the theorem. In spite of that it is possible to find examples of generalized separation, as will be shown at the end of the chapter.

We shall next discuss whether or not property (7.21) of Theorem (7.17) (the perfect correlation property) can also arise under assumptions completely different from those of Theorem (7.17), and in particular for the case in which $\tilde{V}$ is nonsingular. From the result of Theorem (4.43) it clearly emerges that if $\tilde{V}$ is nonsingular, then it will never occur that there exists a pair of perfectly linearly correlated boundary portfolios, which, as shown in Theorem (10.14), is a necessary and sufficient condition for all (but one) boundary portfolios to be perfectly correlated. And from the results of Chapters 6 and 8, we can see that a necessary and sufficient condition for the perfect linear correlation of the boundary portfolios is that the boundary be a straight line. Indeed, in the case for which condition (8.15) is satisfied and in which B^{n+1} is not a straight line even if it is singular, the boundary portfolios are not perfectly linearly correlated. Let us now proceed with a formal complete proof of the above statement.

(10.20) **Theorem**

The necessary and sufficient condition for perfect linear correlation among all (but one) boundary portfolios is that the boundary of the region of admissible portfolios in the space (σ, π) be a ray.

Proof

Assume that the allocation vector $x(\pi)$ on B^n is represented by the following linear function of π

$$x(\pi) = \bar{a}\pi + \bar{b}. \tag{10.21}$$

Assume in addition that V is diagonal. This assumption clearly will not affect the result since it affects only the particular form of $x(\pi)$ and not the form of B^n.

Using the representation of the variance–covariance matrix (see (A.8)),

$$V = S'CS, \tag{10.22}$$

which in the case for which V is diagonal becomes simply

$$V = S'S, \tag{10.23}$$

consider the transformed vectors

$$a = \bar{a}S, \qquad b = \bar{b}S; \tag{10.24}$$

then the boundary of the region of admissible portfolios B^n corresponding to (10.21) takes the simple form

$$v = x'S'Sx = \pi^2\left(\sum_{i=1}^{n} a_i^2\right) + 2\pi\left(\sum_{i=1}^{n} a_i b_i\right) + \sum_{i=1}^{n} b_i^2. \tag{10.25}$$

Clearly, this boundary (10.25) will be a ray in the plane (σ, π) if and only if (10.25) is a perfect square, i.e., if and only if there exist real numbers χ and δ such that

$$\begin{aligned} \sum_{i=1}^{n} a_i^2 &= \chi^2, \\ \sum_{i=1}^{n} a_i b_i &= \chi\delta, \\ \sum_{i=1}^{n} b_i^2 &= \delta^2, \end{aligned} \tag{10.26}$$

which lead to the condition

$$\left(\sum_{i=1}^{n} a_i^2\right)\left(\sum_{i=1}^{n} b_i^2\right) = \left(\sum_{i=1}^{n} a_i b_i\right)^2. \tag{10.27}$$

Some algebraic computation shows that (10.27) is equivalent to

$$\sum_{i \neq j = 1}^{n} (a_i b_j - a_j b_i)^2 = 0, \tag{10.28}$$

which is then the necessary and sufficient condition for the boundary B^n to be a ray. Consider next the conditions under which any two boundary portfolios $x(\pi)$, $y(\pi)$ are perfectly linearly correlated. We have

$$\frac{(x'Vy)^2}{x'Vx \cdot y'Vy} = 1, \tag{10.29}$$

from which

$$(x'Vy)^2 = x'Vx \cdot y'Vy \tag{10.30}$$

and

$$\left(\sum_{i=1}^{n} x_i y_i\right)^2 = \left(\sum_{i=1}^{n} x_i^2\right)\left(\sum_{i=1}^{n} y_i\right)^2, \tag{10.31}$$

which is equivalent to the condition

$$\sum_{i \neq j = 1}^{n} (x_i y_j - x_j y_i)^2 = 0. \tag{10.32}$$

Assume next that

$$x_i = (a\pi_1 + b)_i, \qquad y_i = (a\pi_2 + b)_i. \tag{10.33}$$

After some algebraic computation, using (10.32), we obtain the condition

$$\sum_{i \neq j = 1}^{n} (a_i b_j - a_j b_i)^2 = 0, \tag{10.34}$$

which is identical to condition (10.28) and proves the theorem.

EXAMPLES, NOTES, AND REFERENCES

The concept of generalized separation was introduced by Szegö (1976).

Clearly, when $n = 2$, generalized separation holds; thus in order to obtain a nontrivial example, we must consider the case for which $n \geq 2$. Consider the portfolio problem

$$V = \begin{bmatrix} 1 & 2 & 0 \\ 2 & 2 & 0 \\ 0 & 0 & 3 \end{bmatrix}, \qquad r = \begin{bmatrix} 1 \\ 1 \\ 2 \end{bmatrix}.$$

For this system the first two investments ($m = 2$) satisfy condition (10.16). Indeed, we have

$$x_1(\pi) = x_2(\pi) = 0 \qquad \text{for} \quad \pi = 2,$$

while

$$x_3(\pi) = 0 \qquad \text{for} \quad \pi = 1.$$

Thus the boundary of the region of admissible portfolios B^3 of the three investments is equivalent to the boundary of the two nonintersecting portfolios, defined by the point $\pi = 1$ to which there corresponds the portfolio $(x_1, x_2, 0)$ and by the point $\pi = 2$ to which there corresponds the portfolio (0, 0, 1). Clearly, the boundary is a parabola, and the two nonintersecting portfolios are not perfectly correlated; still, certain other properties hold, in particular at the point $\pi = 1$. The boundary B^3 is tangent to the boundary B^2 relative to the portfolio problem relative only to the first two investments, the boundary that in this particular example is degenerate (Fig. 10.1).

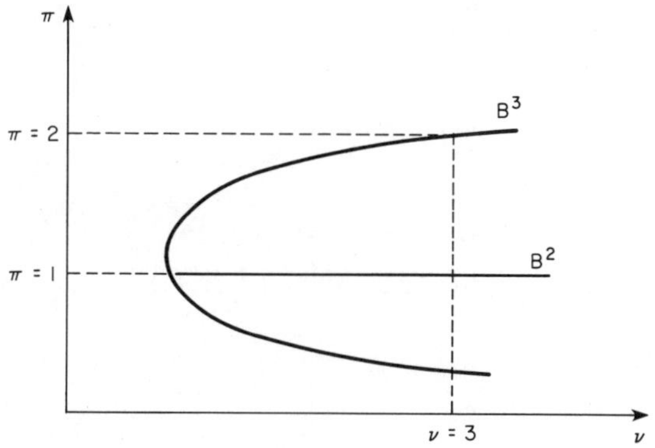

Figure 10.1

We have seen that in comparison with the properties of separation together with linearity, the properties of generalized separation are rather tenuous. On the other hand, from the practical point of view, even this property implies that the portfolio problem can be solved in two steps. It will be seen in more advanced portfolio problems such as the bank asset management problem that separation even in such weak form is very useful.

CHAPTER 11

MULTIPLE SINGULARITIES AND MULTIPLE DOMINANCE

In Chapters 5–9 we presented all possible cases which arise by adding the $(n+1)$th investment to a set of n investments characterized by a nonsingular $n \times n$ variance–covariance matrix V. This elementary typology has allowed us to identify, describe, and analyze all possible situations that may occur. In spite of the rich variety of cases that have been investigated, we have not yet fully completed our analysis. Indeed, we must take into account the possibility that to the original set of n investments we add further m investments such that the new enlarged $(n+m) \times (n+m)$ variance–covariance matrix is singular and its rank can then be any integer r with $n \leq r \leq n+m$. In addition, it may also happen that for some of the additional m investments some of the behaviors described in Chapter 5 can arise, namely, that these investments can either be dominated or semidominated by other investments or dominate or semidominate others. A second equivalent approach to identify all possible situations would be that of relaxing the assumption on the nonsingularity of the matrix V and then isolating all possible behaviors.

We shall use this second approach and then discuss the situations that may arise. With this aim in mind, let us assume that the matrix V has rank

$$r = n - m \qquad \text{with} \quad n > m, \quad n \geq 0. \tag{11.1}$$

The first step for the analysis is then to decompose the matrix V in the form

$$V = \begin{bmatrix} V_1 & K \\ K' & V_2 \end{bmatrix}, \tag{11.2}$$

where V_1 is a nonsingular $(n-m) \times (n-m)$ matrix (V_1 has rank $n-m$), K is an $(n-m) \times m$ matrix, K' is its transpose, and V_2 is an $m \times m$ square matrix. The essential point of the decomposition (11.2) is that it is not unique since V_1 is any one of the nonsingular minors of rank $n-m$ of the matrix V. Since in general there may be many such minors, it is also true that in general the decomposition is not unique.

It is clear that regardless of the nonuniqueness of (11.2), the boundary B^n of the region of admissible portfolios in the plane (v, π) as well as the corresponding boundary in the n-dimensional space X is uniquely defined. This does not apply to other properties and procedures, and in particular to the sign properties, as will be shown in the next chapter (see Examples, Notes, and References of Chapter 12).

We shall adopt the decomposition (11.2) not only in the case for which V is singular and has rank r, but also in the case for which m of the n investments are dominated by the remaining set of $n - m$ investments in a sense that will be better defined in this chapter. When dealing with the simultaneous presence of an $n \times n$ matrix, whatever its properties may be, and the riskless asset, we shall on the other hand use decomposition (6.1) of the enlarged $(n + 1) \times (n + 1)$ matrix $\tilde{V}$, where we assume, however, that V is further decomposed according to (11.2).

If we consider the different combinations of possible elementary situations that may arise (dominance, semidominance, existence of a riskless asset, existence of general singularities of various kinds), we notice that each of these elementary situations, with the exception of the presence of a riskless asset, can be related to more than one investment. We must then conclude that the number of such different combinations is practically boundless. We shall therefore limit our analysis to those particular combinations that have a certain impact on the main results obtained in the previous chapters, namely, on the uniqueness of the $(v, \pi) \to x$ mapping on B^n and on the existence of a unique optimal combination of risky assets x^*. We shall emphasize these particular cases in an attempt to explain within the framework and the limitations of our model why not all investors use the same portfolio of risky assets, which fact contradicts the basic result of Chapters 6 and 7.

We shall begin our investigation by considering the case for which there exists a riskless asset (the $(n + 1)$th investment) with return ρ, but for which at the same time one of the original n risky investments, say the kth investment, is dominated by the remaining $n - 1$ risky investments. An analogous situation will arise when the kth investment is semidominated by the remaining $n - 1$ risky investments.

In other words, we shall combine the results of Chapter 5 with those of Chapter 6. Before giving a necessary and sufficient condition that is similar to the one presented in Theorem (5.14), we shall give the following.

(11.3) **Definition**

Assume that decomposition (6.1) and conditions (6.2) hold, and denote by ρ the return on the riskless asset. Consider the set A_{n-1}^k of $n - 1$ investments obtained when the kth investment is deleted from the original set of

n risky investments. Then the kth investment is said to be dominated with respect to ρ (or ρ-dominated) by the set A_{n-1}^k of $n-1$ investments if

$$\tilde{x}_k(\pi) \equiv 0 \quad \text{on} \quad B^{n+1}, \tag{11.4}$$

where again B^{n+1} denotes the boundary of the region of admissible portfolios relative to problem (6.1), i.e., if and only if (see Theorem (7.17)

$$x_k(\pi^*) = x_k^* = 0, \tag{11.5}$$

where we have denoted again by $\tilde{x}$ and x the allocation vector associated with the $n+1$ and n (risky) investments, respectively.

Considering expressions (6.10), (6.11), (6.55), and (6.58), we immediately reach the conclusion that (11.5) is possible if and only if

$$(V^{-1}r)_k = \rho(V^{-1}e)_k. \tag{11.6}$$

If we consider again the results (presented in Chapter 3) on the sign properties of the allocation vector, we notice that while condition (3.7), i.e.,

$$(V^{-1}r)_k = (V^{-1}e)_k, \tag{11.7}$$

which proved that the kth investment is dominated by the set A_{n-1}^k of the remaining $n-1$ investments, defined a rather abnormal case, condition (11.6) just says that the point $\pi = \pi_k$ such that

$$x_k(\pi_k) = 0 \tag{11.8}$$

satisfies the condition

$$\pi_k = \pi^*. \tag{11.9}$$

It therefore follows that the kth investment can be dominated with respect to ρ by the set A_{n-1}^k of $n-1$ investments without being dominated by the set A_{n-1}^k, i.e., even when

$$x_k(\pi) \not\equiv 0 \quad \text{on} \quad B^n, \tag{11.10}$$

where B^n denotes again the boundary of the region of admissible portfolios relative to the set of n risky investments.

With the reservation expressed in the Examples, Notes, and References of Chapter 3, it is therefore also possible that more than one investment may be dominated with respect to the riskless asset ρ.

Having discussed the meaning and the limitation of the concept of dominance with respect to the riskless asset, we shall next prove the following necessary and sufficient condition, which extends Theorem (5.14) to our case.

(11.11) **Theorem**

The following four statements are equivalent:

(11.12) The kth investment is dominated with respect to the riskless interest rate ρ by the set of $n-1$ investments A_{n-1}^{k}.

(11.13) The set of $n+1$ investments is equivalent to the set of n investments obtained by deleting the kth investment, i.e., the straight lines defining B^{n+1} and those defining the boundary of the region of admissible portfolios relative to the set of n investments obtained by deleting the kth investment coincide. Also the respective tangency points (σ^*, π^*) and $(\underset{\sim}{\sigma}^*, \underset{\sim}{\pi}^*)$ with the hyperbolas B^n and B^{n-1} coincide.

(11.14) The components $\tilde{x}_1^*, \ldots, \tilde{x}_{k-1}^*, \tilde{x}_{k+1}^*, \ldots, \tilde{x}_{n+1}^*$ of the $(n+1)$-vector $\tilde{x}^*$ are, respectively, equal to the components $x_1^*, \ldots, x_{k-1}^*, x_k^*, \ldots, x_n^*$ of the n-vector x^* obtained by deleting the kth investment.

(11.15)
$$r_k = \underset{\sim}{b}'\underset{\sim}{V}^{-1}\underset{\sim}{r} - \rho\underset{\sim}{b}'\underset{\sim}{V}^{-1}\underset{\sim}{e} + \rho,$$

where for simplicity we have first reordered the matrix V (see (6.1)) in the form $\bar{V}$ in such a way that $k = n$, and we have introduced the notations

(11.16)
$$\bar{V} = \begin{bmatrix} \underset{\sim}{V} & \underset{\sim}{b} \\ \underset{\sim}{b}' & \underset{\sim}{\varepsilon} \end{bmatrix}, \qquad r = \begin{bmatrix} \underset{\sim}{r} \\ r_k \end{bmatrix}, \qquad e = \begin{bmatrix} \underset{\sim}{e} \\ 1 \end{bmatrix}, \qquad x = \begin{bmatrix} \underset{\sim}{x} \\ x_k \end{bmatrix}.$$

Proof

After the reordering (11.16) of the problem, condition (11.6) takes the form

(11.17)
$$(\rho\bar{V}^{-1}e)_n = (\bar{V}^{-1}r)_n.$$

Following the same technique as in the proof of Theorem (5.14), we shall express the matrix $\bar{V}^{-1}$ in the form

(11.18)
$$\bar{V}^{-1} = \begin{bmatrix} W & c \\ c' & \delta \end{bmatrix}.$$

Applying the results of Appendix E, we have

(11.19)
$$W = \underset{\sim}{V}^{-1} + \underset{\sim}{V}^{-1}\underset{\sim}{b}\underset{\sim}{b}'\underset{\sim}{V}^{-1}/D,$$

(11.20)
$$c = -\underset{\sim}{V}^{-1}\underset{\sim}{b}/D,$$

(11.21)
$$\delta = 1/D,$$

and

(11.22)
$$D = \det V/\det \underset{\sim}{V} = \underset{\sim}{\varepsilon} - \underset{\sim}{b}'\underset{\sim}{V}^{-1}\underset{\sim}{b}.$$

Condition (11.17) then becomes

$$\rho(-\underset{\sim}{b}'\underset{\sim}{V}^{-1}\underset{\sim}{e}+1) = -\underset{\sim}{b}'\underset{\sim}{V}^{-1}\underset{\sim}{r}+r_k, \tag{11.23}$$

from which (11.15) follows.

In order to proceed further with the proof of the theorem, we must investigate the relationships which exist between the coefficients α, β, and γ relative to the original set of n risky investments and the coefficients $\underset{\sim}{\alpha}$, $\underset{\sim}{\beta}$, and $\underset{\sim}{\gamma}$ corresponding to the set of $n-1$ investments obtained by deleting the kth investment. We can easily prove that

$$\alpha = \underset{\sim}{\alpha} + \rho^2(\underset{\sim}{b}'\underset{\sim}{V}^{-1}\underset{\sim}{e}-1)^2/D, \tag{11.24}$$

$$\beta = \underset{\sim}{\beta} + \rho(\underset{\sim}{b}'\underset{\sim}{V}^{-1}\underset{\sim}{e}-1)^2/D, \tag{11.25}$$

$$\gamma = \underset{\sim}{\gamma} + (\underset{\sim}{b}'\underset{\sim}{V}^{-1}\underset{\sim}{e}-1)^2/D, \tag{11.26}$$

where again D is given by (11.22). Now we can compare the vector x^* relative to the original set of n risky investments with the vector $\underset{\sim}{x}^*$ that corresponds to the set of $n-1$ investments obtained by deleting the kth investment. We have

$$\underset{\sim}{x}^* = \frac{\rho\underset{\sim}{V}^{-1}\underset{\sim}{e} - \underset{\sim}{V}^{-1}\underset{\sim}{r}}{\rho\underset{\sim}{\gamma} - \underset{\sim}{\beta}}, \tag{11.27}$$

while from (11.24)–(11.26) it follows that

(11.28)

$$x^* = \frac{\rho V^{-1}e - V^{-1}r}{\rho\gamma - \beta} = \frac{\rho V^{-1}e - V^{-1}r}{\rho[\underset{\sim}{\gamma} + (\underset{\sim}{b}'\underset{\sim}{V}^{-1}\underset{\sim}{e}-1)^2/D] - [\underset{\sim}{\beta} + \rho(\underset{\sim}{b}'\underset{\sim}{V}^{-1}\underset{\sim}{e}-1)^2/D]}.$$

After some algebraic manipulation it follows that indeed

$$\underset{\sim}{x}^* = x^*. \tag{11.29}$$

Similarly, expressions (11.24)–(11.26) allow us to prove the identity between the boundaries of the two problems, i.e., between the pair of straight lines

$$\pi = \rho \pm \sigma[\rho^2\underset{\sim}{\gamma} - 2\rho\underset{\sim}{\beta} + \underset{\sim}{\alpha}]^{1/2} \tag{11.30}$$

and the pair

$$\pi = \rho \pm \sigma[\rho^2\gamma - 2\rho\beta + \alpha]^{1/2}. \tag{11.31}$$

The use of relationships (11.24)–(11.26) allows us to prove another interesting partial inverse of Theorem (11.5), as shown by the following theorem, which we state without proof.

(11.32) **Theorem**

If the pair of straight lines defining B^{n+1} coincides with the pair of straight lines defining B^n corresponding to the set of n investments obtained by deleting the kth risky investment and if the matrix $\bar{V}$ (11.16) is nonsingular, then the kth investment is dominated.

From the results that we have presented so far, the exact meaning of the concept of dominance with respect to ρ must be clear. The main consequence is the identity of the boundaries B^{n+1} and $\underset{\sim}{B}^n$, i.e., the property

$$B^{n+1} \equiv \underset{\sim}{B}^n, \tag{11.33}$$

where $\underset{\sim}{B}^n$ denotes the boundary of the set of n investments obtained by deleting the kth ρ-dominated investment from the enlarged set of $n+1$ investments while, on the other hand, we have

$$B^n \not\equiv B^{n-1}, \tag{11.34}$$

where we have denoted by B^n and B^{n-1} the boundary of the region of admissible portfolios relative to the set of n risky investments and to its subset A_{n-1}^k, respectively.

Clearly, however, the boundaries B^n and B^{n-1} are tangent at the point π^*, where they are both tangent to one of the straight lines B^{n+1}. Note also that the allocation vector, defining the optimal combination of risky assets $x^* = \underset{\sim}{x}^*$, is uniquely defined, so even if the boundaries B^n and B^{n+1} are different, the uniqueness property of x^* and therefore of $\tilde{x}(\pi)$ is still verified.

The geometrical properties that we have previously outlined suggest the investigation of the properties of the locus of all possible boundaries B^{n-1} (hyperbolas) that correspond to ρ-dominated investments. We state without proof the following:

(11.35) **Theorem**

The locus of the vertices of all the hyperbolas B^{n-1} that are tangent to one straight line of the pair B^{n+1} (see (11.37)) at the point (σ^*, π^*) is given in the plane (σ, π) by the parabola (see Fig. 11.1)

$$\pi = \rho + (\underset{\sim}{\beta} - \rho\underset{\sim}{\gamma})\sigma^2. \tag{11.36}$$

(11.37) **Remarks**

A treatment analogous to that done in the previous pages for the case of ρ-dominance can be easily derived also for the case of ρ-semidominance.

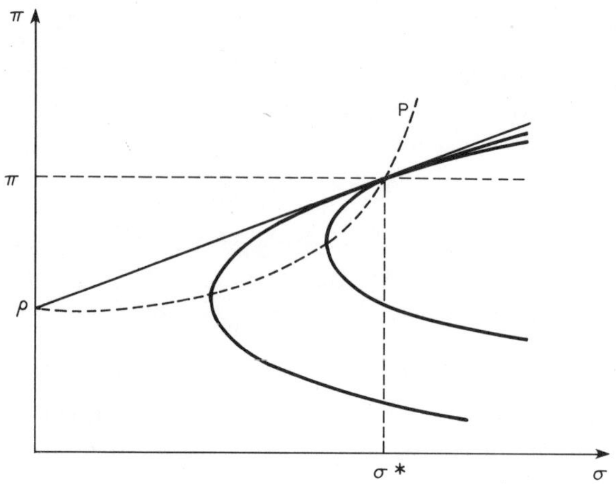

Figure 11.1

In the previous Theorem (11.35), as well as in the investigation leading to the identification of the basic condition (11.6), we were induced to consider the possibility of many investments being dominated, ρ-dominated, semidominated, or ρ-semidominated. The details of the analysis in all possible cases can be derived by the reader. We merely wish to mention that if we assume that the original $n \times n$ matrix V has been decomposed in the form (11.2) and V_1 is nonsingular, we can derive conditions under which the last m investments are either dominated or ρ-dominated by the first $n - m$ investments. The basic feature of this generalization of the concepts of dominance and ρ-dominance that was defined for the case of a single investment is the following theorem, which we state without proof.

(11.38) **Theorem**

If m risky investments are dominated (ρ-dominated) by the complementary set of $n - m$ risky investments A_{n-m}, then each one of these m investments is dominated (ρ-dominated) by the set of investments A_{n-m}.

This theorem, the proof of which is based on a generalization of the results presented in Appendix E to the inversion of a general partitioned matrix, allows us to obtain a set of necessary and sufficient conditions that extend conditions (5.18) and (11.15) to cover this more general case. Again the multiplicity of dominated or ρ-dominated investments does not destroy the uniqueness properties of x^*.

Having exhausted the analysis of the combinations of existence of a riskless asset and dominance, we must next consider in order to complete our analysis the cases of multiple singularities (rank $V < n - 1$) and of the combination of general singularities with dominance. Since we have shown that dominance and ρ-dominance do not affect the problem of the uniqueness of x^*, we shall not discuss this any longer but shall take into account only the case of multiple singularities. In order to do that, we must recall the following classification of simple singularities that can be derived from the results of Chapters 6–9. Indeed, when an $(n + 1)$th investment is added to a set of n investments characterized by an $n \times n$ nonsingular variance–covariance matrix V while the enlarged matrix V is singular, consider the general partition (8.11). The following four cases may occur:

$$a = \emptyset; \tag{11.39}$$

then the $(n + 1)$th investment is riskless, and the results of Chapters 6 and 7 apply.

$$e'a \neq 1; \tag{11.40}$$

the boundary is still a pair of straight lines through the point $(0, \bar{\rho})$.

$$e'a = 1 \quad \text{and} \quad \rho \neq r'a; \tag{11.41}$$

the boundary becomes a vertical straight line.

$$e'a = 1 \quad \text{and} \quad \rho = r'a; \tag{11.42}$$

the boundary B^{n+1} coincides with the boundary B^n, but the corresponding allocation vector $x(\pi)$ is not unique. The only case in which the vector $x(\pi)$ is not unique is that in which condition (11.42) is met, i.e., that in which the added $(n + 1)$th investment is a linear combination of the previous n investments (mutual fund). If we introduce the concept of multiple singularities and in particular that of the addition of an $(n + 1)$th riskless asset to a set of n investments such that the corresponding $n \times n$ variance–covariance matrix V is singular and has rank $n - m$, and the decomposition (11.2) with V_1 nonsingular is taken into account, various combinations of the three types of singular cases (11.40)–(11.42) are possible. Some combinations would give rise to the possibility of riskless arbitrage, such as the case in which the matrix V can be decomposed in such a way that condition (11.40) holds, while the return on the riskless asset ρ is different from that on $\bar{\rho}$. This is equivalent to assuming the existence of two riskless assets with different returns, which (see also Chapter 16) in the framework of the model we are discussing must be ruled out. Similar pathological cases occur when case (11.41) is combined with the riskless asset or case (11.40). The only interesting case, on the other hand, takes place when one or more investments that satisfy condition (11.42), i.e., that are linear combinations of other investments, are considered. In this case indeed the allocation vector $x(\pi)$ on B^{n+1}

or B^n is not uniquely defined. If the boundary is composed of straight lines, x^* is therefore not uniquely defined. This is the only case that can occur when no nonnegativity constraints are taken into account, when different investors can have different optimal combinations of risky assets. We shall discuss another type of nonuniqueness in the next chapter when nonnegativity constraints will be taken into account.

EXAMPLES, NOTES, AND REFERENCES

If V is singular, we know that decomposition (11.2), where V_1 is nonsingular, may be and in general is nonunique. We have shown that this fact does not affect the identification of B^n, which is uniquely defined, but on the other hand it affects the internal structure of R^n. This can be shown in the following example, which will be used also in the next chapter.

Consider the portfolio problem with the data

$$V = \begin{bmatrix} 1 & \frac{1}{2} & \frac{3}{4} \\ \frac{1}{2} & 4 & -\frac{21}{4} \\ \frac{3}{4} & -\frac{21}{4} & 9 \end{bmatrix}, \qquad r = \begin{bmatrix} 1 \\ 2 \\ 4 \end{bmatrix}. \tag{11.43}$$

Note that the 3×3 matrix V has rank 2 and satisfies condition (11.40). The matrix V admits three different decompositions; these decompositions will, in turn, define a different transformation matrix K. Assume that a different component of the transformed allocation vector y is riskless and leads to the following three equivalent systems:

$$\begin{aligned} \pi &= \tfrac{11}{2} y_1 + 2y_2 + 4y_2, \\ v &= 4y_2^2 + 9y_3^2 - \tfrac{21}{2} y_2 y_3, \\ 1 &= y_1 + y_2 + y_3, \end{aligned} \tag{11.44}$$

$$\begin{aligned} \pi &= y_1 + \tfrac{11}{2} y_2 + 4y_3, \\ v &= y_1^2 + 9y_3^2 + \tfrac{2}{3} y_2 y_3, \\ 1 &= y_1 + y_2 + y_3, \end{aligned} \tag{11.45}$$

$$\begin{aligned} \pi &= y_1 + 2y_2 + \tfrac{11}{2} y_3, \\ v &= y_1^2 + 4y_2^2 + y_1 y_2, \\ 1 &= y_1 + y_2 + y_3. \end{aligned} \tag{11.46}$$

As predicted from our previous theoretical treatment, all three models (11.44)–(11.46) generate the same equivalent riskless asset

$$\bar{\rho} = \tfrac{11}{2} \tag{11.47}$$

and the same boundary B^{n+1}, which is defined in the plane (σ, π) by the pair of straight lines defined by the equations

$$\pi = \pm \sigma \sqrt{\tfrac{62}{3}} + \tfrac{11}{2} \qquad \text{with} \quad \sigma \geq 0. \tag{11.48}$$

On the other hand, the boundaries of the region of admissible portfolios corresponding to the three equivalent models (11.44)–(11.46) are different. In the half plane (σ, π), $\sigma \geq 0$, they are,

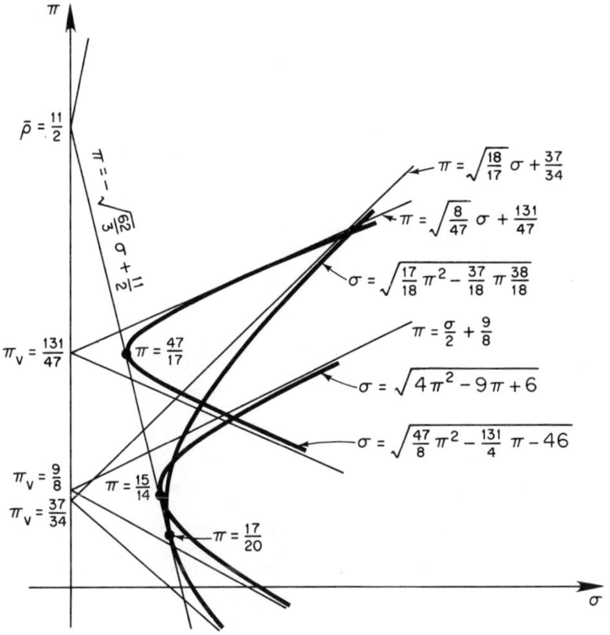

Figure 11.2

respectively, defined by the following branches of hyperbolas:

(11.49) $$\sigma = [4\pi^2 - 9\pi + 6]^{1/2},$$

(11.50) $$\sigma = [\tfrac{17}{18}\pi^2 - \tfrac{37}{18}\pi + \tfrac{19}{9}]^{1/2},$$

(11.51) $$\sigma = [\tfrac{47}{8}\pi^2 - \tfrac{131}{4}\pi + 46]^{1/2},$$

whose asymptotes and vertices are respectively given by the relationships

(11.52) $$\pi = \pm\sigma/2 + 9/\pi, \qquad \sigma = \sqrt{\tfrac{15}{4}}, \qquad \pi = \tfrac{9}{8},$$

(11.53) $$\pi = \pm\sigma\sqrt{\tfrac{18}{17}} + \tfrac{37}{4}, \qquad \sigma = \sqrt{\tfrac{405}{406}}, \qquad \pi = \tfrac{37}{34},$$

(11.54) $$\pi = \pm\sigma\sqrt{\tfrac{8}{47}} + \tfrac{131}{47}, \qquad \sigma = \sqrt{\tfrac{135}{376}}, \qquad \pi = \tfrac{131}{47}.$$

As a further confirmation of our theory, note that all three branches of hyperbolas (11.49)–(11.51) are tangent to the straight line (11.48) that defines the boundary B^{n+1} at the points

(11.55) $$\pi = \tfrac{15}{14},$$

(11.56) $$\pi = \tfrac{17}{20},$$

(11.57) $$\pi = \tfrac{47}{17},$$

respectively. The structure of the example is shown in Fig. 11.2.

The same example (11.43) will be analyzed again in the next chapter from the point of view of the sign properties of the allocation vector x.

CHAPTER 12

THE PORTFOLIO PROBLEM WITH NONNEGATIVITY CONSTRAINTS

In this chapter we shall discuss the properties of the region of admissible portfolios in the case in which this region is parametrically defined by the set of equations

$$(12.1) \qquad v = x'Vx, \qquad \pi = r'x, \qquad 1 = e'x, \qquad x \geq 0.$$

With respect to the original set of Eqs. (2.1), we have added here the nonnegativity constraint on the vector x. Before discussing the properties of the boundary of the region of admissible portfolios (12.1), we must point out one basic difference between system (12.1) and system (2.1).

In the case of system (2.1) the boundary turned out to be a parabola, i.e., the region of admissible portfolios is an unbounded portion of the plane (v, π) or (σ, π), allowing the investor to obtain portfolios characterized by arbitrarily large values of π and v. This is of course impossible when the nonnegativity constraint on the allocation vector is taken into account. Indeed, as pointed out in Chapter 3, there must always exist at least one component $x_i(\pi)$ of the vector $x(\pi)$ on the boundary of the region of admissible portfolios that is not constant, i.e., is such that there exists one value $\pi = \pi_i$ on which this component vanishes. It is therefore impossible that on the whole boundary B^n the nonnegativity constraint is satisfied, while of course (see again Chapter 3) it is quite possible that it is satisfied on an arc of the boundary. Thus the boundary of the region of admissible portfolios with nonnegativity constraints on the allocation vector x, which will be denoted by $\bar{B}^n$, has a completely different character from the boundary B^n, and in particular it can never coincide with B^n.

On this basic problem the following theorem can be proved:

(12.2) **Theorem**

The boundary $\bar{B}^n$ of the region of admissible portfolios (12.1) in the plane (v, π) (or in the plane (σ, π)) is a bounded arc that has as extremals the points $P_{\min} = (v_{\min}, \pi_{\min})$ and $P_{\text{Max}} = (v_{\text{Max}}, \pi_{\text{Max}})(P_{\min} = (\sigma_{\min}, \pi_{\min})$ and $P_{\text{Max}} = (\sigma_{\text{Max}}, \pi_{\text{Max}}))$, where $\pi_{\min} = r_{\min}$ and $\pi_{\text{Max}} = r_{\text{Max}}$ are the smallest and the largest of the expected returns on the n investments, respectively, and $v_{\min}$ and v_{Max} are the corresponding variances. If there exists more than one investment to which there correspond the expected returns $r_{\min}$ and r_{Max}, then we shall call $v_{\min}$ and v_{Max} the smallest of the corresponding variances.

Proof

Consider the second equation of system (12.1):

$$\pi = r'x \tag{12.3}$$

and the nonnegativity constraint

$$x \geq 0. \tag{12.4}$$

Clearly, since (12.4) does not allow short selling and borrowing, the largest value of π can be achieved by investing the whole unit capital in the investment with the largest expected return r_{Max}, while the smallest value of π can correspondingly be reached only by investing the whole unit capital in the investment with the smallest expected return $r_{\min}$.

If there exists more than one investment with the same extremal value of the expected return ($r_{\min}$ or r_{Max}), it will belong to the boundary, the one to which it corresponds, the smallest value of v.

Thus regardless of the particular shape of $\bar{B}^n$, this boundary will be a bounded arc (see Fig. 12.1). Nothing of course has been said about the fact that the extremals $P_{\min}$ and P_{Max} of $\bar{B}^n$ may in some cases belong to B^n. In this case

(12.5) **Corollary**

If the extremal investments $P_{\min} = (v_{\min}, \pi_{\min})$ and $P_{\text{Max}} = (v_{\text{Max}}, \pi_{\text{Max}})$ belong to the boundary B^n of the region of admissible portfolios of the unconstrained portfolio problem (2.1), then $\bar{B}^n$ is the arc of B^n between $P_{\min}$ and P_{Max}.

Note that from what we have pointed out in Chapter 3 (Examples, Notes, and References), it is quite unlikely that Corollary (12.5) may be used for

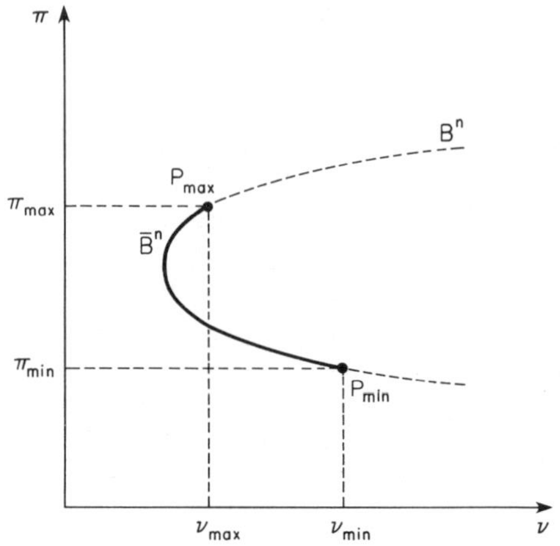

Figure 12.1

the identification of $\bar{B}^n$ when $n > 2$. On the other hand

(12.6) **Corollary**

If $n = 2$, $\bar{B}^2 \subset B^2$ is the part of B^2 lying between the two investments. Indeed, as we pointed out in Chapter 3, when $n = 2$, both investments belong to B^2 and Corollary (12.5) can then be applied.

Since Corollary (12.5) can only very rarely be applied to the identification of $\bar{B}^n$, we shall next devote ourselves to the further analysis of the quantitative properties of $\bar{B}^n$ and at the end of the chapter discuss the numerical algorithm for its identification.

For that, following the procedure presented in Chapter 3, we shall consider the boundary B^n to see if there exists an interval of type (3.2), i.e., an interval

$$\pi_m \leq \pi \leq \pi_M \tag{12.7}$$

such that for all π with

$$\pi_m < \pi < \pi_M \tag{12.8}$$

the corresponding boundary allocation vector satisfies the inequality

$$x(\pi) > 0, \tag{12.9}$$

while for $\pi = \pi_m$ and $\pi = \pi_M$ at least one component of the vector $x(\pi)$ vanishes. We shall assume for the time being that exactly one component of $x(\pi)$ vanishes at each of the extremals of the interval (12.7) and shall denote these components by $x_m(\pi)$ and $x_M(\pi)$, respectively (see Fig. 12.2). Thus

$$x_m(\pi_m) = 0 \qquad \text{and} \qquad x_M(\pi_M) = 0. \tag{12.10}$$

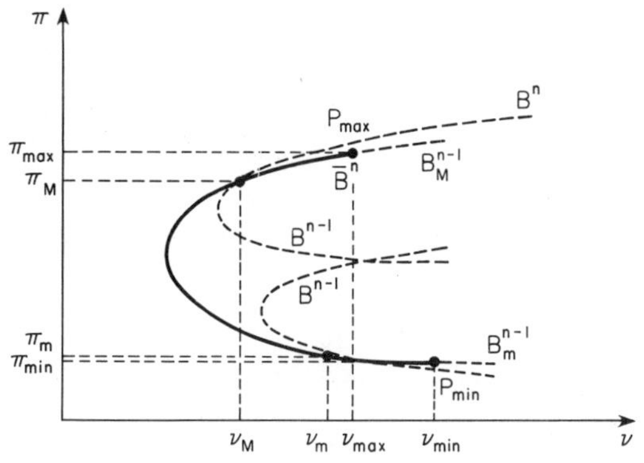

Figure 12.2

Now if it does not occur that $\pi_m \neq \pi_{\min}$ and $\pi_m \neq \pi_{\mathrm{Max}}$, the boundary $\bar{B}^n$ does not coincide with the arc of B^n within the interval (12.7), even if this arc must clearly belong to $\bar{B}^n$. We must therefore identify the remaining parts of $\bar{B}^n$.

In order to do that, we notice that at the point (v_m, π_m) on B^n, the boundary B^n coincides with the boundary B_m^{n-1} of the region of admissible portfolios relative to the set of $n-1$ investments obtained by deleting from the original set of n investments the investment x_m, while at the point (v_M, π_M) on B^n the boundary B^n coincides with the boundary B_M^{n-1} of the region of admissible portfolios relative to the set of $n-1$ investments obtained by deleting from the original set of n investments the investment x_M.

Note in addition that the parabolas B_m^{n-1} and B_M^{n-1} are completely contained in the region of admissible portfolios R^n. Thus at the point (v_m, π_m), B_m^{n-1} is tangent to B^n, while at the point (v_M, π_M), B_M^{n-1} is tangent to B^n.

If $\pi_m \neq \pi_{\min}$, and the assumptions are made that in (v_m, π_m) only x_m vanishes and that in (v_M, π_M) only x_M vanishes, the continuity properties of $x(\pi)$ on B^{n-1} allow us to conclude that there must exist an interval

$$\pi_{m1} < \pi < \pi_m \tag{12.11}$$

such that within this interval on the boundary B_m^{n-1} the allocation vector $x^{n-1}(\pi)$ relative to the set of $n-1$ investments, obtained by deleting from the original set of m investments the investment x_m, satisfies the inequality

$$x^{n-1}(\pi) > 0, \tag{12.12}$$

while there exists at least one component of x^{n-1} that vanishes at the point (v_{m1}, π_{m1}) of B^{n-1}. We shall again assume that this vanishing component is unique and denote it by x_{m1}. Thus

$$x_{m1}^{n-1}(\pi_{m1}) = 0. \tag{12.13}$$

In a similar fashion, if $\pi_M \neq \pi_{\text{Max}}$, then there must exist an interval

$$\pi_M < \pi < \pi_{M1} \tag{12.14}$$

such that within this interval on the boundary B_M^{n-1} the allocation vector $x^{n-1}(\pi)$, obtained by deleting the investment x_M from the original set of n investments, satisfies the inequality

$$x^{n-1}(\pi) > 0, \tag{12.15}$$

while there exists at least one component of $x^{n-1}(\pi)$ that vanishes at the point (v_{M1}, π_{M1}) of B^{n-1}. We shall again assume that there exists only one investment that vanishes at such a point and denote it by x_{M1}. Thus

$$x_{M1}^{n-1}(\pi_{M1}) = 0. \tag{12.16}$$

Now it could happen that $\pi_{m1} = \pi_{\min}$ as well as $\pi_{M1} = \pi_{\text{Max}}$ and therefore $\bar{B}^n$ would have been identified; or it could happen that either $\pi_{m1} = \pi_{\min}$ or $\pi_{M1} = \pi_{\text{Max}}$, and in this case only one of the extremals of $\bar{B}^n$ would have been identified. Finally, it could happen that neither $\pi_{m1} = \pi_{\min}$ nor $\pi_{M1} = \pi_{\text{Max}}$. In all cases for which $\bar{B}^n$ is not identified, one would proceed further by iterating the same procedure until after a finite number of steps one would find the extremals π_{mi}, π_{Mj} such that $\pi_{mi} = \pi_{\min}$ and $\pi_{Mj} = \pi_{\text{Max}}$.

Before reaching a conclusion regarding the qualitative behavior of $\bar{B}^n$, we must first dispose of two particular cases. The first is the case in which there does not exist any arc of B^n within the interval (12.7) such that on (12.8), (12.9) is true; the second case is that in which during the construction of the sequences $\{\pi_{mi}\}$ and $\{\pi_{Mj}\}$ one finds one value in which more than one component of $x(\pi)$ simultaneously vanish. In both of these particular cases while the basic technique remains unchanged, its implementation requires a much greater effort. Indeed, in the first critical case in which B^n does not admit any arc with properties (12.7)–(12.9), one must analyze the boundaries B^{n-1} of all possible sets of $n-1$ investments, obtained by deleting from the original set of n investments all investments one by one and then comparing the results, and if necessary, proceed further with the analysis of the boundaries B^{n-2} of the region of admissible portfolios of all possible sets of $n-2$ investments, etc. In the second critical case one must compute the boundaries of the region of admissible portfolios obtained by the previous set by deleting first one then the other of the investments, which simultaneously vanish, and then proceeding on the boundary to which for the same value of π there corresponds the smallest value of v. In all circumstances, however, it follows that

(12.17) **Theorem**

The boundary $\bar{B}^n$ of the region of admissible portfolios with nonnegativity constraints on the allocation vector parametrically defined by system (12.1) is represented on the plane (v, π) by a continuously differentiable curve composed of a sequence of arcs of parabolas each of which belongs to the boundary of the region of admissible portfolios of a subset of the set of n investments.

The continuous differentiability of $\bar{B}^n$ follows from the fact that in constructing the sequence of boundaries B^n, $B^{n-1}, \ldots$, each of these boundaries is fully contained in the region of admissible portfolios R^n, $R^{n-1}, \ldots$, of the preceding set. Thus their common points (v_{mi}, π_{mi}) are true tangency points.

We have investigated the effect of the nonnegativity constraints in the case in which the problem is nonsingular. Something must, however, be said regarding the solutions of the singular cases arising when the enlarged $(n+1) \times (n+1)$ matrix V is singular (cases that were investigated in Chapters 6–9) or when V itself is singular (Chapter 11). The key result for solving this problem in a methodical fashion is Theorem (6.43), from which we shall deduce the following.

(12.18) **Corollary**

Let the matrix $\tilde{V}$ of the enlarged problem be singular and satisfy condition (6.2) and decomposition (6.1). Consider the straight line (6.44) joining a point (σ_r, π_r) that belongs to the region of admissible portfolios with the point of the plane (σ, π) corresponding to the riskless asset. Then if the allocation vector x_r corresponding to the point (σ_r, π_r) is positive, all points on (6.44) satisfy the nonnegativity constraint (12.19) and the straight line (6.44) is fully contained in the region of admissible portfolios of the enlarged problem satisfying the nonnegativity constraint.

If we compare Corollary (12.18) with Theorem (6.43) and in particular with the considerations contained in Remark (6.50) regarding the form (6.53) of the allocation vector corresponding to the point $(\sigma_r, 2\rho - \pi_r)$, it then follows that if (σ_r, π_r) is on the boundary of the region of admissible portfolios, the allocation vector x corresponding to the point $(\sigma_r, 2\rho - \pi_r)$ will always violate such sign constraints. It then follows that while in the nonsingular case it is possible that $\bar{B}^n \subset B^n$, this will never happen in the singular case.

We must next be more precise on the nonnegativity conditions, i.e., we must distinguish between the case in which the sign constraints act only on the n original investments, i.e., the case

$$x \geq 0 \tag{12.19}$$

and the case in which we rule out borrowing in any form, and then we must consider the stronger constraints

$$x \geq 0, \qquad \tilde{x}_{n+1} \geq 0. \tag{12.20}$$

The form of the boundary of the region of admissible portfolios changes drastically in the two cases. In the first case (12.19) we must have an unbounded region of admissible portfolios. In the second the boundary of the region will begin and end at the extremal investments defined in Theorem (12.2) and relative to the enlarged set of $n + 1$ investments. We can then prove the following:

(12.21) **Theorem**

The boundary $\bar{B}^{n+1}$ relative to the set of $n + 1$ investments when decomposition (6.1) and condition (6.2) hold and when nonnegativity constraints on the allocation vector are included has the following properties. In the case of constraint (12.19) the boundary is composed of two straight lines through the point $(0, \rho)$ corresponding to the riskless asset and tangent, respectively, from above and below to the boundary $\bar{B}^n$ of the original n investments. In the case of constraint (12.20) $\bar{B}^{n+1}$ is then composed of the two straight line segments, having one extremal at $(0, \rho)$ and the other at the respective contact point with $\bar{B}^n$.

Proof

For case (12.19) in which the nonnegativity constraints act only on the first n components of the allocation vector, the result follows immediately from Corollary (12.18). Indeed, since the point $(0, \rho)$ belongs to $\bar{B}^{n+1}$ and all straight lines joining it with any point in $\bar{B}^n$ belong to $\bar{R}^{n+1}$, then clearly the region between the two tangent lines defined in (12.21) belongs to $\bar{R}^{n+1}$ and indeed it is the largest subset of $\bar{R}^{n+1}$ with linear boundaries. We must finally show that there do not exist any points of $\bar{R}^{n+1}$ outside the area between the two straight lines. This can be proved for instance again from (12.18) since it follows that $\bar{R}^{n+1}$ must be convex and have linear boundaries.

In the second case in which we impose stronger nonnegativity constraints (12.20) on our problem, since the first n constraints are already satisfied on the straight lines that we have defined above, we must only identify on these two straight lines the subset on which also the additional requirement $\tilde{x}_{n+1} \geq 0$ is satisfied; since at the point $(0, \rho)$ we have $\tilde{x}_{n+1} = 1$ and $x = 0$, it follows that the boundary $\bar{B}^{n+1}$ in this case is identified by the two segments lying on the straight lines previously defined and having one extremal at the point $(0, \rho)$ and the other at the contact points between $\bar{B}^n$ and the straight lines.

(12.22) **Remark**

In Theorem (12.21) we purposely used the words "contact points" instead of "tangency points." Indeed, a point may not be a tangency point in a strict sense when it is one of the extremal investments, i.e., one of the extremals of $\bar{B}^n$ which we recall is an arc and not an infinite curve. The two situations arising in this case are shown in Fig. 12.3.

Note that in this case the concept of optimal combination of risky assets has degenerated. Indeed, if no short sales are allowed, i.e., in the case for which the nonnegativity constraints (12.19) hold, if ρ is sufficiently large there is no relationship betweeen the composition of the allocation vector at the contact point and ρ.

The problem of finding the boundary $\bar{B}^{n+1}$ even with only the nonnegativity constraints (12.19) becomes rather complicated in the case in which the enlarged matrix is singular, but the added investment is risky (the case investigated in Chapter 8) particularly in the case in which condition (8.12) is satisfied and B^{n+1} is given by two straight lines through the point $(0, \bar{\rho})$, where $\bar{\rho}$ is defined by (8.14). In all other cases arising in Chapter 8 the identification of $\bar{B}^{n+1}$ follows the normal type of analysis performed at the beginning of this chapter.

In the case of condition (8.12) we know that the minimum variance portfolio defined by Eq. (8.53) may not satisfy the inequality constraints (12.19), while the basic results regarding the continuous differentiability of $\bar{B}^{n+1}$

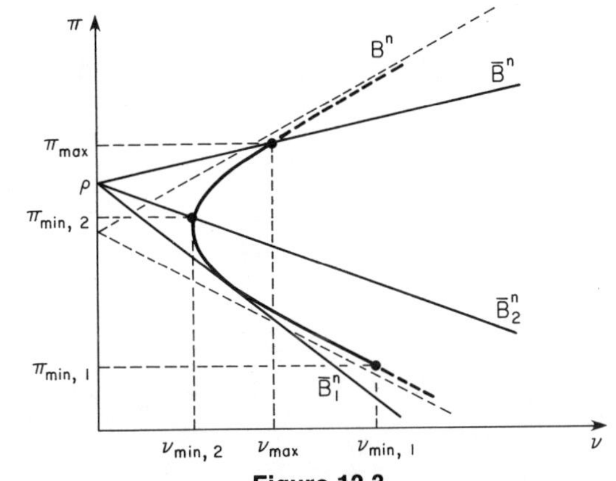

Figure 12.3

still guarantee the results obtained in Theorem (12.21), results which allow us to construct $\bar{B}^{n+1}$ by means of the simplified technique of constructing $\bar{B}^n$ first. This technique cannot be used in the case for which $x_{n+1}(\bar{\rho})$ (8.53) is negative. When this happens, we must apply the technique developed in the first part of this chapter to the above set of $n+1$ investments. Note however that since Corollary (12.18) still holds, it will be very unlikely that we shall be able to find an admissible interval with the properties (12.7)–(12.9) corresponding to a segment of the boundary $\bar{B}^{n+1}$ (two straight lines through $(0, \bar{\rho})$). We are then left to investigate the sign properties of all possible boundaries $\bar{B}^n$ corresponding to all possible nonsingular $n \times n$ minors of $\tilde{V}$ in order to find the boundary, which in general will contain some line segment.

It is important to point out that the presence of a line segment in the boundary $\bar{B}^{n+1}$ may destroy the concept of optimal combination of risky assets. Indeed (see Fig. 12.4), when we add an $(n+2)$th riskless investment to a set of $n+1$ investments that have the boundary B^{n+1} containing a line segment, if the intersection of the straight line containing this segment with the $\sigma = 0$ axis coincides with the point $(0, \rho)$, it then follows that with non-negativity constraints there does not exist a unique optimal combination of risky assets.

The problem of constructing the boundary $\bar{B}^n$, or $\bar{B}^{n+1}$ if n is sufficiently large ($n > 3$), must usually be solved by numerical techniques. In the non-critical case in which V is nonsingular and there exists an interval (12.7), (12.8) on B^n, then one can develop a numerical or analytical–numerical technique which makes full use of the particular properties of the problem and is quite superior to general purpose quadratic programming codes.

In the more critical cases in which the interval (12.7), (12.8) cannot be identified on B^n and one must analyze the properties of all subsets of the $n-1$ investments and their boundaries, as well as in the singular case (8.12)

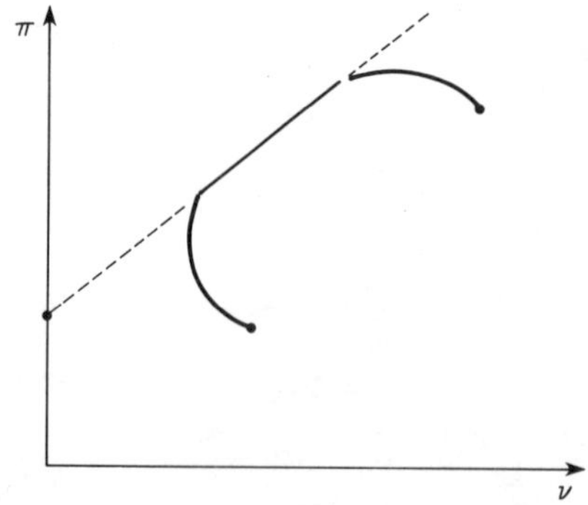

Figure 12.4

when the minimum variance portfolio (8.53) does not satisfy nonnegativity constraints, the use of general purpose quadratic programming algorithms may on the contrary be mandatory.

EXAMPLES, NOTES, AND REFERENCES

The technique used in the proof of Theorem (12.17) can indeed be used practically for the construction of $\bar{B}^n$ if no critical case occurs. Indeed, when a critical case arises, one must in general use a variation of this approach, which is more suited for numerical purposes.

The use of the approach in a noncritical case can be shown by considering again Example (3.61) investigated in Chapter 3.

The equation of its boundary B^3 is defined by the parabola

$$v = 3 - 3\pi + \tfrac{11}{12}\pi^2, \tag{12.23}$$

while the components of the allocation vector $x(\pi)$ are given by

$$\begin{aligned} x_1(\pi) &= -\tfrac{7}{12}\pi + \tfrac{3}{2}, \\ x_2(\pi) &= \tfrac{1}{6}\pi, \\ x_3(\pi) &= \tfrac{5}{12}\pi - \tfrac{1}{2}. \end{aligned} \tag{12.24}$$

Thus

$$\begin{aligned} x_1(\pi) &\geq 0 \quad \text{iff} \quad \pi \leq \tfrac{18}{7}, \\ x_2(\pi) &\geq 0 \quad \text{iff} \quad \pi \geq 0, \\ x_3(\pi) &\geq 0 \quad \text{iff} \quad \pi \geq \tfrac{6}{5}, \end{aligned} \tag{12.25}$$

from which we deduce that on B^3 there exists an arc such that for all values with

$$\pi_{\min} = \tfrac{6}{5} \leq \pi \leq \tfrac{18}{7} = \pi_{\max} \qquad \text{we have} \quad x(\pi) \geq 0. \tag{12.26}$$

At the point

$$\pi = \pi_3 = \tfrac{6}{5} \qquad \text{we have} \quad x_3(\pi) = 0,$$

while at the point

$$\pi = \pi_1 = \tfrac{18}{7} \qquad \text{we have} \quad x_1(\pi) = 0.$$

At the point $\pi = \frac{6}{5}$ we shall consider the boundary B^2 of the region of admissible portfolios obtained by deleting the investment x_3 from the set of three investments. This boundary is given by the parabola (3.68)

$$v = 3\pi^2 - 8\pi + 6, \tag{12.27}$$

and the two components of the allocation vector have the form

$$x_1(\pi) = -\pi + 2, \qquad x_2(\pi) = \pi - 1, \tag{12.28}$$

which clearly vanish for $\pi = 1$ and $\pi = 2$, respectively, the expected returns on the two investments. At the point $\pi = \frac{18}{7}$ we shall instead consider the boundary B^2 of the region of admissible portfolios obtained by deleting the investment x_1 from the set of three investments.

This boundary is given by the parabola (3.66)

$$v = 5\pi^2 - 24\pi + 30, \tag{12.29}$$

while the two components of the allocation vector have the form

$$x_2(\pi) = -\pi + 3, \qquad x_3(\pi) = \pi - 2, \tag{12.30}$$

which vanish for $\pi = 3$ and $\pi = 2$, respectively, the expected returns on the two investments. Since we had

$$\pi_{\min} = 1, \qquad \pi_{\max} = 3,$$

the boundary $\bar{B}^3$ is therefore fully identified (see Fig. 12.5).

The situation in which we have $x(\bar{\rho}) < 0$ and in which, therefore, Theorem (12.21) cannot be applied to the construction of $\bar{B}^{n+1}$ arises for instance in Example (11.43) in which the matrix V has the form

$$\tilde{V} = \begin{bmatrix} 1 & \frac{1}{2} & \frac{3}{4} \\ \frac{1}{2} & 4 & -\frac{21}{4} \\ \frac{3}{4} & -\frac{21}{4} & 9 \end{bmatrix}. \tag{12.31}$$

Now it is easy to check that all three second-order minors of (12.31) are nonsingular. We recall that therefore matrix (12.31) admits three different partitions and that it belongs to the class of matrices for which condition (8.12) is satisfied.

If we consider the partition

$$V = \begin{bmatrix} a'Va & Va \\ a'V' & V \end{bmatrix} \tag{12.32}$$

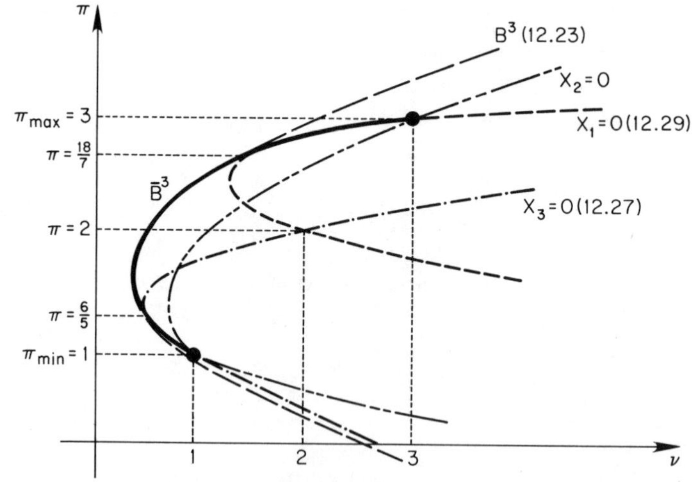

Figure 12.5

with

$$V = \begin{bmatrix} 4 & -\frac{21}{4} \\ -\frac{21}{4} & 9 \end{bmatrix}, \tag{12.33}$$

we have

$$a' = [1, \tfrac{2}{3}]. \tag{12.34}$$

Thus

$$e'a = 1 + \tfrac{2}{3} = \tfrac{5}{3} \neq 1, \tag{12.35}$$

satisfying (8.12).

Consider next the minimum variance allocation vector (8.53); we have

$$\begin{aligned} x_1(\bar{\rho}) &= \frac{1}{1 - e'a} = -\frac{3}{2}, \\ x_2(\bar{\rho}) &= \frac{-a_1}{1 - e'a} = \frac{3}{2}, \\ x_3(\bar{\rho}) &= \frac{-a_2}{1 - e'a} = 1. \end{aligned} \tag{12.36}$$

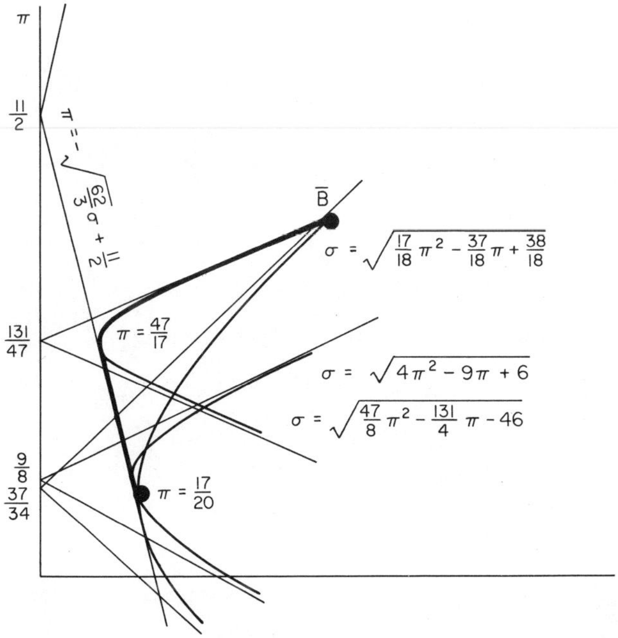

Figure 12.6

Thus the minimum variance portfolio does not satisfy the nonnegativity constraints. We must then consider all second-order minors of $\tilde{V}$, not just (12.32), and consider the boundaries B_1^2, B_2^2, and B_3^2 given by (11.49)–(11.51).

On these boundaries we must identify the arcs (12.7)–(12.8) satisfying the nonnegativity constraints.

Note that since $n = 2$, such arcs always exist and their extremals are the three given investments. We can then construct the boundary of the region of admissible portfolios with nonnegativity constraints as shown in Fig. 12.6, which is derived from Fig. 11.2 and which shows the behavior of the boundary of the region of admissible portfolios relative to Example (11.43).

Note that the boundary contains a line segment.

CHAPTER 13

DIAGONAL AND LINEAR MODELS

It has been shown in the previous chapters that one of the most useful properties that a variance–covariance matrix V may have is to be diagonal.

Indeed, in this case not only is the "technical" problem of matrix inversion trivial, but also one can derive very useful properties of the sign of the allocation vector x on the boundary B^n (see Chapter 3). Thus in Chapter 4 (Theorem (4.83)) we discussed how to find a set of portfolios such that if one replaces the original set of n investments by such a set of portfolios, the region of admissible portfolios is unchanged but the corresponding variance–covariance matrix is diagonal. This idea of orthonormalization of the problem, which transforms the general n portfolio selection problem into a diagonal n portfolio selection problem, even if it has a strong theoretical appeal, is not very practical.

Sharpe (1962) suggested an approximate technique for constructing a diagonal model at the cost of increasing by one the number of investments and the number of constraints. This technique has a strong practical appeal, but it also has some rather unpleasant side effects.

Some further simplified models defined by a constrained linear problem can also be obtained.

As a first step in the construction of the diagonal model, we shall proceed by performing a linear regression between the random variable R_i, representing the return on the ith investment, and the random variable I, which represents the return on a suitably chosen market index. Thus

$$R_i = a_i + b_i I + c_i. \tag{13.1}$$

In this relationship the coefficients a_i and b_i are real numbers characterizing the linear regression line, while c_i is the random variable which accounts for the residuals of the linear regression. Thus

$$E(a_i) = a_i, \qquad E(b_i) = b_i, \qquad E(c_i) = 0, \tag{13.2}$$

while

$$v(a_i) = 0, \qquad v(b_i) = 0, \qquad v(c_i) = \sigma_i^2. \tag{13.3}$$

We shall make the simplifying assumption

$$\operatorname{cov}(c_i, c_j) = 0, \qquad i \neq j = 1, \ldots, n, \tag{13.4}$$

and use the notation

$$E(I) = \bar{I}, \qquad v(I) = \sigma_I^2. \tag{13.5}$$

Thus

$$r_i = a_i + b_i \bar{I} \tag{13.6}$$

and

$$r = a + b\bar{I}, \tag{13.7}$$

where a and b are n column vectors whose elements are a_i and b_i, respectively, and r is as usual the expected return vector. Note that in the original model, one needs $\frac{1}{2}n(n + 3)$ data to be measured and stored, while if one performs the linear regression (13.1) first, one needs only $3n + 2$ data.

Consider again the region of admissible portfolios of the given set of n investments without nonnegativity constraints

$$v = x'Vx, \qquad \pi = x'r, \qquad 1 = x'e. \tag{13.8}$$

Using the representation (13.1)–(13.7), system (13.8) becomes

$$\begin{aligned} v &= x'V^c x + x'bb'x\sigma_I^2, \\ \pi &= x'a + x'b\bar{I}, \\ 1 &= x'e, \end{aligned} \tag{13.9}$$

where we have denoted by V^c the $n \times n$ diagonal matrix whose elements are the variances of the residuals c_i of the linear regression (13.1).

We can represent system (13.8) in the more compact form

$$\begin{aligned} v &= x'[V^c + bb'\sigma_I^2]x \doteq x'\bar{V}x, \\ \pi &= x'[a + b\bar{I}] \doteq x'\bar{r}, \\ 1 &= x'e. \end{aligned} \tag{13.10}$$

Note that the equivalent variance–covariance matrix $\bar{V}$ in this system is not diagonal. If $\bar{V}$ is nonsingular and the components of $\bar{r}$ are not identical, then from (13.9) we derive results that are formally identical to the result of Chapter 2, and similarly for the other cases investigated in the following chapters. We must, however, point out that there exists a formula for the inversion of the matrix $\bar{V}$, which was defined in the first equation of (13.10), which allows the computation of $\bar{V}^{-1}$ as a perturbation of the diagonal matrix $(V^c)^{-1}$. We have (see Appendix I for the derivation)

$$\bar{V}^{-1} = (V^c)^{-1} - \frac{\sigma_I^2 (V^c)^{-1} b b' (V^c)^{-1}}{1 + \sigma_I^2 b' (V^c)^{-1} b} \tag{13.11}$$

This formula clearly allows a simplification of the computation of $\bar{V}^{-1}$, but not a complete analytical solution when n is large.

A possible simplification can be achieved by proceeding with the construction of the "diagonal model" as suggested by Sharpe.

In order to do that, we shall add another $(n + 1)$th investment to the set of n investments by letting

$$x_{n+1} = b'x. \tag{13.12}$$

Now system (13.9) becomes

$$\begin{aligned} v &= x' V^c x + x_{n+1}^2 \sigma_I^2, \\ \pi &= x'a + x_{n+1} \bar{I}, \\ 1 &= x'e, \\ 0 &= x'b - x_{n+1}. \end{aligned} \tag{13.13}$$

If we now let

$$\bar{V} = \begin{bmatrix} V^c & \emptyset \\ \emptyset' & \sigma_I^2 \end{bmatrix}, \quad \bar{a} = \begin{bmatrix} a \\ \bar{I} \end{bmatrix}, \quad \bar{e} = \begin{bmatrix} e \\ 0 \end{bmatrix}, \quad \bar{b} = \begin{bmatrix} b \\ -1 \end{bmatrix}, \quad \bar{x} = \begin{bmatrix} x \\ x_{n+1} \end{bmatrix}, \tag{13.14}$$

system (2.13) takes the form

$$\begin{aligned} v &= \bar{x}' \bar{V} \bar{x}, \\ \pi &= \bar{x}' \bar{a}, \\ 1 &= \bar{x}' \bar{e} = x'e, \\ 0 &= \bar{x}' \bar{b}, \end{aligned} \tag{13.15}$$

which has the property that V is an $n + 1$ diagonal matrix with respect to the original problem. We note that $\bar{e}$ is not the unit vector (in $(n + 1)$-dimensional space) and that in the problem a third constraint (the last equation of system (13.15)) is introduced. Proceeding with the identification of the boundary of the region of admissible portfolios, we define the usual minimization problem of the first equation of system (13.15) subject to the last three equations of system (13.15) acting as constraints. Consider for that the Lagrangian function

$$L = \bar{x}'\bar{V}\bar{x} - \lambda_1(\bar{a}'\bar{x} - \pi) - \lambda_2(\bar{e}'\bar{x} - 1) - \lambda_3\bar{b}'\bar{x}$$
$$= x'V^c x + x_{n+1}^2\sigma_I^2 - \lambda_1(a'x + \bar{I}x_{n+1} - \pi)$$
$$-\lambda_2(e'x - 1) - \lambda_3(b'x - x_{n+1}). \tag{13.16}$$

Differentiating L with respect to $\bar{x}$, λ_1, λ_2, and λ_3, and equating each partial derivative to zero, we obtain

$$\begin{aligned} 2\bar{x}'\bar{V} - \lambda_1\bar{a}' - \lambda_2\bar{e}' - \lambda_3\bar{b}' = 0 &= \partial L/\partial\bar{x}, \\ -\bar{a}'\bar{x} + \pi = 0 &= \partial L/\partial\lambda_1, \\ -\bar{e}'\bar{x} + 1 = 0 &= \partial L/\partial\lambda_2, \\ -\bar{b}'\bar{x} = 0 &= \partial L/\partial\lambda_3. \end{aligned} \tag{13.17}$$

Assume next that $\bar{V}$ is nonsingular and that the determinant of the coefficients of system (13.17) is not zero, i.e.,

$$\begin{vmatrix} \bar{V} & \bar{a} & \bar{e} & \bar{b} \\ \bar{a}' & 0 & 0 & 0 \\ \bar{e}' & 0 & 0 & 0 \\ \bar{b}' & 0 & 0 & 0 \end{vmatrix} \neq 0. \tag{13.18}$$

Then from the first equation of system (13.17) we have

$$\bar{x} = \tfrac{1}{2}(\lambda_1\bar{V}^{-1}\bar{a} + \lambda_2\bar{V}^{-1}\bar{e} + \lambda_3\bar{V}^{-1}\bar{b}). \tag{13.19}$$

By premultiplying the vector $\bar{x}$ by $\bar{a}$, $\bar{e}$, and $\bar{b}$, respectively, and introducing the resulting relationship into the last three equations of system (13.17), we obtain the linear system

$$C\lambda = p, \tag{13.20}$$

where

$$C = \begin{bmatrix} \bar{a}\bar{V}^{-1}\bar{a} & \bar{e}\bar{V}^{-1}\bar{a} & \bar{b}\bar{V}^{-1}\bar{a} \\ \bar{a}'\bar{V}^{-1}\bar{e} & \bar{e}\bar{V}^{-1}\bar{e} & \bar{b}\bar{V}^{-1}\bar{e} \\ \bar{a}'\bar{V}^{-1}\bar{b} & \bar{e}\bar{V}^{-1}\bar{b} & \bar{b}\bar{V}^{-1}\bar{b} \end{bmatrix}, \quad \lambda = \begin{bmatrix} \lambda_1 \\ \lambda_2 \\ \lambda_3 \end{bmatrix}, \quad p = \begin{bmatrix} \pi \\ 1 \\ 0 \end{bmatrix}. \tag{13.21}$$

Because of the assumptions made, C is nonsingular and its determinant is always positive. Thus from (13.21) we get

$$\lambda = C^{-1}p. \tag{13.22}$$

Substituting (13.22) into (13.19) allows us to compute the equation of the boundary of the region of admissible portfolios

$$v = \bar{x}'\bar{V}\bar{x}. \tag{13.23}$$

After some computation, we get the result

$$v = p'C^{-1}p, \tag{13.24}$$

which is again as before a second-order equation (parabola) as a function of π. For further applications it is advisable to obtain an explicit solution of (13.22)–(13.23). If we introduce for the matrix C (13.21) the notation

$$C = [c_{ij}], \tag{13.25}$$

we have

$$\begin{aligned} \lambda_1 &= 2(\pi c_{22}c_{33} + c_{13}c_{23} - \pi c_{23}^2 - c_{12}c_{33})/\Delta, \\ \lambda_2 &= 2(c_{11}c_{33} + \pi c_{13}c_{23} - c_{13}^2 - \pi c_{12}c_{33})/\Delta, \\ \lambda_3 &= 2(\pi c_{12}c_{23} + c_{12}c_{13} - \pi c_{22}c_{13} - c_{11}c_{23})/\Delta, \end{aligned} \tag{13.26}$$

where

$$\Delta = c_{11}c_{22}c_{33} - 2c_{12}c_{13}c_{23} - c_{13}^2c_{22} - c_{23}^2c_{11} - c_{12}^2c_{33} > 0. \tag{13.27}$$

Thus

$$\begin{aligned} \bar{x}(\pi) = [&(\pi c_{22}c_{33} + c_{13}c_{23} - \pi c_{23}^2 - c_{12}c_{33})\bar{V}^{-1}\bar{a} \\ &+ (c_{11}c_{33} + \pi c_{13}c_{23} - c_{13}^2 - \pi c_{12}c_{33})\bar{V}^{-1}\bar{e} \\ &+ (\pi c_{12}c_{23} + c_{12}c_{13} - \pi c_{22}c_{13} - c_{11}c_{23})\bar{V}^{-1}\bar{b}]/\Delta. \end{aligned} \tag{13.28}$$

In order to check the consistency of the results, it is interesting to compute the form of the component $\bar{x}_{n+1}$, i.e., of $b'x$. From (13.28) we have

$$\bar{x}_{n+1}(\pi) = b'x = \tfrac{1}{2}\lambda_1(\bar{V}^{-1}\bar{a})_{n+1} + \tfrac{1}{2}\lambda_2(\bar{V}^{-1}\bar{e})_{n+1} + \tfrac{1}{2}\lambda_3(\bar{V}^{-1}\bar{b})_{n+1}, \tag{13.29}$$

and substituting (13.14) into (13.29), we obtain

$$\bar{x}_{n+1}(\pi) = \frac{\lambda_1}{2}\frac{\bar{I}}{\sigma_I^2} - \frac{\lambda_3}{2}\frac{1}{\sigma_I^2} \tag{13.30}$$

where λ_1, λ_3 are given by Eqs. (13.26).

In this derivation we have assumed that $\bar{V}$ is nonsingular and that I is a completely arbitrary index. We have also treated x_{n+1} as an additional investment, even if the introduction of the last constraint (13.13) clarifies its special role.

The main point is that the index I is not an independent variable, but is a weighted average of the returns on all (risky) securities in the market. Thus

$$I = w'R \tag{13.31}$$

and

$$\bar{I} = w'r, \tag{13.32}$$

while

$$\sigma_I^2 = w'Vw. \tag{13.33}$$

Substituting into (13.32) and (13.33), in place of r and V, the expressions derived from the application of the linear regression (13.1), we can replace $\bar{I}$ and σ_I^2 by

$$\bar{I} = \frac{w'a}{1 - w'b} \tag{13.34}$$

and

$$\sigma_I^2 = \frac{w'V^c w}{1 - w'bb'w}. \tag{13.35}$$

If we introduce (13.28) and (13.29) into the basic system (13.14) and its solution (13.23) and (13.28), the system takes a very particular form. Before performing the substitution, it is important to perform the normalization

$$w'e = 1 \tag{13.36}$$

and recall that it has been proved that the set of weights w, which minimizes the residual error, is

$$w = b. \tag{13.37}$$

Introducing this particular structure into (13.30), we obtain

$$\bar{x}_{n+1}(\pi) = \frac{\lambda_1}{2}\frac{(1 + b'b)b'a}{b'V^c b} - \frac{\lambda_3}{2}\frac{1 - (b'b)^2}{b'V^c b}. \tag{13.38}$$

Note, however, that elements (13.34) and (13.35) must be substituted also into λ_1 and λ_3.

We shall next devote ourselves to the analysis of the possible singular cases.

If we consider the various possible situations arising when the original $n \times n$ variance–covariance matrix is singular, we see that most of these situations cannot occur. Even in the pathological case in which two investments are characterized by identical returns, the matrix $\bar{V}$ is not singular. The same result is evident when instead of the diagonalized system (13.13) we consider system (13.10).

We can therefore conclude that most of the singular cases in the original problem arise because

$$\operatorname{cov}(c_i, c_j) \neq 0. \tag{13.39}$$

Note in particular that when we consider among the elements of the set of n investments two investments with identical returns $r_i = r_j$, clearly

$$\text{cov}(c_i, c_j) = 1, \tag{13.40}$$

and assumption (13.4) is no longer true. This fact gives a measure of the approximation (13.4).

Thus the only important case that must be discussed is that in which to the previous set of n investments we add a "riskless" investment, i.e., an investment such that

$$c_i = 0. \tag{13.41}$$

Note that in this category of investment we do not consider only the true riskless investment, i.e., an investment with

$$\sigma_i = b_i = c_i = 0, \tag{13.42}$$

but also any risky investment that is perfectly correlated with the market index for which we have

$$c_i = 0 \qquad \text{and} \qquad b_i \neq 0. \tag{13.43}$$

If we denote by ρ the return on the investment x_ρ, instead of (13.13), we are led to consider the system

$$\begin{aligned} v &= x'V^c x + x_{n+1}\sigma_I^2, \\ \pi &= x'a + x_\rho \rho + \bar{x}_{n+1}\bar{I}, \\ 1 &= x'e + x_\rho, \\ 0 &= x'b - \bar{x}_{n+1}. \end{aligned} \tag{13.44}$$

Proceeding as before, we construct the Lagrangian function

$$L = \bar{x}'\bar{V}x - \lambda_1(\bar{a}'\bar{x} + x_\rho \rho - \pi) - \lambda_2(\bar{e}'\bar{x} + x_\rho - 1) - \lambda_3 \bar{b}'\bar{x}. \tag{13.45}$$

Differentiating L with respect to $\bar{x}$, x_ρ, λ_1, λ_2, and λ_3 leads to the system

$$\begin{aligned} 2\bar{x}'\bar{V} - \lambda_1\bar{a}' - \lambda_2\bar{e}' - \lambda_3\bar{b}' &= 0 = \partial L/\partial \bar{x}, \\ -\lambda_1\rho - \lambda_2 &= 0 = \partial L/\partial x_\rho, \\ -\bar{a}'\bar{x} - x_\rho\rho + \pi &= 0 = \partial L/\partial \lambda_1, \\ -\bar{e}'\bar{x} - x_\rho + 1 &= 0 = \partial L/\partial \lambda_2, \\ -\bar{b}'\bar{x} &= 0 = \partial L/\partial \lambda_3. \end{aligned} \tag{13.46}$$

The first equation of (13.46) can be solved, leading to

$$\bar{x} = \tfrac{1}{2}(\lambda_1\bar{V}^{-1}\bar{a} + \lambda_2\bar{V}^{-1}\bar{e} + \lambda_3\bar{V}^{-1}\bar{b}), \tag{13.47}$$

while from the second equation of (13.46) we have

$$\lambda_2 = -\lambda_1 \rho. \tag{13.48}$$

The substitution of (13.47) and (13.48) into the last three equations of (13.46) leads to

$$\begin{aligned} \tfrac{1}{2}(\lambda_1 \bar{a}'\bar{V}^{-1}\bar{d} + \lambda_3 \bar{a}'\bar{V}^{-1}\bar{b}) + \rho x_\rho &= \pi, \\ \tfrac{1}{2}(\lambda_1 \bar{e}'\bar{V}^{-1}\bar{d} + \lambda_3 \bar{e}'\bar{V}^{-1}\bar{b}) + x_\rho &= 1, \\ \tfrac{1}{2}(\lambda_1 \bar{b}'\bar{V}^{-1}\bar{d} + \lambda_3 \bar{b}'\bar{V}^{-1}\bar{b}) &= 0, \end{aligned} \tag{13.49}$$

wherc

$$\bar{d} = \bar{a} - \rho \bar{e}. \tag{13.50}$$

System (13.48) can be written in matrix form as

$$C_\rho \lambda_\rho = p, \tag{13.51}$$

where

$$C_\rho = \begin{bmatrix} \frac{1}{2}\bar{a}'\bar{V}^{-1}\bar{d} & \rho & \frac{1}{2}\bar{a}'\bar{V}^{-1}\bar{b} \\ \frac{1}{2}\bar{e}'\bar{V}^{-1}\bar{d} & 1 & \frac{1}{2}\bar{e}'\bar{V}^{-1}\bar{b} \\ \frac{1}{2}\bar{b}'\bar{V}^{-1}\bar{d} & 0 & \frac{1}{2}\bar{b}'\bar{V}^{-1}\bar{b} \end{bmatrix}, \qquad \lambda_\rho = \begin{bmatrix} \lambda_1 \\ x_\rho \\ \lambda_3 \end{bmatrix}. \tag{13.52}$$

Thus if

$$\det C_\rho \neq 0, \tag{13.53}$$

then

$$\lambda_\rho = C_\rho^{-1} p. \tag{13.54}$$

In detail, we have

$$\begin{aligned} \lambda_1 &= 2(\pi - \rho)\bar{b}'\bar{V}^{-1}\bar{b}/\Delta, \\ x_\rho &= \bar{d}'(\bar{V}^{-1}\bar{b}\bar{e}'\bar{V}^{-1} - \bar{V}^{-1}\bar{e}\bar{b}'\bar{V}^{-1})\bar{b}/\Delta, \\ \lambda_3 &= 2(\pi - \rho)\bar{b}'\bar{V}^{-1}\bar{d}/\Delta, \end{aligned} \tag{13.55}$$

where

$$\Delta = 2\rho \bar{d}'(\bar{V}^{-1}\bar{b}\bar{e}'\bar{V}^{-1} - \bar{V}^{-1}\bar{e}\bar{b}'\bar{V}^{-1})\bar{b}. \tag{13.56}$$

Thus

$$\begin{aligned} x(\pi) &= \tfrac{1}{2}(\lambda_1 \bar{V}^{-1}\bar{a} - \lambda_1 \rho \bar{V}^{-1}\bar{e} + \lambda_3 \bar{V}^{-1}\bar{b}) \\ &= \tfrac{1}{2}(\lambda_1 \bar{V}^{-1}\bar{d} + \lambda_3 \bar{V}^{-1}\bar{b}) \\ &= [(\pi - \rho)\bar{b}'\bar{V}^{-1}\bar{b}\bar{V}^{-1}\bar{d} + (\rho - \pi)\bar{b}'\bar{V}^{-1}\bar{d}\bar{V}^{-1}\bar{b}]/\Delta, \end{aligned} \tag{13.57}$$

(13.58) $$Vx(\pi) = \tfrac{1}{2}(\lambda_1 \bar{d} + \lambda_3 \bar{b}),$$

(13.59) $$\begin{aligned} x'(\pi)Vx(\pi) &= \tfrac{1}{4}(\lambda_1^2 \bar{d}'\bar{V}^{-1}\bar{d} + 2\lambda_1\lambda_3 \bar{d}'\bar{V}^{-1}\bar{b} + \lambda_3^2 \bar{b}'\bar{V}^{-1}\bar{b} \\ &= [(\pi - \rho)^2(\bar{b}'\bar{V}^{-1}\bar{b})^2 \bar{d}'\bar{V}^{-1}\bar{d} \\ &\quad + 2(\pi - \rho)(\rho - \pi)(\bar{d}'\bar{V}^{-1}\bar{b})^2 \bar{b}'\bar{V}^{-1}\bar{b} \\ &\quad + (\rho - \pi)^2(\bar{b}'\bar{V}^{-1}\bar{d})^2 \cdot \bar{b}'\bar{V}^{-1}\bar{b}]/\Delta^2. \end{aligned}$$

Thus

(13.60) $$\sigma = \frac{(\pi - \rho)}{\Delta}[(\bar{b}'\bar{V}^{-1}\bar{b})(\bar{b}'\bar{V}^{-1}\bar{b} \cdot \bar{d}'\bar{V}^{-1}\bar{d} - \bar{d}'\bar{V}^{-1}\bar{b} \cdot \bar{d}'\bar{V}^{-1}\bar{b})]^{1/2},$$

which is again the equation of a straight line in the plane (σ, π). Results similar to those obtained in Chapters 6 and 7 can then also be derived.

Note that the procedure starts to pay for $n > 3$ because for $n = 3$ we have to invert a 3×3 symmetric matrix C anyway in order to find the boundary! This is caused by the increase in the difficulty of the Lagrangian system.

It is of interest to analyze the case in which we solve the original problem without the constraint

(13.61) $$x_{n+1} = x'b,$$

and after having obtained a solution, we seek conditions under which such additional constraint holds. We can prove that this can never happen. Indeed, if in (13.16) we let

(13.62) $$\lambda_3 = 0,$$

after some computation we find the explicit solution

(13.63) $$x = [(\gamma\pi - \beta)V^{-1}a + (\alpha - \beta\pi + \bar{I}^2/\sigma_I^2)V^{-1}e]/(\alpha\gamma - \beta^2 + \bar{I}^2/\sigma_I^2)$$

and

(13.64) $$x_{n+1} = [(\gamma\pi - \beta)\bar{I}/\sigma_I^2]/(\alpha\gamma - \beta^2 + \bar{I}^2/\sigma_I^2).$$

We must next see under what conditions Eq. (13.61) is satisfied, i.e., if

(13.65) $$(\gamma\pi - \beta)b'V^{-1}a + (\alpha - \beta\pi + \bar{I}^2/\sigma_I^2)b'V^{-1}e = (\gamma\pi - \beta)\bar{I}/\bar{\sigma}_I^2.$$

Since this equation must be satisfied for all values of π, we can derive from it two equations independent of π, which can be combined, leading to the condition

(13.66) $$\alpha\gamma - \beta^2 + \sigma_I^2(b'V^{-1}a - (\beta/\gamma)b'V^{-1}e)^2 = 0,$$

which is never satisfied since $(\alpha\gamma - \beta^2) > 0$.

Proceeding in the same way in the case of a "riskless" asset, after some computation we are led to the condition

$$b'V^{-1}a - \rho b'V^{-1}e = \bar{I}/\sigma_I^2, \tag{13.67}$$

which is also never satisfied.

The case of the "riskless" asset for which condition (13.43) holds warrants some further analysis since its comparison with the general critical cases analyzed in Chapter 8 may throw some light on the extent of the approximation (13.4). Condition (13.43) holds for the case of investments that are perfectly correlated to the market index I. Now we have pointed out that the market index I is a particular linear combination of investments. Thus while in the exact problem every time there exists among the n investments one the variance of which is a linear combination of the variance of the other $n-1$ investments, the corresponding matrix V is singular (see Chapter 8 for detailed conditions); now in this simplified diagonal model the singularity of the problem occurs only for the particular linear combination I.

CHAPTER 14

THE CAPITAL ASSET PRICING MODEL

The major result obtained in Chapter 6, i.e., in the case for which there exists in the market a riskless asset, was the identification of the optimal risky portfolio x^*, i.e., of a certain combination of risky assets that will be used by all mean-variance investors. Thus this combination will fix the *relative demand* of the various assets under the assumption that the expected return on each investment is given and that the variance–covariance matrix of the investment is also given.

On the other hand, we observe on the market a certain *supply* of investment opportunities, which are defined by their daily prices.

The capital asset pricing theory reaches some important results by equating demand, expressed by the vector x^*, and supply, defined by the relative price of each security observed on the market under the assumption that the market is in equilibrium.

This result can be achieved under three basic assumptions on the market:

(a) Each investor acting on the market is a risk averter with the same probability beliefs, which enable him to make his investment decisions on the (σ, π) plane. Clearly, each investor will have different parameters in his (quadratic) utility function.

(b) The market is perfect and in equilibrium. In particular, no transaction costs occur and therefore the returns on lending and borrowing (or selling short) are the same.

(c) There exists one (and only one!) riskless asset with rate of return ρ. Thus all investors will divide their capital between the riskless asset and the optimal combination of risky assets x^*. Clearly, such an optimal risky portfolio x^* is the same for all investors.

Assume that there exist h investors acting on the market and consider the kth investor ($k = 1, \ldots, h$). Let W_0^k be the capital of the kth investor. Then

$$d^k = (e'x^*\eta_k)W_0^k \tag{14.1}$$

is the capital invested by the kth investor in the optimal combination of risky assets, while

$$d_\rho^k = x_\rho^k W_0^k = (1 - e'x^*\eta_k)W_0^k \tag{14.2}$$

is the capital invested by the kth investor in the riskless asset. Thus

$$W_0^k = d^k + d_\rho^k. \tag{14.3}$$

In (14.1) η_k is the scaling factor relative to the kth investor (see Chapter 6). The two quantities d^k and d_ρ^k represent the demand of the optimal risky portfolio and of the riskless asset originated by the kth investor ($k = 1, \ldots, h$). The aggregated demand will then be

$$\begin{aligned} W &= \sum_{k=1}^{h} W_0^k = \sum_{k=1}^{h} (d^k + d_\rho^k) \\ &= \sum_{k=1}^{h} (e'x^*\eta_k)W_0^k + (1 - e'x^*\eta_k)W_0^k. \end{aligned} \tag{14.4}$$

Note that given W and given the total demand of the risky portfolio, the total demand of the riskless asset is uniquely defined. Now in an equilibrium situation the total demand of the risky portfolio must be equal to the total supply. The total supply must be equal to the market value M of the aggregate of risky securities. Thus

$$\sum_{k=1}^{h} (e'x^*\eta_k)W_0^k = M. \tag{14.5}$$

Now we can disaggregate M into its components and let

$$M = \sum_{i=1}^{n} N_i P_i, \tag{14.6}$$

where we denote by P_i the current (equilibrium) price per share of the ith security and by N_i the number of outstanding shares of the ith security. Thus the percentage market value of the ith security is

$$x_i^M = \frac{N_i P_i}{M} = \frac{N_i P_i}{\sum_{i=1}^{n} N_i P_i}. \tag{14.7}$$

In equilibrium then

$$\sum_{k=1}^{h} (e'x^*\eta_k)W_0^k = \sum_{i=1}^{n} N_i P_i, \tag{14.8}$$

which equates the total demand to the total supply. For each security we must also have

(14.9) $$x_i^M = x_i^*,$$

and, recalling (14.7) and (6.58),

(14.10) $$\frac{N_i P_i}{\sum_{i=1}^n N_i P_i} = \frac{(V^{-1}d)_i}{e'V^{-1}d}.$$

The fundamental relationship (14.10) equates P_i, the observed price, to r_i, σ_i, and ρ_{ij}, i.e., the expected return, standard deviation, and covariance of the ith security measured in an equilibrium situation. Note first that since

(14.11) $$P_i > 0,$$

the left-hand side of Eq. (14.10) is positive; thus the right-hand side must also be positive. Thus in equilibrium r and V must be such that

(14.12) $$x^* = \frac{V^{-1}d}{e'V^{-1}d} > 0.$$

In our presentation we have so far been concerned with the analysis of the properties of the ith security and of its relations with respect to the market. Clearly, all results presented here can also be applied to the "composite" securities, which are the portfolios.

Indeed, some results, even if applicable to each security, find a more natural interpretation if applied to the case of portfolios.

We shall next proceed with our analysis by assuming that we observe N_i, P_i, and ρ and that we want to derive the equilibrium relation x^* and the other data for all securities.

We shall assume that we have also been able to measure σ_{M} and π_{M}, the standard deviation and the expected return on the market.

If this is true, we can first derive the boundary of the region of admissible portfolios, which in the plane (σ, π) must be a straight line joining the point $(0, \rho)$ with the point $(\sigma_{\mathrm{M}}, \pi_{\mathrm{M}})$. The equation of this straight line is

(14.13) $$\pi = \rho + \chi_e \sigma,$$

where the angular coefficient χ_e has the form

(14.14) $$\chi_e = \frac{\pi_{\mathrm{M}} - \rho}{\sigma_{\mathrm{M}}}.$$

The straight line (14.13) is called the *capital market line.*

We shall now proceed with the identification of relationships that connect the equilibrium return and standard deviation of each security with that of the market.

In an equilibrium situation indeed we can replace v^* with σ_{M}^2 and σ_{ix^*} with $\sigma_{i\mathrm{M}}$. If we apply this identity to Eq. (7.3), we obtain

$$r_i - \rho = b_i(\pi_{\mathrm{M}} - \rho), \tag{14.15}$$

where

$$b_i = \sigma_{i\mathrm{M}}/\sigma_{\mathrm{M}}^2. \tag{14.16}$$

Equation (14.15) relates the expected return on each security, and in particular the "risk premium" d_i, to the expected return on the market, or, more exactly, its risk premium through the angular coefficient (14.16). Indeed, (14.15) becomes

$$d_i = b_i d_{\mathrm{M}}, \tag{14.17}$$

where

$$d_i = r_i - \rho \tag{14.18}$$

and

$$d_{\mathrm{M}} = \pi_{\mathrm{M}} - \rho. \tag{14.19}$$

Equations (14.15) and (14.17) are called *security market lines.*

We can also represent Eq. (14.15) in a way that is formally identical to (14.13), the capital market line. Indeed, from (14.15) we have

$$r_i - \rho = \chi_s \sigma_{i\mathrm{M}}, \tag{14.20}$$

where the angular coefficient χ_s is defined by

$$\chi_s = (\pi_{\mathrm{M}} - \rho)/\sigma_{\mathrm{M}}^2. \tag{14.21}$$

By comparing (14.14) and (14.21), we have

$$\chi_s = \chi_e/\sigma_{\mathrm{M}}. \tag{14.22}$$

In spite of the formal similarities, the capital market line and the security market line have quite different meanings. The first, if the underlying assumptions are satisfied, defines the boundary of the region of admissible portfolios, i.e., the efficient set; the second connects each investment with the market and clearly holds for each investment even if not efficient.

We shall next combine Eq. (14.13) of the capital market line with that of the security market line and obtain the equation

$$\frac{r_i - \rho}{\sigma_{i\mathrm{M}}} = \frac{d_i}{\sigma_{i\mathrm{M}}} = \frac{\chi_e}{\sigma_{\mathrm{M}}} = \frac{\pi_{\mathrm{M}} - \rho}{\sigma_{\mathrm{M}}^2}, \tag{14.23}$$

which can also be represented in the form

$$\frac{d_i}{\chi_e} = \frac{\sigma_{iM}}{\sigma_M} = \sigma_i \rho_{iM}. \tag{14.24}$$

This last equation clarifies the nature of the risk associated with each security and the fact that only in the case of efficient portfolios is it possible to measure the risk only by means of the standard deviation of the portfolio. Indeed, for a fixed ratio d_i/χ_e we can see that the correlation coefficient ρ_{iM} for which σ_i in (14.24) has its minimum value is

$$\rho_{iM} = 1, \tag{14.25}$$

which is true (see properties (7.21) and (10.20)) for efficient portfolios. This again proves that it never pays to use inefficient portfolios.

Let us again consider the security market line (14.15) and proceed with a suitable interpretation of the meaning of the coefficient b_i, which will allow us to connect the result of this chapter with some results of the previous chapter. Consider again the random return on the ith investment and represent it in the form

$$R_i = r_i + f_i, \tag{14.26}$$

where as usual r_i represents the expected return on the ith investment and f_i is a random variable with

$$E(f_i) = 0, \qquad \sigma(f_i) = \sigma_i. \tag{14.27}$$

Let us represent in a similar way the return on the market portfolio, i.e.,

$$R^M = \pi_M + f_M, \tag{14.28}$$

where

$$E(f_M) = 0, \qquad v(f_M) = \sigma_M^2. \tag{14.29}$$

Introducing (14.26) and (14.28) into the security market line (Eq. (14.15)), we have

$$R_i - f_i - \rho = b_i(R^M - f_M - \rho), \tag{14.30}$$

from which

$$\begin{aligned} R_i &= \rho + b_i(R^M - f_M - \rho) + f_i \\ &= \rho(1 - b_i) + b_i R^M + (f_i - b_i f_M). \end{aligned} \tag{14.31}$$

Define

$$a_i = (1 - b_i), \tag{14.32}$$

$$c_i = f_i - b_i f_M, \tag{14.33}$$

where a_i is a real number and c_i is again a random variable with

$$E(c_i) = 0, \qquad v(c_i) = (1 - \rho_{iM})\sigma_i^2. \tag{14.34}$$

Thus from (14.31)

$$R_i = a_i + b_i R^M + c_i. \tag{14.35}$$

Now if we compare (14.35) with Eq. (13.1), we see that if we replace the market return R with the market index return I, they are identical. And if we consider I to be (as it is) a proxy for R^M, then the coefficients (14.32) and (14.33) must be identical with those that appear in Eq. (13.7). The coefficient b_i, which was defined as the ratio (14.16), is then a measure of the *volatility* of the ith investment, i.e., disregarding for the time being the residual c_i, it measures the response of the return on the ith security to a variation of return on the whole market. This coefficient b_i is usually called the "beta" coefficient. Indeed,

$$b_i = \frac{dR_i}{dR^M}. \tag{14.36}$$

Securities with a high value of b_i tend to give a return higher than the market when it is positive and lower than the market when it is negative (Fig. 14.1).

We have so far ignored the presence of the residual c_i. Note that this is correct when we are dealing with portfolios on the efficient frontier that are perfectly linearly correlated with the market.

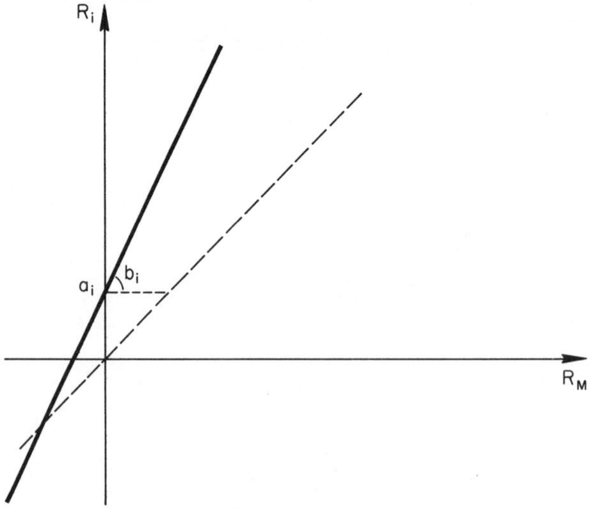

Figure 14.1

From the preceding remarks it follows that it never pays to use an inefficient portfolio; even with an efficient portfolio one has a certain risk, which is associated with the variance of the market and which is measured by

$$b_i(R^{\mathrm{M}} - \pi_{\mathrm{M}}) = b_i f_{\mathrm{M}}. \tag{14.37}$$

This is the so-called *systematic risk*, or market risk, directly associated through the volatility coefficient b_i to the market risk f_{M}. Indeed, the random component of the return on an investment f_i can be expressed (see (14.33)) in the form

$$f_i = b_i f_{\mathrm{M}} - c_i, \tag{14.38}$$

while its variance has the form

$$\sigma_i^2 = b_i^2 \sigma_{\mathrm{M}}^2 + (1 - \rho_{i\mathrm{M}})\sigma_i^2. \tag{14.39}$$

The first part of the right-hand side of (14.39) is the systematic component of the variance, while the second part is the nonsystematic one. Thus comparing (14.39) with the security market line (14.15), it is important to point out that the risk premium $r_i - \rho$ is proportional to b_i and therefore to the *systematic risk*. It is evident once again that even in equilibrium the only way to achieve a higher expected return is to run a higher (systematic) risk, i.e., to use portfolios with higher volatility.

In all results that we have presented so far we have dealt with the case in which there exists in the market a riskless asset with rate of return ρ. On the other hand, the market portfolio x^{M} (14.7) can still be observed, and σ_{M} and π_{M} can be measured. Consider Eq. (14.15) and rewrite it as

$$r_i = r_{n+1} + b_i(\pi_{\mathrm{M}} - \sigma_{n+1}). \tag{14.40}$$

Now the return r_{n+1} is the expected return corresponding to the investment characterized by a zero volatility, i.e.,

$$b_{n+1} = 0. \tag{14.41}$$

If we consider the definition of b_i (14.16), this is the return on a boundary investment that is orthogonal to the market, i.e., such that

$$\sigma_{n+1,\mathrm{M}} = \mathrm{cov}(x_{n+1}(\pi), x^{\mathrm{M}}) = 0. \tag{14.42}$$

Since the market is "efficient," i.e., the point $(v_{\mathrm{M}}, \pi_{\mathrm{M}})$ belongs to the boundary of the region of admissible portfolios, Theorem (4.23) allows us to identify such a portfolio. Indeed, from (4.24)

$$r_{n+1} = \frac{\pi_{\mathrm{M}}\beta - \alpha}{\pi_{\mathrm{M}}\gamma - \beta}. \tag{14.43}$$

Thus in a market without a riskless asset, the security market line becomes

$$(14.44)\qquad r_i - \frac{\pi_M\beta - \alpha}{\pi_M\gamma - \beta} = b_i\left(\pi_M - \frac{\pi_M\beta - \alpha}{\pi_M\gamma - \beta}\right) = b_i\frac{\pi_M^2\gamma - 2\pi_M\beta + \alpha}{\pi_M\gamma - \beta},$$

which has the same formal properties as (14.15).

The results (14.40)–(14.44) concerned with the case in which there do not exist any riskless assets can be obtained directly from the general result (4.91) by replacing $x(\pi)$ with x^M. Indeed, in this case we obtain expression

$$(14.45)\qquad r_i - \pi_0 = b_i(\pi_M - \pi_0),$$

where π_0 is the return on the portfolio that is orthogonal to x^M.

EXAMPLES, NOTES, AND REFERENCES

The capital asset pricing model first proposed by Sharpe (1964) has been further extended from both the theoretical and the experimental point of view by many authors (see Jensen (1972a) and Ross (1976)).

It is important to mention that its most useful applications are concerned with the identification of the correct "equilibrium" opening selling price of new securities and of the evaluation of possible choices among risky industrial ventures as to the level of insurance, etc.

The technique starts with the observation of the price per share of the security of the firm that is evaluating the project and the identification of the level of risk/return associated with this firm on the market. By observing the various possible new risk/return levels associated with the various projects, one can derive the equilibrium price that the market would associate with the company shares according to the various choices, allowing the identification of the project that maximizes the present value of the firm's total equity.

The most important result of portfolio theory, i.e., the capital asset pricing model, even if it is an interesting speculation, destroys investment theory per se. The idea that since all the investors are rational and risk averters, the market is always right and correctly gives a premium expected return and penalizes risk, clearly leads to a tautology and to the disappearance of the professions of investors, advisors, and financial managers.

The only possible justification for the remaining practical interest in the subject may lie in the facts that investors do not behave only according to mean variance, information is not shared, and, finally, the time structure of investments cannot be disregarded.

A quite interesting theoretical and "central" result of portfolio selection, i.e., the capital asset pricing model, has recently been subjected to deep critical investigation. The papers by Roll (1977) and Ross (1976) demolish all previous empirical tests that were performed notably by Jensen (1972a) and Black *et al.* (1972).

The whole problem has been the subject of a recent important review paper by Ross (1978). Ross (1976, 1978) has also proposed one interesting alternative theory, called the arbitrage theory of capital asset pricing. In the notes and references of Chapters 2 and 6 we provided the theoretical framework (the case $W_0 = 0$) for an arbitrage theory.

The capital asset pricing theory, or the arbitrage theory, essentially provides a quantification of the return/risk equilibrium relationship and, if the investors behave only according to a return/risk rationale, in such a way that market imperfections, i.e., investments that have an undervalued return/risk ratio will promptly increase their value, may indeed provide an investment tool. Clearly, this is not the case, and the role of other considerations may be equally important in identifying investment opportunities.

Along these lines the capital asset pricing model can be used in a variety of different applications that are not strictly confined to the area of finance. Indeed, each time there exists a market in which risky assets are traded and this market is thought to move only according to a return/risk criterion, an equilibrium condition can be found and a cost attached to each risky decision. For instance, in the areas of corporate finance, capital investments, and budget, in which firms must choose among different forms of financing risky ventures, the influence of the various opportunities on the equity value can be investigated and the optimal solution identified. Similarly, in the area of insurance, which is even more closely related to "chance" than are stocks and bonds, the desired level of risk and therefore the reinsurance level can be identified by these techniques.

A word of warning can, however, be included for the inexperienced reader; if the markets would indeed behave only according to return/risk criteria and if the adjustment of temporary disequilibria would take place instantaneously, then there would not exist any investment opportunities. Clearly, even if we believe that markets are risk/return efficient, the analysis of the dynamic properties of the return to equilibria, i.e., the investigation of the time behavior of prices, a topic that has been absolutely ignored so far, would be of crucial importance.

CHAPTER 15

PORTFOLIO SELECTION IN AN INFLATIONARY OR MULTICURRENCY ENVIRONMENT

This chapter is meant to be more a comment and an interpretation under a different light of the results presented in the previous chapters than a presentation of new results. Indeed, in spite of the importance of the problem, the static model that we present is not suited, unless drastic approximations are made, to deal with the major problems involved in the theory of portfolio selection in an inflationary or multicurrency environment. While some results are indeed available, the basic problem of selecting the optimal portfolio that would take into consideration the real return from the investments and would distinguish between the risk (uncertainty) connected with the investment and the uncertainty of the inflation is mathematically rather difficult to solve.

The problem of one investor who computes the return on his investment in the currency of a certain country, but is allowed to make risky investments in other currency is mathematically also very similar to the inflationary problem and presents the same difficulties.

The analysis even of the simplest problem in which the returns on the investments are directly measured in real quantities or in one currency shows that the results are very instructive and account for the care with which we took into account and analyzed in detail the situation in which among the n investments there does not exist a riskless one (Chapters 2, 3) and the particular case for which an investment is dominated or semidominated (Chapter 5).

This, however, is not true in the case for which portfolios are chosen according to the returns evaluated in real terms. Consider for instance the case for the boundary of the region of admissible portfolios, evaluated in monetary terms, when there exists a riskless asset with return $\pi = \rho$. The

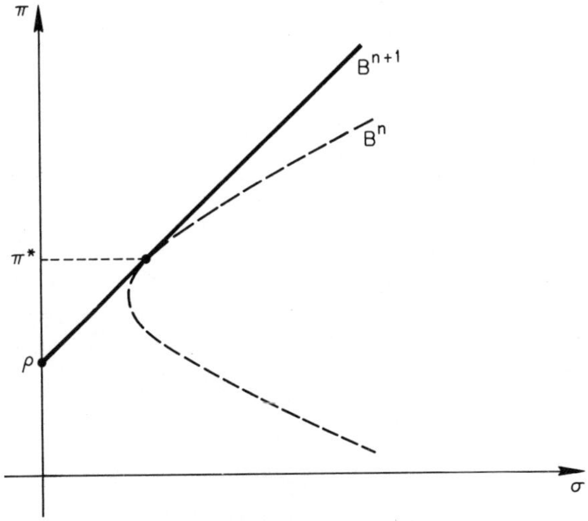

Figure 15.1

situation was analyzed in Chapter 6 and is shown in its most typical configuration in Fig. 15.1, where we have assumed that conditions (6.68) hold.

Let us now consider the same set of investments, but analyze their returns in real terms and construct the boundary of the region of admissible portfolios based on these returns.

In purely qualitative terms the boundary takes the form shown in Fig. 15.2, where we have denoted by π_r and σ_r the expected value of the portfolio return

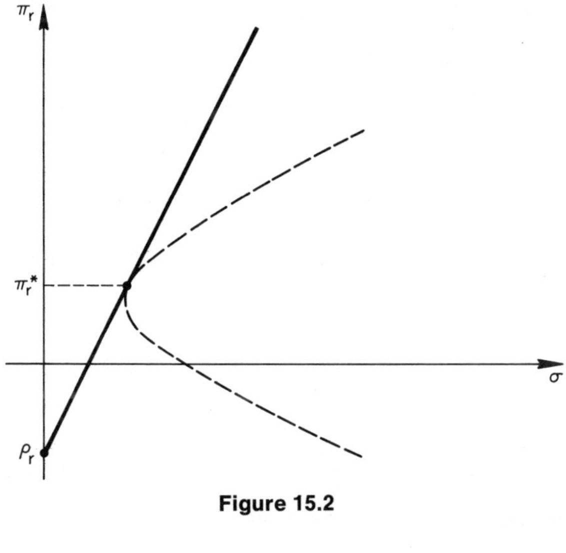

Figure 15.2

and its standard deviation, respectively, when the returns are measured in real terms. Now we notice the following relationship between the boundary portfolios belonging to B and those belonging to B_r. The investment that was riskless in monetary terms, shown in Fig. 15.1 by the point $(0, \rho)$, becomes a risky investment, and as such it will almost certainly (see Chapter 3, Examples, notes, and References) be in the interior R_r of the region of admissible portfolios and not on the boundary B_r.

In this case it becomes interesting to investigate experimentally the properties of the minimum variance portfolio of B_r. This portfolio, which as we know does not depend on the expected return vector in real terms, contains useful information.

In what follows we shall discuss a simple static model that will enable us to analyze partly analytically and partly numerically a simple portfolio selection problem in which the time horizon is divided into two intervals (at the end of the first interval the portfolio can be reallocated) in which we take into account investment opportunities in two different currencies. Clearly, this model can then be expanded into a multiperiodic multicurrency model. In this investigation we have modified and extended some preliminary results obtained on the same problem by Levin (1970). In this model we shall maximize a utility function or better investigate the efficient set relative to the total return on the portfolio evaluated at the end of the time horizon and in one currency only. This will imply the need for converting the whole investment into one single currency at the end of the time horizon (for the sake of convenience we can assume the currency to be the national currency of the investor). We assume that the investments available are both risky as well as riskless and that furthermore we have two different classes of "riskless" investments: those with life span over the entire horizon and those that expire at the end of the first half. We also assume the existence of a forward market in the currency exchange as well as in the riskless investments in each currency allowing the possibility of a complete hedge against exchange risk.

We next define the following variables:

- x_{no}^{01} the sum invested in riskless national assets expiring at the end of the first half-period,
- r_{no}^{01} the corresponding interest rate;
- x_{no}^{12} the sum invested in riskless national assets from the beginning to the end of the second half-period,
- r_{no}^{12} the corresponding interest rate;
- x_{no}^{02} the sum invested in riskless national assets at the beginning of the whole period and expiring at the end;
- r_{no}^{02} the corresponding interest rate.

Denote by $\bar{x}^{ij}_{\text{no}}$ the corresponding borrowed amounts in national currency and by $\bar{r}^{ij}_{\text{no}}$ the corresponding interest rates; notice that we do not assume, as in the previous model, that $\bar{r}^{ij}_{\text{no}} = r^{ij}_{\text{no}}$, i.e., that borrowing and lending interest rates are the same. This assumption explains why contrary to what has been done previously we must differentiate between borrowed sums ($\bar{x}^{ij}_{\text{no}}$) and loaned sums (x^{ij}_{no}).

Let us next denote by

x^{01}_{n} the sum invested in risky national investments that expire at the end of the first half-period,
R^{01}_{n} the corresponding interest rate (random), and
r^{01}_{n} its expected value,

while we shall denote by

x^{12}_{n}, x^{02}_{n}, R^{12}_{n}, R^{02}_{n}, r^{12}_{n}, and r^{02}_{n} the analogous national investments with different starting and expiring dates.

The solution of this two-period problem will be clear from the theory presented in the next chapter. It is however important to discuss a simplified one-period model, which will allow us to discuss decision variables relative to the investments in the foreign currency.

The crucial assumption, which will allow us to reach a closed form solution of the problem in a simplified case, is that all investments in foreign currencies are hedged against the exchange risk. This operation can, for instance, be performed by buying forward the investor's own currency (or selling forward the foreign currency). However, if this operation is claimed to be possible in a dynamic framework (see Solnik (1973), pp. 10–28), it is not absolutely clear what can be done in our static context when the return on the investment in the foreign currency is a random variable. In the simplified model we shall present a partial, but feasible solution of the problem.

Proceeding with the presentation of the notation, we shall denote by the subscript f all types of foreign investment operations, in the same way in which we used the subscript n for the case of the national investment.

Finally, we shall denote by the subscript e the corresponding types of investment operations performed only on the exchange market. Notice that our two-period model allows us to take fully into account the forward market operations.

In the simplified model we shall consider the same type of time structure that we used in Chapters 2–14, with the same simplifying assumption that lending and borrowing rates are the same. We shall then define the vector x^{n} of the allocation of capital among the national investments, x^{f} among the international investments, and x^e among speculations on the exchange market, with r^n, r^f, and r^e being the respective expected return vectors. Clearly, while we consider here only a single-period model, we are allowing the possibility of investing in a whole range of possible currencies. We shall assume that the total number of risky investment opportunities (national, foreign, and exchange) is n. The $n \times n$ variance–covariance matrix will describe the random behavior of the investment set. The region of admissible portfolios will again be parametrically defined by the system

$$v = x'Vx, \qquad \pi = x'r, \qquad 1 = x'e, \tag{15.1}$$

where

$$V = \begin{bmatrix} V^n & K^{nf} & K^{ne} & \emptyset^n \\ (K^{nf})' & V^f & K^{fe} & \emptyset^f \\ (K^{ne})' & (K^{fe})' & V^e & \emptyset^e \\ (\emptyset^n)' & (\emptyset^f)' & (\emptyset^e)' & \emptyset \end{bmatrix}, \qquad r = \begin{bmatrix} r^n \\ r^f \\ r^e \\ r^0 \end{bmatrix}. \tag{15.2}$$

Then all the results of the previous chapters can be applied.

We must now clarify exactly the assumptions that have been made. Nothing new has to be said about the vectors x^n, r^n and about the matrix V^n, which correspond to the investments performed in the national currency of the investor. Regarding the investments (risky as well as riskless) in the foreign currency, we shall hedge against the exchange risk the quantity r^f, which is then measured in the national currency of the country of the investor. In this way the investments that are riskless in the foreign currency still remain riskless since in this case the hedging can be performed exactly on the return r_0^f (measured in the foreign currency) since r_0^f is known with certainty at the decision instant. As has already been mentioned, this type of operation cannot be performed on the investments in the foreign currency that are risky. Clearly, the hedging performed on the expected value of this return has the property of reducing the exchange risk on the foreign investment, but on the other hand, it may possibly increase the level of the three foreign currency speculation operation (x^e, r^e, V^e).

These operations cannot be classified under "riskless investments in the foreign currency"; indeed, these operations consist of borrowing or lending (spot) funds in the foreign currency and receiving (or paying) a certain interest rate at the end of the period. Under the heading of foreign exchange currency speculative operations we shall therefore consider all operations on the forward markets. Note that some of these operations in our model are mandatory in order to hedge the expected returns on the foreign investments against the currency exchange risk.

Now clearly a new constraint, setting a lower bound on x^e, must be introduced.

The basic risk intrinsic to the returns on the investments as well as caused by the random character of the exchange market is now completely reflected in the matrix V. We recall that the (partially hedged) returns on the foreign securities are evaluated in the national currency of the investor. This implies that the exchange risk cannot be separated from the intrinsic risk related to the investments that are risky in their own original currency. Of course the off-diagonal blocks K^{fn}, K^{ne}, and K^{fe} of the partitioned matrix V (15.2) will show this dependence. In particular, the block K^{fe}, expressing the covariances between the returns on the foreign investments and the foreign exchange forward market, expresses the exchange risk. Note that in this approach since the riskless investments in foreign currencies are transformed into riskless investments in the national currency through hedging, the matrix V is always singular; in addition, the possibility of arbitrage, allowing infinite riskless profits, cannot be ruled out. This fact is shown in the square matrix block $\emptyset$ and by the rectangular matrix blocks $\emptyset^{\text{n}}$, $\emptyset^{\text{f}}$, and $\emptyset^{\text{e}}$ (15.2).

The second possible solution technique is based on the straightforward analysis of system (15.1) without any additional constraints on x^{e}. This technique avoids any hedging against the exchange risk (thus it does not allow any identification of possible riskless arbitrage opportunities in the foreign exchange market), but simply translates all returns on all investments in the national currency of the investor. Then the investments that are riskless in foreign currencies become risky in the national currency of the investor, and their variability give a measure of the respective exchange risk.

Another more pragmatic approach to the multicurrency portfolio selection problem is based on the preliminary separation of the whole set of possible investments into two groups of investments. The first group contains all investments that are characterized by the exchange risk only (notably bonds in various currencies with maturity at the end of the decision interval). The second group contains all investments that are characterized by an exchange risk as well as by an intrinsic risk. The riskless asset (i.e., the investment, if it exists, riskless in the investor's own currency) will be contained in both groups.

If we denote by V^B, r^B, x^B, and e^B the data relative to the first group of investments, we have the following portfolio problem

$$(15.3) \qquad v = (x^B)'V^Bx^B, \qquad \pi = (r^B)'x^B + \rho x_\rho, \qquad 1 = (e^B)'x^B + x_\rho,$$

where ρ denotes the return on the riskless investment and x_ρ the fraction of wealth invested in it. Denoting by V^I, r^I, x^I, and e^I the data relative to the second group of investments we obtain the following portfolio problem

$$(15.4) \qquad v = (x^I)'V^Ix^I, \qquad \pi = (r^I)'x^I + \rho x_\rho, \qquad 1 = (e^I)'x^I + x_\rho.$$

Both portfolio problems ((15.3) and (15.4)) contain a riskless asset; thus the results of Chapters 6 and 7 apply. In the case of system (15.3) we obtain the optimal combination of assets that are characterized by the exchange risk only, i.e., the portfolio

$$(x^B)^* = \frac{(V^B)^{-1}d^B}{(e^B)'(V^B)^{-1}d^B}, \tag{15.5}$$

where

$$d^B = r^B - \rho e^B. \tag{15.6}$$

In the case of system (15.4) the optimal combination of all the assets characterized by intrinsic risk is the portfolio

$$(x^I)^* = \frac{(V^I)^{-1}d^I}{(e^I)'(V^I)^{-1}d^I}, \tag{15.7}$$

where

$$d^I = r^I - \rho e^I. \tag{15.8}$$

Consider next the portfolio obtained by combining the two "investments" $(x^B)^*$ and $(x^I)^*$. Introducing the allocation vector (15.10), we obtain

$$\begin{aligned} v &= v_B^* x_B + v_I^* x_I + 2\sigma_B^* \sigma_I^* \rho_{BI}^* x_B x_I, \\ \pi &= r_B^* x_B + r_I^* x_I, \\ 1 &= x_B + x_I, \end{aligned} \tag{15.9}$$

where r_B^*, v_B^*, σ_B^* are the data relative to $(x^B)^*$ and r_I^*, v_I^*, σ_I^* the data relative to $(x^I)^*$, while ρ_{BI}^* denotes the correlation coefficient between $(x^B)^*$ and $(x^I)^*$. The boundary of the region of admissible portfolios (15.9) will again be represented in the plane (σ, π) by a branch of a hyperbola B^2 defined by the new two-dimensional allocation vector

$$x = \begin{bmatrix} x_B \\ x_I \end{bmatrix}. \tag{15.10}$$

If we add again the riskless asset (ζ, x_ρ) in the plane (σ, π), the complete boundary will be described by the pair of straight lines (6.8) through the point $(0, \rho)$, which in general will have a tangent point x^* to the hyperbola B^2. This point x^* will be the optimal combination of all risky assets (no matter what the nature of the risk may be).

More important than x^* is the point x^c which is the point belonging to B^2 that is orthogonal to $(x^B)^*$, i.e., such that

$$\operatorname{cov}(x^c, (x^B)^*) = 0. \tag{15.11}$$

This point which can be found by applying the results of Chapter 4, defines a portfolio of investments that is completely hedged against exchange risk. If the portfolio $(x^B)^*$ (which is characterized by the exchange risk only) belongs to B^2, we have a useful "mutual fund" theorem, if it does not, such a mutual fund theorem will exist between x^c (15.10) and its orthogonal portfolio on B^2. Note that in general x^c will contain investments characterized by intrinsic risk as well as by exchange risk, and the "hedging" operation will not therefore be feasible for exchange operations only.

Having investigated the general structure of the problem, the basic theoretical results concerning the two-period model, which has been previously presented, become a particular case of the multiperiod model, which will be presented in the next chapter.

NOTES AND REFERENCES

The subject of portfolio selection in a multicurrency environment has recently received considerable attention in the literature. The basic results are due to Solnik (1973, 1974) who presents an international capital assets pricing model based on a separation theorem. The model used by Solnik is dynamic and follows the technique proposed by Merton (1973). The separation theorem suggests that (Solnik, 1973, pp. 28) "all investors are indifferent between choosing portfolios from the original set of assets or from three funds where a possible choice for these funds is (1) a portfolio of all stocks hedged against exchange risk (the world market portfolio), (2) a portfolio of bonds speculative in the exchange risk dimension, (3) the risk-free asset of their country." As we showed in the previous pages of this chapter, the operation of hedging against the exchange risk cannot practically be performed on an intrinsically risky investment, and a separation theorem of this type cannot stand in a multiperiodic model unless the periods become infinitesimally small.

A more recent paper discussing the theoretical as well as practical implications of foreign exchange risk is due to Makin (1978). Other papers on the whole subject of multicurrency portfolio management are contained in the book edited by Sarnat and Szegö (1979).

The theoretically similar and practically related topic of portfolio selection in an inflationary environment was first investigated by Sarnat (1968) and is the subject of a recent book edited by the same author (Sarnat, 1978). The basic remark regarding the relationship between B and B_r is contained in the note by Sarnat (1968).

The major difficulty in achieving some quantitative results on this problem lies in the fact that the random variable that describes the returns on the investment in real terms is a product of two random variables, the first of which describes the returns in monetary terms and the second the inflationary effect. Now unless drastic simplifications are made, there is no useful way to characterize the first two moments of the product random variable as a function of the first two moments of the two multiplying random variables.

This explains the reason why this type of problem has been investigated and solved by means of dynamic models through which the basic separation theorems were proved (see Solnik (1973, 1975)).

By using the same dynamic model, Fisher (1975) solved the problem of portfolio selection in an inflationary situation and analyzed the role of inflation-indexed bonds. Other more recent results on inflation are contained in the collection of works edited by Sarnat (1978) and devoted to the problem of portfolio selection and investment in an inflationary environment.

Quite recently, Szegö and Rusconi (1980) obtained some results on the composition of the minimum variance portfolio for the Italian investment market. They consider four possible investments; the stock market, the bond market, the real estate market, and the commodity market. Computing the returns on the investments in real terms and using as a measure of inflation a cost of living index, they were able to show that for the period 1970–1976 the stock market was dominated by combinations of the bond market and the commodity market. The estate market turned out to be semidominated, i.e., regardless of the risk aversion level of the investor, the optimal solution suggested that he invests in real estate a fixed proportion of his wealth. The efficient boundary is then generated by combinations of bonds and commodities. The minimum variance portfolio turned out to include a very high percentage of commodities.

CHAPTER 16

BANK ASSETS AND PORTFOLIO MANAGEMENT

All of the preceding chapters of this volume were devoted to the study of the portfolio selection problem and more precisely to the analysis of the properties of the efficient set of the mean variance criterion. This efficient set can be represented by a curve in the plane (σ, π) or (v, π), parametrically defined either by system (2.1) or by system (12.1), where system (2.1) characterizes the unconstrained problem and system (12.1) the problem in which nonnegativity constraints are taken into account.

As pointed out in Chapter 1, the portfolio selection model of the kind that we have been analyzing is a purely static model with the additional constraints that there exists only one riskless investment such that lending and borrowing rates coincide, that the investor does not hold any investment at the decision instant, but only liquid assets, and finally, that at the end of the time horizon all investments must be liquidated. Clearly, even if we limit ourselves to the case of static models, these three constraints are unacceptable if one wants to use the model for the solution of bank assets or portfolio management problems.

When dealing with portfolio problems like the one arising in the management of mutual funds or of bank assets, one is first forced to take into account the simultaneous presence, even on the same time period, of different riskless rates for borrowing and lending. For investors we may assume that the riskless borrowing rate is higher than the riskless lending rate and that the efficient set takes the form shown in Fig. 16.1. Clearly, there does not exist a unique optimal combination of risky assets; but besides this, the efficient set shows only some minor variations with respect to the case investigated in Chapters 6 and 7. However, in the case of banks the situation becomes totally different since the riskless borrowing rate (rate paid on deposits) is always lower than the riskless lending rate (interest on loans). Thus if no

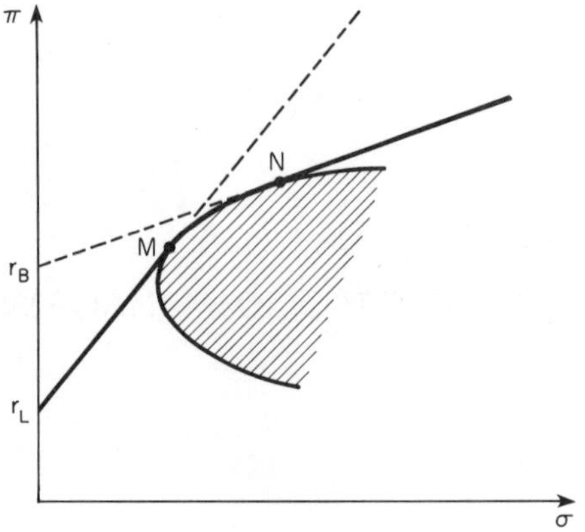

Figure 16.1

other constraints are added to the model, we shall be discussing the situation described in Fig. 16.2, which allows infinite riskless returns.

Clearly, this is not the case since the bank can neither raise infinite deposits with the interest rate r_0 nor allocate infinite loans at the rate r_L. In other words, in order to apply the basic approach of portfolio theory to bank assets management, we must be able to "ration" the level of deposits and loans that can be obtained with the interest rates r_0 and r_L, respectively.

This can be done by assuming that both the deposit and the loan level follow a demand equation that relates the decision variables of the bank, r_0 and r_L, to various exogeneous factors (money supply, interest rates used by competitors, etc.).

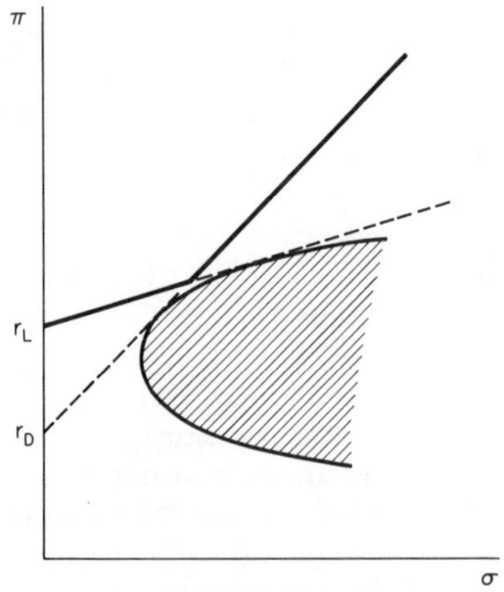

Figure 16.2

The demand equations are assumed to be

$$x_0 = H + kK + a_1R_0 - (1-k)a_2R_{n+1} + q_0, \tag{16.1}$$
$$x_{n+1} = K - a_2R_{n+1} + q_{n+1},$$

where we denote by x_0 and x_{n+1} the deposit and loan level, respectively, and by R_0 and R_{n+1} the corresponding interest rates. Equations (16.1) are connecting random variables in the sense that if we assume at the decision instant what the desired end-of-period deposit and loan level is, then the actual interest rates that we must adopt during the time interval and that will enable us to achieve the desired interest rates are random variables. In addition, we assume that the demand for loans from the public, corresponding to the interest rate R_{n+1}, is always met by the bank, i.e., that the rationing of loans is performed only through R_{n+1}. In Eqs. (16.1) we included the scalar k. This represents the multiplier, connecting loans to deposits through the well-known phenomenon of "autogenesis" of deposits. The size of k depends on the structure of the market in which the bank operates.

Equations (16.1) could represent the result of a linear regression, performed on the data, and while H, K, a_1, and a_2 are real numbers, the variables q_0 and q_{n+1} denote the residuals of the regressions.

From Eqs. (16.1) we have

$$R_0 = \frac{K-H}{a_1} + \frac{1}{a_1}[x_0 - (1-k)x_{n+1}] + \frac{(1-k)q_{n+1} - q_0}{a_1}, \tag{16.2}$$
$$R_{n+1} = \frac{K}{a_2} - \frac{1}{a_2}x_{n+1} + \frac{q_{n+1}}{a_2}.$$

These equations can be written in the simpler form

$$R_0 = r_0 + r_0^*[x_0 - (1-k)x_{n+1}] + \bar{q}_0, \tag{16.3}$$
$$R_{n+1} = r_{n+1} - r_{n+1}^* x_{n+1} + \bar{q}_{n+1},$$

where again $\bar{q}_0$ and $\bar{q}_{n+1}$ are random variables with zero mean. We shall denote their standard deviations by σ_0 and σ_{n+1}, respectively.

The expected values of the interest rates on deposits and loans (R_0 and R_{n+1}) that are needed to reach the end-of-period levels x_0 and x_{n+1} will be denoted by $\bar{r}_0$ and $\bar{r}_{n+1}$, respectively.

Afterward it will be convenient to introduce suitable variables, defined by the equations

$$\tilde{r}_0 = \bar{r}_0 - r_0 = r_0^*[x_0 - (1-k)x_{n+1}], \tag{16.4}$$
$$\tilde{r}_{n+1} = \bar{r}_{n+1} - r_{n+1} = -r_{n+1}^* x_{n+1}.$$

Equations (16.4) are the basic "market equations" of the model: they express the estimate at time $t-1$ of the interest rates that are needed in order that deposits and loans reach the levels x_0 and x_{n+1}, respectively, at time t. The random variables $\overline{q}_0$ and $\overline{q}_{n+1}$ (16.3) express the uncertainty of this estimate.

We must next consider the set of risky investments that the bank must take into account in its assets management problem. We shall again assume that there exist n risky investment opportunities characterized by the expected return vector r, by the variance–covariance matrix of their returns V, and by the n-dimensional allocation vector x. Bearing in mind what was discussed in Chapter 1 concerning the problem of time horizons, we must point out that the n risky investments could be either shares (if the bank regulations so allow) or bonds with a maturity date that comes after the end of the horizon of the investment decision.

In order to be consistent with the definitions of x_0 and x_{n+1}, which contrary to what was done in the previous chapters do not represent percentages but actual levels, the components of the vector x must also represent levels, the monetary value of the ith investment at the decision instant, i.e.,

$$x_i = p_i m_i, \tag{16.5}$$

where p_i is the unit purchase price of investment i $(i = 1, \ldots, n)$ and m_i is the number of unit purchased. For simplicity we shall assume that m_i can be a real number and not just an integer. We shall also assume that the variance–covariance matrix V of the return on the nth risky investment is nonsingular.

At each decision instant the bank must then decide the allocation of its "resources" among loans, deposits, and alternative risky investments.

We must now clarify and define exactly the type and level of the "resources" available at each decision instant, bearing in mind that the structure and composition of these resources change with the evolution of time. In particular, at the 0th decision instant, by which we represent the instant at which the bank starts its operation, the resources are simply given by the bank's own capital W^0 and by the deposit x_0^0. The sum of these two quantities will then be divided between the loans x_{n+1}^0 and the n alternative risky investments x_i^0 $(i = 1, \ldots, n)$ according to the budget constraints

$$e'x^0 + x_{n+1}^0 = W^0 + x_0^0, \tag{16.6}$$

where we denote by e the n-dimensional unit column vector and by e' its transpose and where x_0^0 and x_{n+1}^0 are given by the corresponding demand equations.

The situation changes completely at the general decision instant t.

Since some investments are supposed to have been made at the previous instant $t - 1$, $x^{t-1} \neq 0$, at the tth decision instant the bank either must liquidate part of the ith asset or a new fraction of it must be purchased in order to achieve the new desired level x_i^t $(i = 1, \ldots, n; t = 1, 2, \ldots)$.

If the unit value of the ith investment does not change during the period between the $(t-1)$th and tth decision instants, the variation in monetary value of the ith asset is simply given by the expression

$$|x_i^{t-1} - x_i^t|. \tag{16.7}$$

In general, however, the situation is more involved than that shown by expression (16.7). Since the value of the ith investment varies during each period, the quantity of the ith investment, which must be traded at the tth decision instant, will be given by the expression

$$|a_i^t - x_i^t|, \tag{16.8}$$

where a_i^t represents the book value (quotation at time t of the whole investment in security i decided at time $t-1$). Clearly, in general

$$a_i^t \neq x_i^{t-1}. \tag{16.9}$$

Having clarified the time structure of the decision variables x_i^t and of the modified variable a_i^t, from now on we shall always refer only to the tth decision instant. This will allow us to drop the time index t from the equations and let

$$|a_i - x_i| = k_i x_i \tag{16.10}$$

denote the book value of the transactions performed on the ith investment, i.e., the book value of the amount of the ith investment to be bought or sold at the decision instant t. Quantity (16.10), however, because of transaction and market costs, does not coincide with the amount that will actually be received (or invested) in the sale (or purchase) of the ith investment at the decision instant. Indeed, in order to obtain a usable portfolio management model, we must at this point take into account the transactions and market costs involved in the actual performance of the transaction $a_i - x_i$. This will be done by introducing a random variable c_i, which defines the random costs associated with the trading of one unit of the ith investment. The actual trading cost C_i will be a nonlinear function of the traded quantity, and we shall assume that it is defined by the relationship

$$C_i = c_i(a_i - x_i)^2 = c_i(k_i x_i)^2, \qquad i = 1, \ldots, n. \tag{16.11}$$

Thus at the tth decision instant, $t \neq 0$, the budget constraint can be expressed by the inequality

$$e'x + x_{n+1} \leq e'a + W - M + x_0, \tag{16.12}$$

where W denotes the cash available for investments at the decision instant and M is a constant, which depends in an obvious way on the deposits and loans that exist before the decision instant and that are completely defined by the previous decisions.

The inequality sign in relationship (16.12) is due to the fact that if $x_i \neq a_i$ for some $i = 1, \ldots, n$, this implies a trading (buying or selling) of the amount $|x_i - a_i|$, an operation that carries along the trading cost (16.11).

For instance, if $a_i > x_i$, we shall have to sell the amount $|a_i - x_i|$ of the ith asset. Through this operation, however, we shall not be able to realize the book value $|a_i - x_i|$ of the transaction, but only the quantity

$$|a_i - x_i| - c_i(a_i - x_i)^2, \qquad i = 1, \ldots, n. \tag{16.13}$$

We shall next compute the end-of-period return connected with the reallocation of the assets and liabilities performed at the decision instant.

In order to do that, we shall introduce a new n-dimensional vector y, defined by the relationships

$$y_i = (k_i x_i)^2, \qquad i = 1, \ldots, n. \tag{16.14}$$

This vector will allow us to represent the trading costs in the simpler form

$$C_i = c_i y_i, \qquad i = 1, \ldots, n. \tag{16.15}$$

The actual end-of-period return from each of the n risky alternative investments now becomes

$$R_i x_i - c_i y_i, \qquad i = 1, \ldots, n, \tag{16.16}$$

while the end-of-period return on the whole bank assets portfolio is now given by the relationship

$$\pi = R'x - R_0 x_0 + R_{n+1} x_{n+1} - c'y, \tag{16.17}$$

where we have denoted by R the n-dimensional random return vector associated with n risky alternative investments, by c the n-dimensional random cost coefficient vector with components defined by (16.11), and by R_0 and R_{n+1} the random returns on deposits and loans, respectively, as defined in Eqs. (16.3).

The expected value of the return then takes the form

$$\pi = r'x - \bar{c}'y - \bar{r}_0 x_0 - \bar{r}_{n+1} x_{n+1}, \tag{16.18}$$

where r and $\bar{c}$ denote the expected values of the vectors R and c, respectively, while r_0 and r_{n+1} are defined by Eqs. (16.4).

We shall next compute the variance of the total return. This will be done under the simplifying assumption that the random variables R, q_0, q_{n+1}, and c are uncorrelated. Thus the variance of the return on the whole bank assets portfolio is given by the equation

$$v = x'Vx + \sigma_0^2 x_0^2 + \sigma_{n+1}^2 x_{n+1}^2 + y'V_c y, \tag{16.19}$$

where we have denoted by V and V_c the variance–covariance matrices associated with the returns R on the n risky investments and with the cost coefficient c, respectively, while σ_0 and σ_{n+1} denote the standard deviations of R_0 and R_{n+1}, respectively. We shall assume that V_c is nonsingular.

The last set of relationships that must be considered in order to complete the model is

$$x_0 \geq 0 \qquad x_{n+1} \geq 0 \tag{16.20}$$

and

$$x \geq 0. \tag{16.21}$$

While conditions (16.20) are clearly connected with the definition of the basic variables of the model, the nonnegativity condition (16.21) is suggested by bank regulations, which exist in most countries and prevent the short sale of assets. The model, on the other hand, would still be valid if inequality (16.21) were omitted.

Having defined the bank equations of the model, we shall proceed with the analysis of its properties.

The first problem is to find the region of admissible portfolios in the plane (v, π). This region is defined by the relationships

$$v = x'Vx + \sigma_0^2 x_0^2 + \sigma_{n+1}^2 x_{n+1}^2 + y'V_c y, \tag{16.22}$$

$$\pi = r'x - \bar{c}'y - \tilde{r}_0 x_0 + \tilde{r}_{n+1} x_{n+1}; \tag{16.23}$$

$$e'x + x_{n+1} \leq e'a + W - M + x_0, \tag{16.24}$$

$$x_0 \geq 0, \qquad x \geq 0, \qquad x_{n+1} \geq 0. \tag{16.25}$$

Under suitable conditions, it can be proved that the external boundary B of region (16.22)–(16.25) identifies a convex set.

In what follows, we shall use the simplified notation

$$\begin{aligned} x'Vx + \sigma_0^2 x_0^2 + \sigma_{n+1}^2 x_{n+1}^2 + y'V_c y &\doteq f(x_0, x, x_{n+1}), \\ r'x - \bar{c}'y - \tilde{r}_0 x_0 + \tilde{r}_{n+1} x_{n+1} &\doteq g(x_0, x, x_{n+1}), \\ e'a + W - M &\doteq T. \end{aligned} \tag{16.26}$$

Thus the system (16.22)–(16.25), which parametrically defines the region of admissible portfolios, takes the simpler form

$$v = f(x_0, x, x_{n+1}), \tag{16.27}$$

$$\pi = g(x_0, x, x_{n+1}); \tag{16.28}$$

$$e'x + x_{n+1} \leq T + x_0, \tag{16.29}$$

$$x_0 \geq 0, \qquad x \geq 0, \qquad x_{n+1} \geq 0. \tag{16.30}$$

The boundary B of the region of admissible portfolios limits the region of admissible portfolios from the side of the lowest value of the variance or, equivalently, from the side of the highest value of the expected return. Thus B can be obtained by alternatively solving one of the following two optimization problems (see (16.37)–(16.39) for the notation):

$$\min[v = f(\underline{x})] \tag{16.31}$$

subject to

$$\pi = g(\underline{x}), \tag{16.32}$$

where

$$\underline{x} \in X, \tag{16.33}$$

or

$$\max[\pi = g(\underline{x})] \tag{16.34}$$

subject to

$$v = f(\underline{x}), \tag{16.35}$$

where

$$\underline{x} \in X. \tag{16.36}$$

In problems (16.31)–(16.33) and (16.34)–(16.36) we have set for simplicity

$$\underline{x}' = [x_0, x', x_{n+1}], \tag{16.37}$$

$$X = \{\underline{x} \in R^{n+2}: \underline{x} \geq 0,\ \underline{e}'\underline{x} \leq T\}, \tag{16.38}$$

$$e' = [-1, e, 1]. \tag{16.39}$$

In order to be able to prove the convexity properties of the region of admissible portfolios of problems (16.27)–(16.30), we must next clarify the convexity and concavity properties of the functions $f(\underline{x})$ and $g(\underline{x})$. It is easy to prove that $f(\underline{x})$ and $g(\underline{x})$ are strictly convex and strictly concave functions, respectively, provided that their coefficients satisfy the inequalities

$$r_0^*(1 - k)^2 < r_{n+1}^*, \tag{16.40}$$

where the coefficients r_0^* and r_{n+1}^* are defined by Eqs. (16.3). We see that it is indeed sensible to assume that the inequality constraint (16.40) is always satisfied by the data of the problem.

Having assumed that $f(\underline{x})$ is strictly convex and $g(\underline{x})$ strictly concave, we shall analyze the minimization problem (16.31)–(16.33). We shall do this by replacing it by a sequence of minimization problems.

Let us first introduce the equality-constrained problem

(16.41) $$h(v) = \min_{g(x)=v} f(\underline{x}), \qquad \underline{x} \in X,$$

which can be viewed as the first stage in the solution of problem (16.31)–(16.33). As a second solution step, we shall consider the inequality-constrained problem

(16.42) $$h(\pi) = \min_{v \geq \pi} h(v), \qquad v \in J_v,$$

where

(16.43) $$J_v = \{v : \exists \underline{x} \in X, g(\underline{x}) = v\}.$$

Thus the convex problem

(16.44) $$\min f(\underline{x})$$

with

(16.45) $$g(\underline{x}) \geq \pi, \qquad \underline{x} \in X,$$

is equivalent to the sequence of problems

(16.46) $$\min_{v \geq \pi} \left[\min_{g(\underline{x})=v} f(\underline{x}) \right] \qquad \text{with} \quad v \in J_v, \quad \underline{x} \in X.$$

This reformulation of the original minimization problem (16.31)–(16.33) allows us to remark that the function $h(v)$ is increasing on any subset of J_v corresponding to a part of the domain of g if and only if the constraint (16.45) is active. This, on the other hand, must always be the case since we require that the optimal bank portfolio be efficient. This fact will allow us to conclude that problem (16.44)–(16.45) is equivalent to the original minimization problem (16.31)–(16.33).

Proceeding exactly in the same manner for the maximization problem (16.34)–(16.36), we shall reformulate it as

(16.47) $$H(\nu) = \max_{\substack{f(\underline{x}) \leq \nu \\ \underline{x} \in X}} g(\underline{x}) = \max_{\substack{n \leq \nu \\ n \in I_n}} \left[\max_{\substack{f(\underline{x}) = n \\ \underline{x} \in X}} g(\underline{x}) \right],$$

where

(16.48) $$I_n = \{n : \exists \underline{x} \in X, f(\underline{x}) = n\}.$$

Now consider the two sets

(16.49) $$S_1(\nu) = \{(\underline{x}, \nu, \pi) : \underline{x} \in X, f(\underline{x}) \leq \nu\},$$

(16.50) $$S_2(\pi) = \{(\underline{x}, \nu, \pi) : \underline{x} \in X, g(\underline{x}) \geq \pi\}.$$

That these two sets are convex follows from the following theorem.

(16.51) **Theorem**

Let $f_i(x)$ be a convex function on the S-dimensional space R^S and let α_i be a real number for each $i \in I$, where I is an arbitrary index set. Then the set

$$C = \{x : f_i(x) \leq \alpha_i \text{ for any } i \in I\} \tag{16.52}$$

is convex.

It then also follows that the intersection of S_1 and S_2 is convex, i.e., that

$$\begin{aligned} S(v, \pi) &= S_1(v) \cap S_2(\pi) \\ &= \{(\underline{x}, v, \pi) : x \in X, f(\underline{x}) \leq v, g(\underline{x}) \geq \pi\} \end{aligned} \tag{16.53}$$

is a convex set.

If we project the set $S(v, \pi)$ orthogonally onto the subspace (v, π), we obtain a new set $P(S)$ defined as

$$P(S) = \{(v, \pi) : \exists \underline{x} \in X, f(\underline{x}) \leq v, g(\underline{x}) \geq \pi\}. \tag{16.54}$$

Then problem (16.44)–(16.45) and problem (16.47) can be written in the more compact forms

$$\inf\{v : (v, \pi) \in P(S)\} = h(\pi), \tag{16.55}$$

$$\sup\{\pi : (v, \pi) \in P(S)\} = H(v). \tag{16.56}$$

The following theorem, (16.52) allows us to conclude that $h(\pi)$ is strictly convex with respect to π and $H(v)$ strictly concave with respect to v.

(16.57) **Theorem**

Let F be a convex set in the $(S + 1)$-dimensional space R^{S+1} and let

$$f(x) = \inf\{\mu : (x, \mu) \in F\}, \qquad x \in R. \tag{16.58}$$

Then f is a convex function on R^S. Similar results hold for strictly convex, concave, and strictly concave functions.

Finally, consider the theorem

(16.59) **Theorem**

The orthogonal projection of a convex set C on a subspace L is another convex set.

This result allows us to assume convexity of the sets

$$\begin{aligned} &\{(v, \pi) : (v, \pi) \in P(S), H(v) \geq \pi\}, \\ &\{(v, \pi) : (v, \pi) \in P(S), h(\pi) \leq v\}, \end{aligned} \tag{16.60}$$

and therefore

(16.61) **Theorem**

If condition (16.40) is satisfied, then the region of admissible portfolios of the bank assets management problem, defined by (16.22)–(16.25), in the plane (v, π) is a convex set.

Convexity of the region of admissible portfolios is a sufficient condition for allowing the use of any concave utility function and obtaining a unique optimum portfolio, and it is a standard required condition on the validity of the model. Having performed this basic step, we can now proceed further and try to prove a separation theorem, which for our model should allow the separation between the investment decision in risky assets (the optimal combination of risky assets) and the investment decision in risky assets and liabilities (deposits and loans).

We have

(16.62) **Theorem**

The bank assets management problem (16.22)–(16.25) is equivalent to a selection between two mutual funds, one of which contains only deposits and loans and the other all risky investments.

Proof

The region of admissible portfolios in the plane (v, π) for the n risky investments is parametrically defined by the relationships

(16.63) $$\tilde{v} = x'Vx + y'V_c y,$$

(16.64) $$\tilde{\pi} = r'x - \bar{c}'y,$$

(16.65) $$e'x \leq 1,$$

(16.66) $$x \geq 0, \qquad y \geq 0.$$

The region of admissible portfolios in the plane (v, π) relative to deposits and loans only is parametrically defined by the relationships

(16.67) $$\bar{v} = \sigma_0^2 x_0^2 + \sigma_{n+1}^2 x_{n+1}^2,$$

(16.68) $$\bar{\pi} = r_0^* x_0[x_0 - (1-k)x_{n+1}] - r_{n+1}^* x_{n+1}^2,$$

(16.69) $$x_{n+1} \leq 1 + x_0,$$

(16.70) $$x_0 \geq 0, \qquad x_{n+1} \geq 0.$$

Consider now the upper bound of the other capital available to the bank for investment purposes:

(16.71) $$T = e'a + W - M.$$

This capital will then be divided into two parts ξ and η, of which η will be invested in riskless "assets" (deposits and loans), and ξ will be used for risky investments.

The region of admissible portfolios obtained by dividing the available "resources" between the set of all risky assets (16.63)–(16.66) and the set of riskless assets (16.67)–(16.70) must satisfy the set of relationships

(16.72) $$v = \xi^2\tilde{v} + \eta^2\bar{v},$$

(16.73) $$\pi = \xi\tilde{\pi} + \eta\bar{\pi};$$

(16.74) $$\xi + \eta \leq T,$$

(16.75) $$\xi \geq 0, \qquad \eta \geq 0.$$

If we substitute (16.63)–(16.66) and (16.67)–(16.70) into (16.71)–(16.75), this set of equations becomes

(16.76) $$v = (\xi x)'V(\xi x) + (\xi y)'V_c(\xi y) + \sigma_0^2(\eta x_0)^2 + \sigma_{n+1}^2(\eta x_{n+1})^2,$$

(16.77) $$\pi = r'(\xi x) - \bar{c}'(\xi y) + r_0^*(\eta x_0)[(\eta x_0) - (1-k)(\eta x_{n+1})] - r_{n+1}^*(\eta x_{n+1})^2;$$

(16.78) $$e'(\xi x) + \eta x_{n+1} \leq T + \eta x_0,$$

(16.79) $$x_0 \geq 0, \qquad x \geq 0, \qquad x_{n+1} \geq 0, \qquad \xi \geq 0, \qquad \eta \geq 0,$$

which, by the simple change of variables

(16.80) $$\tilde{x}_i = \xi x_i, \qquad \tilde{y}_i = \xi y_i, \qquad \tilde{x}_0 = \eta x_0, \qquad \tilde{x}_{n+1} = \eta x_{n+1},$$

is identical to (16.22)–(16.25) and proves the theorem.

The separation theorem that we have just proved does not allow the identification of an optimal "combination of risky assets" that would be the same for all banks with the same probability beliefs. Indeed, since each bank is characterized by its own k, in general the optimal values of x_0, x_{n+1}, and x will change from bank to bank.

The result obtained in this chapter can be used as a portfolio management model for investors and investment funds if we abolish the "riskless" assets x_0, x_{n+1} and the corresponding demand equations.

The model, however, allows us to take into account the existence at the decision instant of a set of investments and of the cost of altering the portfolio. With respect to the original portfolio selection model, which was investigated in previous chapters, this model is much more realistic even if one uses considerably more data.

NOTES AND REFERENCES

The first attempt to extend the portfolio selection model to bank assets management was made by Fried (1969). In his model the "rationing" of x_0 and x_{n+1} is achieved by assuming that the deposit level is a random variable.

The idea of developing a complete bank assets management model in which the deposit and loan levels are decision variables was exposed in a monograph by Bertoni and Szegö (1972), following some preliminary ideas by Kareken (1967) and Porter (1961). A detailed presentation of the model and of the exact structure of the constants used in Eqs. (16.1) can be found in the paper by Bertoni *et al.* (1975). In the proof of the theorem presented in this chapter we have followed the technique used by Szegö and Mazzoleni (1976).

The problem of investigating portfolio selection problems with transaction costs has attracted the attention of many authors. A recent paper by Brito (1978) emphasizes some additional aspects of the problem. Previous models that included transaction costs were based on a piecewise-linear approximation of the costs, and they were therefore able to maintain the basic mathematical structure of the original portfolio selection model.

The model proposed here requires, in addition to the statistical data for performing the regressions (16.3) and the usual data on the first two moments of the returns on the risky investments, an estimate of the first two moments of the random variables c_i.

From the point of view of practical application in portfolio management, the problem may be quite simplified by adopting a linear diagonal approximate model and assuming that the transaction cost coefficients are proportional to b_i, the volatility coefficients.

APPENDIX A

THE STRUCTURE OF THE VARIANCE–COVARIANCE MATRIX

The matrix V is an $n \times n$ positive semidefinite symmetric matrix with elements

(A.1) $$V_{ij} = \sigma_i \sigma_j \rho_{ij}, \qquad i, j = 1, \ldots, n.$$

The coefficients σ_i, $i = 1, \ldots, n$, are the standard deviations of the returns on the n investments, and ρ_{ij} are the correlation coefficients between the return on the ith investment and that on the jth investment, $i, j = 1, \ldots, n$. These coefficients satisfy the conditions

(A.2) $$\sigma_i \geq 0, \qquad i = 1, \ldots, n,$$

(A.3) $$|\rho_{ij}| \leq 1, \qquad i \neq j, \quad i, j = 1, \ldots, n,$$

(A.4) $$\rho_{ij} = 1, \qquad i = j, \quad i, j = 1, \ldots, n.$$

Let us next introduce the $n \times n$ symmetric matrix C with elements

(A.5) $$c_{ij} = \rho_{ij}.$$

The matrix C thus has a unit diagonal and all off-diagonal elements that are less than one in absolute value.

Consider also the $n \times n$ diagonal matrix S with elements

(A.6) $$s_{ij} = \sigma_i, \qquad i = j, \quad i, j = 1, \ldots, n,$$

(A.7) $$s_{ij} = 0, \qquad i \neq j, \quad i, j = 1, \ldots, n.$$

The matrix V can then be decomposed in the form

(A.8) $$V = S'CS.$$

Thus, if V is nonsingular

(A.9) $$V^{-1} = (S')^{-1}C^{-1}S^{-1} = U'C^{-1}U,$$

where U is an $n \times n$ diagonal matrix, which is the inverse of S. Thus

(A.10) $$u_{ij} = \sigma_i^{-1}, \qquad i = j, \quad i, j = 1, \ldots, n,$$

(A.11) $$u_{ij} = 0, \qquad i \neq j, \quad i, j = 1, \ldots, n.$$

Clearly, from the computational point of view, the main difficulty in inverting V is the inversion of the matrix C. It is also obvious that a sufficient condition for the singularity of V is that

(A.12) $$\rho_{ij} = 1 \qquad \text{for some} \quad i \neq j, \quad i, j = 1, \ldots, n.$$

The matrix C must satisfy some further conditions, in addition to (A.3) and (A.4). These conditions can be derived by taking into account the multiple correlation coefficient of the return on the ith investment with the returns on all other investments:

(A.13) $$R_i = [1 - |C|/C_{ii}]^{1/2},$$

where we denote by C_{ii} the algebraic complement of the element c_{ii} of the matrix C (A.5) and by $|C|$ the determinant of C. The following properties must hold:

(A.14) $$\begin{aligned} 0 \leq R_i \leq 1, &\qquad i = 1, \ldots, n, \\ |C|/C_{ii} \leq 1, &\qquad i = 1, \ldots, n. \end{aligned}$$

From (A.14) it immediately follows that

(A.15) $$C_{ii}/|C| = c^*_{ii} \geq 1,$$

where we denote by c^*_{ii} the elements of the matrix C^{-1}, if it exists. Hence if C is nonsingular, the elements of the main diagonal of its inverse always satisfy condition (A.15).

As an example of the use of formula (A.9), we shall compute the inverse of matrix V for the case $n = 2$. From (A.9)–(A.11) it follows that

$$V^{-1} = \begin{bmatrix} \dfrac{1}{\sigma_1} & 0 \\ 0 & \dfrac{1}{\sigma_2} \end{bmatrix} \begin{bmatrix} 1 & \rho_{12} \\ \rho_{12} & 1 \end{bmatrix}^{-1} \begin{bmatrix} \dfrac{1}{\sigma_1} & 0 \\ 0 & \dfrac{1}{\sigma_2} \end{bmatrix}$$

$$= \frac{1}{(1 - \rho_{12})^2} \begin{bmatrix} \dfrac{1}{\sigma_1} & 0 \\ 0 & \dfrac{1}{\sigma_1} \end{bmatrix} \begin{bmatrix} 1 & -\rho_{12} \\ -\rho_{12} & 1 \end{bmatrix} \begin{bmatrix} \dfrac{1}{\sigma_1} & 0 \\ 0 & \dfrac{1}{\sigma_2} \end{bmatrix}$$

$$= \frac{1}{(1 - \rho_{12})^2} \begin{bmatrix} \dfrac{1}{\sigma_1^2} & \dfrac{\rho_{12}}{\sigma_1 \sigma_2} \\ -\dfrac{\rho_{12}}{\sigma_1 \sigma_2} & \dfrac{1}{\sigma_2^2} \end{bmatrix}.$$

APPENDIX B

PROOF THAT $\alpha\gamma - \beta^2 > 0$

We shall prove that if

(B.1) $$r_i \neq r_j \quad \text{for some} \quad i, j = 1, \ldots, n$$

and

(B.2) $$\det V \neq 0,$$

then

(B.3) $$\alpha\gamma - \beta^2 > 0.$$

To prove this inequality, consider the $n \times 2$ matrix

(B.4) $$G = (r, e)$$

and notice that

(B.5) $$G'V^{-1}G = \begin{bmatrix} \alpha & \beta \\ \beta & \gamma \end{bmatrix} = F.$$

Clearly, if there does not exist any real number δ with $r = \delta e$, and if (B.2) is satisfied, then

(B.6) $$\text{rank } G = 2,$$

and the vector

(B.7) $$y = Gx$$

is not zero for each $x \neq 0$. From (B.5) and (B.7) we obtain

(B.8) $$x'Fx = x'G'V^{-1}Gx = y'V^{-1}y,$$

which shows that if condition (B.1) is satisfied, then a necessary and sufficient condition for F to be positive definite and for (B.3) to be true is that V^{-1} be positive definite.

The proof that if (B.2) is satisfied, then (B.1) is a necessary and sufficient condition for (B.3) to be true, can also easily be carried out.

PROOF OF PROPERTY (2.15)

We shall next prove that if

(C.1) $$\det V \neq 0,$$

then a necessary and sufficient condition for

(C.2) $$\det L = \begin{vmatrix} 2V & r & e \\ r' & 0 & 0 \\ e' & 0 & 0 \end{vmatrix} \neq 0$$

is that

(C.3) $$r_i \neq r_j \qquad \text{for some} \quad i, j = 1, \ldots, n.$$

Indeed, the condition is sufficient since otherwise there exists a real number δ such that

(C.4) $$r = \delta e;$$

hence the last two rows (and columns) of determinant (C.2) are proportional and therefore the determinant is zero.

We shall next prove the necessity of condition (C.3). If $\det L = 0$, there exists a $(n+2)$-dimensional column vector

(C.5) $$\begin{bmatrix} a \\ \mu \\ \rho \end{bmatrix} \neq 0,$$

which satisfies the linear homogeneous system

(C.6) $$\begin{bmatrix} 2V & r & e \\ r' & 0 & 0 \\ e' & 0' & 0 \end{bmatrix} \begin{bmatrix} a \\ \mu \\ \rho \end{bmatrix} = \begin{bmatrix} \emptyset \\ 0 \\ 0 \end{bmatrix},$$

where $\emptyset$ denotes the n-dimensional column zero vector.

In (C.5) a denotes an n-dimensional column vector, while μ and ρ are scalars.

System (C.6) can be written more explicitly in the form

$$\begin{aligned} 2Va + \eta r + \rho e &= 0, \\ r'a &= 0, \\ e'a &= 0. \end{aligned} \tag{C.7}$$

Since V is nonsingular, the first equation of system (C.7) can be solved, leading to

$$a = -\tfrac{1}{2}V^{-1}(\mu r + \rho e). \tag{C.8}$$

This expression can then be substituted into the second and third equations of system (C.7), giving the system

$$\begin{aligned} \mu\alpha + \rho\beta &= 0, \\ \mu\beta + \rho\gamma &= 0. \end{aligned} \tag{C.9}$$

This system has a nonzero solution (μ, ρ) if and only if the determinant of its coefficients vanishes, i.e., if and only if

$$\alpha\gamma - \beta^2 = 0, \tag{C.10}$$

which is ruled out by the result of Appendix B. Thus the only solution of system (C.9) is

$$\mu = \rho = 0, \tag{C.11}$$

and from (C.8) it also follows that

$$a = 0. \tag{C.12}$$

Thus the only solution of system (C.6) is the trivial solution (C.11), (C.12), which contradicts our assumption (C.5).

Similar arguments prove that if condition (C.3) is satisfied, then a necessary and sufficient condition for (C.2) is that (C.1) be true.

APPENDIX D

THE EXISTENCE OF AN ORTHONORMAL BASIS

The transformation (2.61)

(D.1) $$Ky = x,$$

where (2.60)

(D.2) $$k_{ij} = x_j^i$$

and x_j are admissible portfolios, is in many cases very useful if the n admissible linearly independent vectors x^i ($i = 1, \ldots, n$), which provide a new basis for the allocation problem, are V-orthogonal, i.e., if such vectors satisfy the system of

(D.3) $$\frac{n!}{2!(n-2)!} + n,$$

equations in n^2 unknowns (the components x_j^i)

(D.4) $$(x^i)' V x^j = 0, \qquad i \neq j = 1, \ldots, n,$$

(D.5) $$e' x^i = 1, \qquad i = 1, \ldots, n.$$

We shall briefly describe the problem of the existence of the vectors x^i ($i = 1, \ldots, n$), satisfying (D.4) and (D.5), i.e., the problem of the existence of a particular orthonormal basis (D.4), (D.5) by examining the problem for the case $n = 2$.

In this particular case we obtain from Eq. (D.4) the relationship

(D.6) $$\frac{x_1^1}{x_2^1} = \frac{(x^2)' V e^2}{(x^2)' V e^1},$$

where we denote by e^i ($i = 1, 2$) the column vector with the elements

$$e_j^i = \begin{cases} 1 & \text{for} \quad i = j, \\ 0 & \text{for} \quad i \neq j. \end{cases} \tag{D.7}$$

Combining (D.5) and (D.6), we obtain the solution

$$x_1^1 = \frac{(x^2)'Ve^2}{(x^2)'Ve}, \qquad x_2^1 = \frac{(x^2)'Ve^1}{(x^2)'Ve}, \tag{D.8}$$

provided that

$$(x^2)'Ve \neq 0. \tag{D.9}$$

Thus in this case, once the vector x^2 is chosen, the vector x^1 is completely identified. As n increases, the number of vectors that satisfy the system (D.4), (D.5) increases, and even when one of the vectors is arbitrarily chosen, the remaining $n - 1$ vectors satisfying (D.4), (D.5) are in general nonunique.

APPENDIX E

THE INVERSE OF A PARTITIONED MATRIX

In this appendix we shall give a detailed proof of the inversion formulas (5.19)–(5.23). The proof will be carried out for the more general case of a nonsymmetric matrix. These formulas provide an obvious numerical technique for matrix inversion that may be superior to other known techniques in the case in which one must invert a symmetric matrix which is positive (or negative) definite, allowing a simultaneous solution of the inversion problem and of the analysis of the sign properties of the matrix (see, for instance, Faddeev and Faddeeva (1963)). Consider the $(n+1) \times (n+1)$ matrix

$$\tilde{V} = \begin{bmatrix} V & a \\ b' & \varepsilon \end{bmatrix}, \tag{E.1}$$

where V is an $n \times n$ matrix, a and b are n-column vectors, ε a scalar, and we denote by b' the transpose of b. Assume that $\det V \neq 0$; we want to compute $\tilde{V}^{-1}$ under the assumption that V^{-1} is known. Now a necessary and sufficient condition for the existence of $\tilde{V}^{-1}$ is

$$\det \tilde{V} \neq 0, \tag{E.2}$$

and a necessary and sufficient condition for (E.2) not to be satisfied is the existence of a nonzero $n+1$ column vector $\tilde{h}$, which is the solution of the linear homogeneous equation

$$\tilde{h}'\tilde{V} = \tilde{\emptyset}', \tag{E.3}$$

where $\tilde{\emptyset}$ is the $n+1$ column zero vector.

If we represent the vector h in the form

$$\tilde{h} = \begin{bmatrix} h \\ \theta \end{bmatrix} \neq \emptyset, \tag{E.4}$$

where h is an n-column vector and θ a scalar, Eq. (E.3) leads to the system

$$h'V + \theta b' = \emptyset', \tag{E.5}$$

$$h'a + \theta\varepsilon = 0, \tag{E.6}$$

where $\emptyset$ is the n-column zero vector.

From Eq. (E.5), since V is nonsingular, we obtain

$$h' = -\theta b'V^{-1} \tag{E.7}$$

and from (E.6) and (E.7)

$$-\theta b'V^{-1}a + \theta\varepsilon = 0. \tag{E.8}$$

This equation admits a solution $\theta \neq 0$ if and only if

$$-b'V^{-1}a + \varepsilon = 0. \tag{E.9}$$

Note from Eq. (E.7) that $\theta = 0$ implies $h = \emptyset$. Thus (E.9) is a necessary and sufficient condition for the existence of $\tilde{h} \neq \emptyset$, which is the solution of Eq. (E.3). Hence (E.2) is true if and only if

$$D = \varepsilon - b'V^{-1}a \neq 0. \tag{E.10}$$

Consider next the $(n + 1) \times (n + 1)$ matrix

$$\tilde{W} = \begin{bmatrix} W & c \\ d' & \delta \end{bmatrix}, \tag{E.11}$$

where W is an $n \times n$ matrix, c and d are n-column vectors, and δ is a scalar. We want to compute the elements of $\tilde{W}$ such that

$$\tilde{V}\tilde{W} = \tilde{W}\tilde{V} = \tilde{I}, \tag{E.12}$$

where we denote by $\tilde{I}$ the $(n + 1)$ identity matrix. If (E.12) is satisfied, $\tilde{W}$ is, by definition, the inverse of $\tilde{V}$.

If we introduce into (E.12) the representations (E.1) and (E.11) of V and W, respectively, we have

$$\begin{bmatrix} V & a \\ b' & \varepsilon \end{bmatrix}\begin{bmatrix} W & c \\ d' & \delta \end{bmatrix} = \begin{bmatrix} W & c \\ d' & \delta \end{bmatrix}\begin{bmatrix} V & a \\ b' & \varepsilon \end{bmatrix} = \begin{bmatrix} I & \emptyset \\ \emptyset' & 1 \end{bmatrix}. \tag{E.13}$$

If we perform the block multiplications shown in (E.13), we obtain the set of equations

$$VW + ad' = I, \tag{E.14}$$

$$Vc + \delta a = \emptyset, \tag{E.15}$$

$$b'W + \varepsilon d' = \emptyset', \tag{E.16}$$

$$b'c + \varepsilon\delta = 1, \tag{E.17}$$

(E.18) $$WV + cb' = I,$$

(E.19) $$Wa + \varepsilon c = \emptyset,$$

(E.20) $$d'V + \delta b' = \emptyset',$$

(E.21) $$d'a + \delta\varepsilon = 1.$$

The solution of Eqs. (E.14)–(E.21) will allow us to identify the unknowns W, c, d, and δ. From (E.15) we have

(E.22) $$c = -\delta V^{-1}a,$$

which, substituted into (E.17), gives

(E.23) $$-\delta b'V^{-1}a + \varepsilon\delta = 1,$$

from which, because of (E.10), we obtain

(E.24) $$\delta = 1/(\varepsilon - b'V^{-1}a) = -1/D.$$

From (E.20) we have

(E.25) $$d' = -\delta b'V^{-1},$$

which, substituted into (E.14), gives

(E.26) $$W = \delta V^{-1}ab'V^{-1} + V^{-1}.$$

It is easy to show that expressions (E.22), (E.24), (E.25), and (E.26) also satisfy the remaining Eqs. (E.16), (E.18), (E.19), and (E.21) and hence are a solution of the system (E.14)–(E.21) and (E.13).

It is then proved that

(E.27) $$\tilde{V}^{-1} = \tilde{W} = \begin{bmatrix} W & c \\ d' & \delta \end{bmatrix},$$

where W, c, d', and δ are given by (E.26), (E.22), (E.25), and (E.24), respectively.

From known results on matrix theory, we also have

(E.28) $$D = 1/\delta = \det \tilde{V}/\det V.$$

In the particular case for which the matrix V is symmetric, i.e., for the decomposition (E.1), V is symmetric and

(E.29) $$a = b.$$

The inverse of $\tilde{V}$ becomes

(E.30) $$\tilde{V}^{-1} = \tilde{W} = \begin{bmatrix} W & c \\ c' & \delta \end{bmatrix},$$

where

(E.31) $$W = V^{-1} + V^{-1}bb'V^{-1}/D,$$

(E.32) $$c = -b'V^{-1}/D,$$

and again

(E.33) $$\delta = -1/D.$$

The results can easily be extended to a block partition of the matrix V.

APPENDIX F

PROOF OF CONDITION (6.17)

We shall prove that if

(F.1) $$\det V \neq 0,$$

then a necessary and sufficient condition for (6.17) to be true is that

(F.2) $$r_i \neq r_j \qquad \text{for some} \quad i, j = 1, \ldots, n.$$

To prove this statement, we recall that if (6.17) is not true, then there exists an $(n + 3)$-dimensional column vector f with

(F.3) $$f = \begin{bmatrix} b \\ \eta \\ \mu \\ \delta \end{bmatrix} \neq 0,$$

which satisfies the linear homogeneous system

(F.4) $$\begin{aligned} 2Vb + r\mu + e\delta &= 0, \\ \rho\mu + \delta &= 0, \\ r'b + \rho\eta &= 0, \\ e'b + \eta &= 0. \end{aligned}$$

Now because of (F.1), we can solve the first equation of (F.4) and derive

(F.5) $$b = -\tfrac{1}{2}V^{-1}(r\mu + e\delta),$$

while from the second equation of (F.4), we have

(F.6) $$\delta = -\rho\mu.$$

Introducing (F.5) and (F.6) into the last two equations of (F.4), we obtain the system

$$\text{(F.7)} \qquad \begin{aligned} \mu\alpha - \rho\mu\beta - 2\rho\eta &= 0, \\ \mu\beta - \rho\mu\gamma - 2\eta &= 0, \end{aligned}$$

from which, if we eliminate η, we derive the equation

$$\text{(F.8)} \qquad \mu(\rho^2\gamma - 2\rho\beta + \alpha) = 0.$$

Now the expression in parenthesis is the value of v, corresponding to B'' evaluated at the point $\pi = \rho$, which is different from zero because of (F.1). Thus (F.8) has a unique solution $\mu = 0$, which if substituted into (F.7), (F.6), and (F.5), gives a unique solution of the system

$$\text{(F.9)} \qquad \mu = \eta = \delta = b = 0,$$

which contradicts assumption (F.3) and proves the theorem.

APPENDIX G

CONSTRUCTION OF THE TRANSFORMATION MATRIX K

We shall show how the transformation matrix K, defined by (8.19), can be built. Consider to this end the general matrix

$$\tilde{K} = \begin{bmatrix} A & d \\ c' & \varepsilon \end{bmatrix} \tag{G.1}$$

and the corresponding product $\tilde{K}'\tilde{V}\tilde{K}$, where $\tilde{V}$ is given by (8.11), i.e.,

$$\tilde{K}'\tilde{V}\tilde{K} = \begin{bmatrix} A' & c \\ \dot{d}' & \varepsilon \end{bmatrix} \begin{bmatrix} V & Va \\ a'V & a'Va \end{bmatrix} \begin{bmatrix} A & d \\ c' & \varepsilon \end{bmatrix}. \tag{G.2}$$

If we perfom the multiplication in (G.2) and impose that

$$\tilde{K}'\tilde{V}\tilde{K} = \begin{bmatrix} V & \emptyset \\ \emptyset' & 0 \end{bmatrix}, \tag{G.3}$$

we obtain the equations

$$\begin{aligned} A'VA + ca'VA + A'Vac' + ca'\,Vac' &= V, \\ d'VA + \varepsilon a'VA + \varepsilon a'Vac' + d'Vac' &= \emptyset', \\ \varepsilon^2 a'Va + 2\varepsilon a'Vd + d'Vd &= 0. \end{aligned} \tag{G.4}$$

Now the third equation of (G.4) can be written in the form

$$(d + \varepsilon a)'V(d + \varepsilon a) = 0, \tag{G.5}$$

and since V is positive definite, the *only* solution of (G.5) is

$$d = -\varepsilon a. \tag{G.6}$$

If we substitute (G.6) into the second equation of (G.4), this is satisfied for all values of c. The first equation of (G.4) can be written as

$$(A + ac' - I)'V(A + ac' - I) = 0, \tag{G.7}$$

and since V is positive definite again, the *only* solution of (G.7) is

$$A + ac' = I. \tag{G.8}$$

The solution

$$A = I \qquad \text{and} \qquad c = \emptyset, \tag{G.9}$$

which was used in (8.19), satisfies (G.8), but it is clearly not the only possible solution of the problem.

APPENDIX H

PROOF OF CONDITION (8.49)

We shall prove that if

$$r_{n+1} \neq r'a \tag{H.1}$$

and condition (8.2) is satisfied, then (8.49) is true.

Proceeding by contradiction, assume that (8.49) is not true, i.e., that

$$\det L = 0. \tag{H.2}$$

Then there exists a nonzero $(n + 3)$-dimensional row vector

$$\tilde{\tilde{b}}' = (b', \varepsilon, \eta, \theta) \tag{H.3}$$

such that the linear homogeneous system

$$L\tilde{\tilde{b}} = \emptyset \tag{H.4}$$

is satisfied, i.e., such that

$$\begin{aligned} Vb - r\eta - e\theta &= \emptyset, \\ \eta r_{n+1} &= 0, \\ -r'b + \varepsilon r_{n+1} &= 0, \\ -e'b &= 0. \end{aligned} \tag{H.5}$$

From the second equation of (H.5), if $r_{n+1} \neq 0$, we have

$$\eta = 0, \tag{H.6}$$

from which the first equation of (H.5) gives

$$b = \theta V^{-1} e, \tag{H.7}$$

which can be substituted into the last equation of (H.5), giving

$$\theta e' V^{-1} e = 0. \tag{H.8}$$

Now since V^{-1} is positive definite, (H.8) implies that

$$\theta = 0, \tag{H.9}$$

from which (H.7) and the third equation of (H.5) give, respectively,

$$b = \emptyset, \qquad \varepsilon = 0. \tag{H.10}$$

Thus if $r_{n+1} \neq 0$, we have proved that the only solution of system (H.4) is

$$\tilde{\tilde{b}} = \tilde{\tilde{\emptyset}}, \tag{H.11}$$

which contradicts the assumption made on $\tilde{\tilde{b}}$. Now in the particular case in which $a = \emptyset$, condition (H.1) simply becomes $r_{n+1} \neq 0$. Our thesis has therefore been proved.

APPENDIX I

ON THE NUMERICAL CONSTRUCTION OF THE BEST FIT INDEX

We assume that we have a set of prices $p_{i,j}$ for each item i at a series of times t_j and that in all there are N items and M instants of time. We do not make any assumptions about the intervals between the successive instants of time, but assume that those chosen do adequately represent the variations in the price over the whole period. In particular, M must be greater than N.

We also assume that the index is to be a weighted average of the $p_{i,j}$ at each instant of time, but that the weights remain constant over the whole period, i.e., the index is given by

$$I(t_j) = I_j = \sum_{i=1}^{N} w_i p_{ij} \qquad \text{for} \quad j = 1, \ldots, M \tag{I.1}$$

and the N weights w_i have to be determined.

For a given set of weights it is possible to calculate for each item i, M pairs of values I_j, p_{ij}. On an (I, p) plot these would appear as M points (see Fig. I.1), and a straight line could be approximated to them.

If the line is $p = a_i + b_i I$, we can choose a_i, b_i by the conventional regressional methods, i.e., we calculate a_i, b_i to minimize the sum of the squares of the residuals:

$$R = \sum_j (a_i + b_i I_j - p_{ij})^2, \tag{I.2}$$

$$\frac{\partial R}{\partial a} = M a_i + b_i \sum_j I_j - \sum_j p_{ij} = 0,$$
$$\frac{\partial R}{\partial b} = a_i \sum_j I_j + b_i \sum_j I_j^2 - \sum_j I_j p_{ij} = 0. \tag{I.3}$$

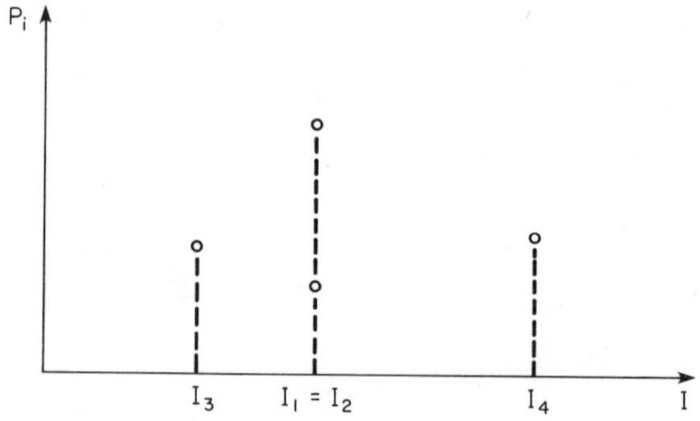

Figure I.1

Writing

$$\text{(I.4)} \qquad \bar{P}_i = \frac{1}{M}\sum_j p_{ij}, \qquad \bar{I} = \frac{1}{M}\sum_j I_j,$$

and defining

$$\text{(I.5)} \qquad q_{ij} = p_{ij} - \bar{P}_i, \qquad d_j = I_j - \bar{I},$$

system (I.3) gives

$$a_i = \bar{P}_i - b_i\bar{I}.$$

Then substituting this value of a_i in expression (I.2) for R, we obtain

$$\begin{aligned} R &= \sum_j (\bar{P}_i - b_i\bar{I} + bI_j - p_{ij})^2 \\ &= \sum_j [b_i(I_j - \bar{I}) - (p_{ij} - \bar{P}_i)]^2 \\ &= \sum_j (b_i d_j - q_{ij})^2. \end{aligned}$$

The minimization of R gives

$$\frac{\partial R}{\partial b_i} = \sum_j (b_i d_j - q_{ij}) d_j = 0,$$

that is,

$$b \sum_j d_j^2 - \sum_j q_{ij} d_j = 0,$$

and finally, we obtain b_i as a function of the new variables q_{ij} and d_j:

(I.6) $$b_i = \sum_j q_{ij} d_j \Big/ \sum_j d_j^2 .$$

Note that R expressed in these new variables has the term corresponding to a_i equal to zero.

The sum of the squares of the residuals is

(I.7) $$R = \sum_j q_{ij}^2 - \left(\sum_j q_{ij} d\right)^2 \Big/ \sum_j d_j^2 .$$

We define the best index as that which minimizes the sum of all these residuals over all items. In other words, we must determine the weights w_i such that

(I.8) $$F = \sum_i \sum_j q_{ij}^2 - \sum_i \left(\sum_j q_{ij} d_j\right)^2 \Big/ \sum_j d_j^2$$

is a minimum.

There are several ways of expressing F. For example, it can be written as

(I.9) $$F = \sum_i (1 - r_i^2) \sum_j q_{ij}^2 ,$$

where

(I.10) $$r_i = \sum_j q_{ij} d_j \Big/ \sqrt{\left(\sum_j q_{ij}^2\right)\left(\sum_j d_j^2\right)} .$$

This shows that the minimization is equivalent to maximizing a weighted sum of the squares of the correlation coefficients between each price p_{ij} and the index I_j (after removal of the means).

Further, if the column vectors D, and W and the matrix Q are defined as

(I.11) $$D = [d_i], \qquad W = [w_i], \qquad Q = [q_{ij}],$$

then since $d_j = \sum_i w_i p_{ij} - \sum_i w_i \bar{P}_i$,

(I.12) $$D = Q'W,$$

(I.13) $$\sum_j d_j^2 = W'QQ'W,$$

(I.14) $$\sum_i \left(\sum_j q_{ij} d_j\right)^2 = D'Q'QD,$$

and

(I.15) $$F = \sum_i \sum_j q_{ij}^2 - \frac{W'(QQ')^2 W}{W'(QQ')W} .$$

Now the second term is a ratio of two quadratic forms in the variables w_i, and if λ is an eigenvalue of QQ', λ^2 is an eigenvalue of $(QQ')^2$. Moreover, this term assumes its maximum value when the vector W corresponds to the largest of the eigenvalues.

Assuming now that the elements in W have these values and are normalized such that $\sum_i w_i^2 = 1$, the vector $B = [b_i]$ is then

$$B = \frac{QD}{D'D} = \frac{QQ'W}{W'QQ'W} = \frac{\lambda W}{\lambda \sum w_i^2} = W \tag{I.16}$$

and

$$r_i = \frac{(QD)_i}{\sqrt{D'D \sum_j q_{ij}^2}} \tag{I.17}$$

$$= \frac{(QQ'W)_i}{\sqrt{\lambda}\sqrt{\sum_j q_{ij}^2}}$$

$$= \sqrt{\lambda}\frac{w_i}{\sqrt{\sum_j q_{ij}^2}},$$

where $(QD)_i$ is the ith element in the vector QD.

In addition, note that the variance of index I_j $(j = 1, \ldots, M)$ for the optimal index is the maximum eigenvalue of QQ'.

REFERENCES

K. J. Arrow (1972). "Aspects of the Theory of Risk-Bearing." Yrjö Jahnssonin Säätiö, Helsinki, 1965 (reprinted by North-Holland Publ., Amsterdam).

W. J. Baumol (1963). An expected gain-confidence limit criterion for portfolio selection, *Management Science* **10**, 174–181.

A. Bertoni and G. P. Szegö (1972). "Metodologie Quantitative per la Gestione delle Banche di Deposito." Giuffrè, Milan.

A. Bertoni, P. Mazzoleni, and G. P. Szegö (1975). On the analytical identification of the optimal loan and deposit interest rates of a commercial bank, *Metroeconomica* **27**, 44–67.

F. Black, M. Jensen, and M. Scholes (1972). The capital asset pricing model: some empirical tests, *in* "Studies in the Theory of Capital Markets" (M. Jensen, ed.), pp. 79–121. Praeger, New York.

K. H. Borch (1968). "The Economics of Uncertainty." Princeton Univ. Press, Princeton, New Jersey.

K. H. Borch (1969a). A note on uncertainty and indifference curves, *Review of Economic Studies* **36**, 1–4.

K. H. Borch (1978). Portfolio theory is for risk lovers, *Journal of Banking and Finance* **2**, 179–181.

N. O. Brito (1978). Portfolio selection in an economy with marketability and short sales restrictions, *Journal of Finance* **33**, 589–601.

G. Debreu and I. N. Herstein (1953). Nonnegative square matrices, *Econometrica* **21**, 597–607.

D. K. Faddeev and V. N. Faddeeva (1963). "Computational Methods of Linear Algebra." W. H. Freeman & Co., San Francisco, California.

E. F. Fama (1965). Portfolio analysis in a stable paretian market, *Management Science* **11**, 404–419.

M. S. Feldstein (1969). Mean variance analysis in the theory of liquidity preference and portfolio selection, *Review of Economic Studies* **36**, 5–11.

S. Fisher (1975). The demand for index bonds, *Journal of Public Economics* **83**, 509–534.

J. Fried (1969). A Generalized Markowitz Model of Bank Portfolio Selection, Ph.D. Thesis. Northwestern Univ., Evanston, Illinois.

M. Friedman and L. J. Savage (1948). The utility analysis of choice involving risk, *The Journal of Political Economy* **61**, 279–304.

I. Friend and J. Bicksler (eds.) (1976). "Risk and Return in Finance." Ballinger, Cambridge, Massachusetts.

B. Gavish (1977). A relaxation algorithm for building undominated portfolios, *Journal of Banking and Finance* **1**, 143–150.

G. Hanoch and H. Levy (1969). The efficiency analysis of choices involving risk, *Review Economic Studies* **36**, 335–346.

I. N. Herstein and J. Milnor (1953). An axiomatic approach to measurable utility, *Econometrica* **21**, 291–297.

S. E. Hersom, C. Sutti, and G. P. Szegö (1973). On best linear fit index, Numerical Optimization Centre Tech. Rep. No. 46. Hatfield Polytechnic, Hatfield, United Kingdom.

W. W. Hogan and J. M. Warren (1972). Computation of the efficient boundary in the *E-SV* portfolio selection model, *Journal of Financial and Quantitative Analysis* **7**, 1881–1896.

W. W. Hogan and J. M. Warren (1974). Toward the development of an equilibrium capital market model based on semivariance, *Journal of Financial and Quantitative Analysis* **9**, 1–11.

M. Jensen (1972a). Capital markets: theory and evidence, *Bell Journal of Economics and Management Science* **3**, 151–174.

M. Jensen (ed.) (1972b). "Studies in the Theory of Capital Markets." Praeger, New York.

V. J. Kareken (1967). Commercial banks and the supply of money: a market determined demand deposit rate, *Federal Reserve Bulletin* **53**, 1699–1711.

D. Kira and W. T. Ziemba (1977). Equivalence among alternative portfolio selection criteria, *in* "Financial Decision Making under Uncertainty" (H. Levy and M. Sarnat, eds.). Academic Press, New York.

J. H. Levin (1970). Forward exchange and internal-external equilibrium, *University of Michigan International Business Studies* **12**.

H. Levy and M. Sarnat (1972). "Investment and Portfolio Analysis." Wiley, New York.

H. Levy and M. Sarnat (eds.) (1977). "Financial Decision Making under Uncertainty." Academic Press, New York.

J. Lintner (1965). The valuation of risk assets and the selection of risky investments in stock portfolios and capital budgets, *Review of Economics and Statistics* **47**, 13–37.

J. H. Makin (1978). Portfolio theory and the problem of foreign exchange risk, *Journal of Finance* **33**, 517–532.

H. M. Markowitz (1952). Portfolio selection, *Journal of Finance* **7**, 77–91.

H. M. Markowitz (1959). "Portfolio Selection." Wiley, New York.

H. M. Markowitz (1977). An algorithm for finding undominated portfolios, *in* "Financial Decision Making under Uncertainty" (H. Levy and M. Sarnat, eds.). Academic Press, New York.

R. C. Merton (1971). Optimal consumption and portfolio rules in a continuous time model, *Journal of Economic Theory* **3**, 373–413.

R. C. Merton (1972). An analytic derivation of the efficient portfolio frontier, *Journal of Financial and Quantitative Analysis* **7**, 1851–1872.

R. C. Merton (1973). An intertemporal capital asset pricing model, *Econometrica* **41**, 867–887.

R. C. Merton (1975). Theory of finance from the perspective of continuous time, *Journal of Financial and Quantitative Analysis* **10**, 659–674.

R. C. Merton (1977). On the Microeconomic Theory of Investment under Uncertainty, Sloan School of Management, M.I.T., Work. Pap. WP 958–77.

J. Mossin (1973). "Theory of Financial Markets." Prentice-Hall, Engewood Cliffs, New Jersey.

J. A. Ohlson (1975). The asymptotic validity of quadratic utility as the trading interval approaches zero, *in* "Stochastic Optimization Models in Finance" (W. T. Ziemba and R. G. Vickson, eds.). Academic Press, New York.

R. C. Porter (1961). A model of bank portfolio selection, *Yale Economic Essay* **1**, 322–359.

R. Roll (1977). A critique of the asset pricing theory's tests—part I, *Journal of Financial Economics* **4**, 129–176.

R. Roll and B. H. Solnik (1975). A Pure Foreign Exchange Asset Pricing Model, *Helsinki Conference on Monetary Mechanism in Open Economies.*

S. Ross (1976). Return risk and arbitrage *in* "Risk and Return in Finance" (I. Friend and J. Bicksler, eds.), pp. 189–218. Ballinger Cambridge, Massachusetts.

S. Ross (1978). The current status of the capital asset pricing model, *Journal of Finance* **33**, 885–902.

M. Rusconi (1975). Problemi di equivalenza e dominanza nella teoria matematica della selezione degli investimenti, *Bollettino Unione Matematica Italiana* **12** (Ser.V), 1–11.

P. A. Samuelson (1970). The fundamental approximation theorem of portfolio analysis in terms of means, variances and higher moments, *Review of Economics Studies* **36**, 537–542.

M. Sarnat (ed.) (1978). "Inflation and Capital Markets." Ballinger, Cambridge, Massachusetts.

M. Sarnat (1973). Purchasing power, risk, portfolio analysis, and the case of index-linked bonds, *Journal of Money, Credit, and Banking* **5**, 836–845.

M. Sarnat and G. P. Szegö (eds.) (1979). "International Investment and Trade." Ballinger, Cambridge, Massachusetts.

W. F. Sharpe (1964). Capital asset prices: a theory of market equilibrium under condition of risk, *Journal of Finance* **19**, 425–442.

B. H. Solnik (1973). "European Capital Markets: Towards a General Theory of International Investment." Lexington Books, Lexington, Massachusetts.

B. H. Solnik (1974). An equilibrium model of the international capital market, *Journal of Economic Theory* **8**, 500–524.

B. H. Solnik (1978). Inflation and optimal portfolio choices, *Journal of Financial and Quantitative Analysis* **13**, 903–912.

S. Stefani and G. P. Szegö (1976). Formulazione analitica della funzione utilita' dipendente da media e semivarianza mediante il principio dell'utilità attesa, *Bollettino Unione Matematica Italiana* **13**, 157–162.

B. K. Stone (1970). "Risk, Return, and Equilibrium." M.I.T. Press, Cambridge, Massachusetts.

J. Stiglitz (1972). Portfolio allocation with many risky assets, *in* "Mathematical Methods in Investment and Finance" (G. P. Szegö and K. Shell, eds)., pp. 76–128. North-Holland Publ., Amsterdam.

G. P. Szegö (1970). Sulla Selezione Ottima del Portafoglio. Rendiconti per il Potenziamento in Venezia degli Studi Economici, CEDAM, Padova, Vol. 3, pp. 3–24.

G. P. Szegö (ed.) (1972a). "Modelli Analitici di Gestione Bancaria." Tamburini, Milan.

G. P. Szegö (1972b). "Nuovi Risultati Analitici nella Teoria della selezione del Portafoglio." Tamburini, Milan.

G. P. Szegö (1976). Séparation généralisée dans le théorie du portefeuille, *in* "Institutions et Marchés Financiers," CERESSEC, Cergy.

G. P. Szegö (1978a). A note on covariance properties of efficient portfolios, *Journal of Banking and Finance* **2**, 399–401.

G. P. Szegö (1978b). The effect of bankruptcy risk on the financial structure of the firm, Fifth Ann. Meeting of the European Finance Assoc., Bergamo.

G. P. Szegö, P. Mazzoleni, and G. Zambruno (1972). Modelli analitici di gestione bancaria, *in* "Modelli Analitici di Gestione Bancaria" (G. P. Szegö, ed.). Tamburini, Milan.

G. P. Szegö and P. Mazzoleni (1976). Bank asset management via portfolio theory: some analytic results, Proc. E.F.A. 1975 Meeting, pp. 455–472. North-Holland Publ., Amsterdam.

G. P. Szegö and M. Rusconi (1980). La struttura del mercato finanziario italiano in termini reali negli anni '70, *Rivista di Statistica Applicata* **13** (to be published).

J. Tobin (1958). Liquidity preference as behaviour towards risk, *Review of Economic Studies* **25**, 65–86.

J. Tobin (1969). Comments on Borch and Feldstein, *Review of Economic Studies* **36**, 13–14.

J. Von Neumann and D. Morgenstern (1944). "Theory of Games and Economic Behavior." Princeton Univ. Press, Princeton, New Jersey.

G. M. Zambruno (1975). On the Dominance of Investments in the Portfolio Selection Theory, *Bollettino Unione Matematica Italiana* **12** (Ser. IV) 88–96.

W. T. Ziemba and R. G. Vickson (eds.) (1975). "Stochastic Optimization Models in Finance." Academic Press, New York.

INDEX

R

S

T

U

V

ECONOMIC THEORY, ECONOMETRICS, AND MATHEMATICAL ECONOMICS

Consulting Editor: Karl Shell

UNIVERSITY OF PENNSYLVANIA
PHILADELPHIA, PENNSYLVANIA

Franklin M. Fisher and Karl Shell. **The Economic Theory of Price Indices: *Two Essays on the Effects of Taste, Quality, and Technological Change***

Luis Eugenio Di Marco (Ed.). **International Economics and Development: *Essays in Honor of Raúl Presbisch***

Erwin Klein. **Mathematical Methods in Theoretical Economics: *Topological and Vector Space Foundations of Equilibrium Analysis***

Paul Zarembka (Ed.). **Frontiers in Econometrics**

George Horwich and Paul A. Samuelson (Eds.). **Trade, Stability, and Macroeconomics: *Essays in Honor of Lloyd A. Metzler***

W. T. Ziemba and R. G. Vickson (Eds.). **Stochastic Optimization Models in Finance**

Steven A. Y. Lin (Ed.). **Theory and Measurement of Economic Externalities**

David Cass and Karl Shell (Eds.). **The Hamiltonian Approach to Dynamic Economics**

R. Shone. **Microeconomics: *A Modern Treatment***

C. W. J. Granger and Paul Newbold. **Forecasting Economic Time Series**

Michael Szenberg, John W. Lombardi, and Eric Y. Lee. **Welfare Effects of Trade Restrictions: *A Case Study of the U.S. Footwear Industry***

Haim Levy and Marshall Sarnat (Eds.). **Financial Decision Making under Uncertainty**

Yasuo Murata. **Mathematics for Stability and Optimization of Economic Systems**

Alan S. Blinder and Philip Friedman (Eds.). **Natural Resources, Uncertainty, and General Equilibrium Systems: *Essays in Memory of Rafael Lusky***

Jerry S. Kelly. **Arrow Impossibility Theorems**

Peter Diamond and Michael Rothschild (Eds.). **Uncertainty in Economics: *Readings and Exercises***

Fritz Machlup. **Methodology of Economics and Other Social Sciences**

Robert H. Frank and Richard T. Freeman. **Distributional Consequences of Direct Foreign Investment**

Elhanan Helpman and Assaf Razin. **A Theory of International Trade under Uncertainty**

Edmund S. Phelps. **Studies in Macroeconomic Theory, Volume 1: *Employment and Inflation.* Volume 2: *Redistribution and Growth.***

Marc Nerlove, David M. Grether, and José L. Carvalho. **Analysis of Economic Time Series: *A Synthesis***

Thomas J. Sargent. **Macroeconomic Theory**

Jerry Green and José Alexander Scheinkman (Eds.). **General Equilibrium, Growth and Trade: *Essays in Honor of Lionel McKenzie***

Michael J. Boskin (Ed.). **Economics and Human Welfare: *Essays in Honor of Tibor Scitovsky***

Carlos Daganzo. **Multinomial Probit: *The Theory and Its Application to Demand Forecasting***

L. R. Klein, M. Nerlove, and S. C. Tsiang (Eds.). **Quantitative Economics and Development: *Essays in Memory of Ta-Chung Liu***

Giorgio P. Szegö. **Portfolio Theory: *With Application to Bank Asset Management***

In preparation

M June Flanders and Assaf Razin. **Development in an Inflationary World**

Thomas G. Cowing and Rodney E. Stevenson (Eds.). **Productivity Measurement in Regulated Industries**